16th BLUE BOOK

Dolls & Values®

by Jan Foulke

#1 Best Seller

30 years

Photographs by
Howard Foulke

Antique Section — Pages 19 to 204.
Modern Section — Pages 205 to 311.

Published by

Hobby
House
Press

Hobby House Press, Inc.
Grantsville, Maryland
www.hobbyhouse.com

Additional copies of this book may be purchased at
$19.95 (plus postage and handling) from
Hobby House Press, Inc.
1 Corporate Drive
Grantsville, MD 21536
1-800-554-1447
www.hobbyhouse.com

Using This Book

Welcome to the Doll Collecting World! If you have any interest in dolls, whether you are new to dolls, or an old hand at them, the **Blue Book of Dolls & Values** was written for you. It can help you identify and learn more about your dolls or dolls you are thinking of purchasing. It can help you evaluate or appraise your dolls or guide you on prices for future additions to your collection. It puts, right at your fingertips, in a well-organized easy-to-use format, a great amount of information that you will need to know in order to build your doll collection. The great success of the **Blue Book of**

Dolls & Values, through 16 revisions since 1974, speaks for itself as it fills the needs of doll lovers, collectors, dealers, appraisers and estate executors who return to buy the latest editions.

For convenience in locating a doll more quickly, the **Blue Book** is divided into two color-coded sections: *Antique & Vintage Dolls* in the blue section; *Modern & Collectible Dolls* in the pink section. Generally, the dolls in the *Antique Section* are the older dolls made from wood, wax, papier-mâché, china, bisque and cloth. Most of the dolls in the *Modern Section* are made

22½in (57cm) early Jumeau portrait doll with extreme almond or wrap-around eyes. For additional information, see page 105. *Private Collection.*

26in (66cm) Sonneberg Täufling. For additional information, see page 158. *H & J Foulke, Inc.*

23in (58m) German bisque doll, incised "D.A." For additional information, see page 51. *H & J Foulke, Inc.*

of composition, hard plastic and vinyl, although there is some unavoidable overlapping. Where certain dolls, such as *Raggedy Ann* and *Kewpie*, were made over very long periods, the modern examples are included with the main entry in the *Antique Section* in order to keep the whole production history of a doll in one place. An extensive index of doll names and manufacturers and an index of mold numbers of bisque and china heads are included at the back of the *Blue Book* to help you find dolls more quickly. Information aids provided are a bibliography of books suggested for in-depth study and a glossary of doll terms.

Within their sections, the dolls presented in the *Blue Book* are listed alphabetically by maker, material or, sometimes, trade name. For the most part, dolls are arranged in chronological order by date within a main entry. For each doll, we have included historical information, physical description, marks and labels, and the retail selling price. Photographs are shown for as many dolls as possible, but since every doll cannot be shown in each edition, you should consult previous *Blue Books* for additional photographs.

As for the doll sizes priced for most of the antique dolls, they are chosen at random, so do not assume that the dolls are made only in the sizes listed. It just is not possible for us to list all sizes of a doll which can range from 6in (15cm) to 42in (106cm). If we do not list your doll's size, you will need to use a little common sense to interpolate a price.

Some of the historical information given for dolls was compiled from original research already published by Dorothy S., Elizabeth A. and Evelyn J. Coleman; Johana G. Anderton; Jürgen and Marianne Cieslik; and Pam and Polly Judd. The Colemans allowed some of the doll marks to be reproduced from their book *The Collector's Encyclopedia of Dolls.*

We gathered the data for compiling the retail prices during 2002 and 2003. We checked prices at antique shops and shows, auctions (including the internet), doll shops and shows, dealers' web sites, advertisements in collectors' periodicals, lists from doll dealers and purchases and sales reported by both collectors and dealers. This information, along with our own valuations and judgments, was computed into the range of prices shown in the *Blue Book*. When we could not find a sufficient number of dolls to be sure of giving a reliable range, we marked those prices with two asterisks (**).

The price range for a doll listed in the *Blue Book* is the retail value of the doll if purchased from a dealer in the condition as noted in the description.

Fine examples, especially those which are all original or boxed with original tags or never played with, can bring a premium of at least 50 percent more than the prices quoted. Sometimes a specific example will bring a premium price because it is particularly cute, sweet, pretty or visually appealing, having an outstanding appearance. There is just no way to factor this aspect into a price guide.

All prices given in the *Blue Book* for antique dolls are for those of good quality and condition, but showing some normal wear and aging. Dolls should be appropriately dressed in old clothing or new clothing made from old fabrics. Bisque or china heads should not be cracked, broken or repaired, but may have slight manufac-

17in (43cm) Ronnaug Petterssen celluloid dolls, all original. For additional information, see page 141. *H & J Foulke, Inc.*

turing imperfections such as speckling, surface lines, darkened mold lines or uneven coloring. Bodies may have repairs but should be old and appropriate to the head. A doll with its original old dress, shoes and wig will generally be valued higher than the quoted prices because these items are in scarce supply and can easily cost more than $85 each, if purchased separately.

Prices given for composition dolls are for those in overall good to excellent condition with original hair and clothing, unless noted otherwise. Composition may be lightly crazed, but should be colorful. Hard plastic and vinyl dolls must be perfect with hair in its original set, crisp original clothes and no mildew or odor. A never-played-with doll in original box with labels would bring a premium price.

When you use the *Blue Book*, please keep in mind that no price guide is the final word about a doll. It cannot provide an absolute answer as to what to pay. It should be used only as an aid to you in purchasing and evaluating a doll. The final decision of whether to buy and what to pay, must be yours personally, for only you are on the scene actually examining the specific doll in question. Also, please remember that no book can take the place of actual field experience. Before you buy, do a lot of looking. Ask lots of questions. You will find most dealers and collectors are glad to talk about their dolls and pleased to share their information.

Happy Dolling!
Jan Foulke
June 2003

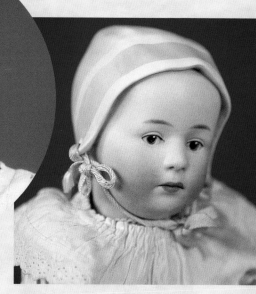

14in (36cm) Schoenhut 308 character girl. For additional information, see page 178. *H & J Foulke, Inc.*

11in (28cm) Gebrüder Heubach 7877 character baby, so-called "Baby Stuart." For additional information, see page 102. *H & J Foulke, Inc.*

19in (48cm) Georgene Novelties *Beloved Belindy*. For additional information, see page 165. *Kay Jensen Antique Dolls.*

Acknowledgements

Many friends, customers, fellow dealers and doll collectors around the world contributed to the *16th Blue Book of Dolls & Values.* We would like to express our appreciation to Connie Blain, Rosemary Kanizer, Floyd Jones, Gloria & Mike Duddlesten, Carmel Doll Shop, Kathy & Terri's Dolls, Linda Kellermann, Laraine & Gangolf Friesberg, Connie & Jay Lowe, Richard Saxman, Greg Montcastle, Sue Kallen, Mary Ann Spinelli, McMasters Harris Premier Doll Auctions, Mary Barnes Kelley, Dr. Carole Stoessel Zvonar, Helen Burton, Dorothy Hunt, Shogun, Nancy A. Smith, Bart Boeckmans, Doodlebug Dolls, Sheila Needle, Kay Jensen, Rae-Ellen Koenig, Sidney Jeffrey, George Bassett, Diane Costa, Pat Vaillancourt, Becky & Andy Ourant and H & J Foulke, Inc., as well as several collectors who wished to remain anonymous.

Also, our thanks to Gary Ruddell of Hobby House Press, Inc., with whom we have worked for 30 years, and Virginia Ann Heyerdahl for editorial assistance.

All of these people helped to make this book possible.

Jan and Howard Foulke
June 2003

Investing In Dolls

Collectors talk about a doll collection being an investment, and it can be a very good one. Unfortunately, there is no guarantee that any particular doll will appreciate consistently year after year. I never advise people to collect dolls strictly as an investment. I think you should collect dolls because you like them and enjoy the hobby. If the doll appreciates in value, consider that as a bonus. We like to think that 20 or 30 years down the road when we get ready to sell our dolls, we will get more for them than we paid and, in general, I think this is true if we have bought wisely. The track record for vintage or antique dolls over 40 years old has been fairly good. Collectible dolls of the past 30 years or so are a more risky market. Most of them bring, on the secondary market, only 10 to 50 percent of their original cost.

Since assembling a doll collection can be rather costly in today's market and most of you have only a limited amount of money to allocate to it, you must be sure that you are spending your dollars to the best advantage. In this chapter, I will provide some suggestions about what to look for and what to consider before buying a doll. My basic tenet is, if you do not have the knowledge to be sure about the doll you are buying, do be sure you are buying it from someone you trust to give you the correct information about it.

21in (53cm) poured wax doll. For additional information, see page 196. *Floyd Jones.*

Marks

Fortunately, most of the antique bisque, some of the papier-mâché, cloth and other types of antique dolls are marked or labeled. Marks and labels give you confidence because they identify the trade name, the maker, the country of origin, the style or mold number, or perhaps even the patent date.

Most composition and modern dolls are marked with the maker's name and sometimes also the trade name of the doll and the date. Some dolls have tags sewn on or into their clothing to identify them; many still retain original hangtags.

Of course, many dolls are unmarked, but after you have seen quite a few dolls, you begin to notice their individual characteristics and can often determine what a doll possibly is. When you have had some experience buying dolls, you begin to recognize an unusual face or an especially fine quality doll, and the lack of a mark may be less important. The doll has to speak for itself, and the price must be based upon your frame of doll reference. That is, you must relate the face and quality to those of a known doll maker and make price judgments from that point.

Quality

The mark does not tell you everything about a doll. Two examples from the same mold could look entirely different and carry vastly different prices because of the quality of the work done on the doll, which can vary from head to head, even with dolls made from the same mold by one firm. To command top price, a bisque doll should have lovely bisque, decoration, eyes and hair. Before purchasing a doll, you should determine whether the example is the best available of that type. Even the molding of one head can be much sharper with more delineation of such details as dimples or locks of hair. The molding detail is especially important to notice when purchasing dolls with character faces or molded hair.

The quality of the bisque should be smooth; dolls with bisque which is pimply, peppered with tiny black specks or unevenly colored, or which has noticeable firing lines on the face, would be second choices at a lower price. However, collectors must keep in mind that porcelain factories sold

10in (25cm) Arranbee hard plastic *Littlest Angel,* all original. For additional information, see page 225. *Rosemary Kanizer.*

many heads with small manufacturing defects because companies were in business for profit and were producing expendable play items, not works of art. Small manufacturing defects do not devalue a doll. It is perfectly acceptable to have light speckling, light surface lines, firing lines in inconspicuous places, darkened mold lines, a few black specks, or cheek rubs. The absolutely perfect bisque head is a rarity.

Since doll heads are hand-painted, you should examine the artistry of the decoration. The tinting of the complexion should be subdued and even, not harsh and splotchy. Artistic skill

5¾in (14cm) French all-bisque *Mignonette,* all original. For additional information, see page 21. *H & J Foulke, Inc.*

should be evident in the portrayal of the expression on the face and in details such as the lips, eyebrows and eyelashes, and particularly in the eyes, which should show highlights and shading when they are painted. On a doll with molded hair, individual brush marks to give the hair a more realistic look would be a desirable detail.

If a doll has a wig, the hair should be appropriate if not old. Dynel or synthetic wigs are not appropriate for antique dolls; a human hair or good quality mohair wig should be used. If a doll has glass eyes, they should be old with natural color and threading in the irises to give a lifelike appearance.

If a doll does not meet all of these standards, it should be priced lower than one that does. Furthermore, an especially fine example will bring a premium over an ordinary but nice model.

Condition

Another important factor when pricing a doll is the condition. A bisque doll with a crack on the face or extensive professional repair involving the face would sell for one-quarter or less than a doll with only normal wear. An inconspicuous hairline would decrease the value somewhat, but in a rare doll it would not be as great a detriment as in a common doll. As the so-called better dolls are becoming more difficult to find, a hairline is more acceptable to collectors if there is a price adjustment. The same is true for a doll which has a spectacular face — a hairline would be less important to price in that doll than in one with an ordinary face.

Sometimes a head will have a factory flaw which occurred in the making, such as a firing crack, scratch, piece of kiln debris, dark specks, small bubbles, a ridge not smoothed out or light surface lines. Since the factory was producing toys for a profit and not creating works of art, heads with slight flaws were not all discarded, especially if flaws were inconspicuous or could be covered. If factory defects are not detracting, they have little or no effect on the value of a doll.

It is to be expected that an old doll will show some wear. Perhaps there is a rub on the nose or cheek, a few small "wig pulls" or maybe a chipped earring hole; a Schoenhut doll or a Käthe Kruse may have some scuffs; an old papier-mâché may have a few age cracks; a china head may show wear on the hair; an old composition body may have scuffed toes or missing fingers. This wear is to be expected and does not necessarily affect the value of a doll. However, a doll in exceptional condition will bring more than "book" price.

Unless an antique doll is rare or you particularly want that specific doll, do not pay top price for a doll that needs extensive work: restringing, setting eyes, repairing fingers, replacing body parts, new wig or dressing. All of these repairs add up to a considerable sum at the doll hospital, possibly making the total cost of the doll more than it is really worth.

Composition dolls in perfect condition are becoming harder to find. Because their material is so susceptible to the atmosphere, their condition can deteriorate literally overnight. Even in excellent condition, a composition doll nearly always has some fine crazing or slight fading. It is very difficult to find a composition doll in mint condition

14in (36cm) Alexander *Sonja Henie Bride,* all original. For additional information, see page 211. *H & J Foulke, Inc.*

and even harder to be sure that it will stay that way. However, in order for a composition doll to bring "book" price, there should be a minimum of crazing, very good coloring, original uncombed hair and original clothes in very good condition. Pay less for a doll that does not have original clothes and hair or that is all original but shows extensive play wear. Pay even less for one with heavy crazing and cracking or other damages. For composition dolls that are all original, unplayed-with, in original boxes and with little or no crazing, allow a premium of about 50 percent over "book" price.

Hard plastic and vinyl dolls must be in excellent condition if they are at "book" price. The hair should be perfect, in the original set; clothes should be completely original, fresh and unfaded. Skin tones should be natural with good cheek color. Add a premium of 25 to 50 percent for mint dolls never removed from their original boxes.

Body

In order to command top price, an old doll must have the original or an appropriate old body in good condition. If a doll does not have the correct type of body, you end up not with a complete doll but with parts that may not be worth as much as one whole doll. As dolls are becoming more difficult to find, more are turning up with "put together" bodies. Many dolls are now entering the market from old collections assembled years ago. Some of these contain dolls which were "put together" before there was much information available about correct heads and bodies. Therefore, the body should be checked to make sure it is appropriate to the head, and all parts of the body should be checked to make sure that they are appropriate to each other.

12in (31cm) Eros Italian girl, all original. For additional information, see page 140. *H & J Foulke, Inc.*

A body with mixed parts from several makers or types of bodies is not worth as much as one with correct parts.

Minor damage or repair to an old body does not affect the value of an antique doll. An original body carefully repaired, recovered or even, if necessary, completely repainted is preferable to a new one. An antique head on a new body would be worth only the value of its parts, whatever the price of the head and new body, not the full price of an antique doll. A rule of thumb is that an antique head is generally worth about 40 to 50 percent of the price of the complete doll. A very rare head could be worth up to 80 percent. If there is a choice of body types for the same bisque head, a good quality ball-jointed composition body is more desirable than a crudely made five-piece body or stick-type body with only pieces of turned wood for upper arms and legs. Collectors prefer jointed composition bodies over kid ones for dolly-faced dolls, and pay more for the same face on a composition body.

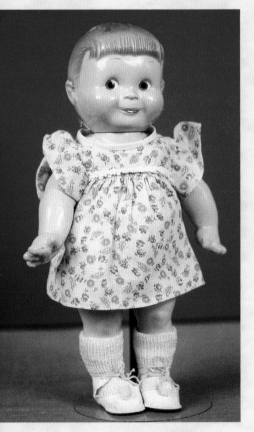

13in (33cm) Cameo composition *Giggles,* all original. For additional information, see page 244. *H & J Foulke, Inc.*

Occasionally, the body adds value to the doll. In the case of bisque heads, a small doll with a completely jointed body, a French fashion-type with a wood-jointed body, a *Tête Jumeau* head on an adult body or a character baby head on a jointed toddler-type body would all be higher in price because of their special bodies.

As for the later modern dolls, a composition doll on the wrong body or with a body that is cracked, peeling and in poor condition would have a greatly reduced value. The same is true of a vinyl doll with replaced parts, body stains or chewed-off fingers.

Clothing

It is becoming increasingly difficult to find dolls in old clothing because, as the years go by, fabrics continue to deteriorate. Consequently, collectors are paying more than "book" price for an antique doll if it has original old clothes, shoes and hair. Even faded, somewhat worn or carefully mended original or appropriate old clothes are preferable to new ones. As collectors become more sophisticated and selective, they realize the value of old doll clothing and accessories. Some dealers are now specializing in these areas. Good old leather doll shoes will bring more than $85 per pair; a lovely Victorian white-work doll dress can easily cost $95; an old dress for a French fashion lady, $300 and more. Good old doll wigs can bring from $25 to $250.

However, when clothing must be replaced and appropriate old clothing cannot be obtained, new clothes should be authentically styled for the age of the doll and constructed of fabrics that would have been available when the doll was produced. There are many reference books and catalog reprints showing dolls in original clothing, and doll supply companies offer patterns for dressing old dolls.

To bring top price, a modern doll must have original clothes. It is usually fairly simple to determine whether or not the clothing is original and factory made. Some makers even placed tags in the doll's clothing. Replaced clothing greatly reduces the price of modern dolls. Without the original clothing, it is often impossible to identify a modern doll because so many were made using the same face mold.

Total Originality

Today totally original antique dolls are becoming rare. It is often

21in (53cm) Simon & Halbig 1079. For additional information, see page 183. *H & J Foulke, Inc.*

difficult to determine whether the head and body and all other parts of a doll, including wig, eyes and clothes, have always been together. Many parts of a doll may have been changed and clothing and accessories could have been added over the years. Many dolls labeled "all original" are simply wearing contemporary clothing and wigs. Some collectors and dealers are "embellishing" more expensive dolls by taking original clothing and wigs from cheaper dolls to further enhance the value of the most costly ones.

Dolls with trunks of clothing should be examined to determine whether or not the clothes actually go with the doll or are an assembled wardrobe. A little common sense goes a long way in deciding whether the clothes are of the proper fit, fabric and style for the dolls. The same is true for accessories.

Boxed sets of dolls and accessories should be examined very carefully as some very charming sets of newly assembled old items are being offered as totally original for very, very high prices. Of course, when these ensembles are genuine, they are the ultimate in doll collecting.

Age

The oldest dolls do not necessarily command the highest prices. A lovely old china head with exquisite decoration and a very unusual hairdo would bring a price of several thousand dollars but not as much as a 20th century German bisque character child. Many desirable composition dolls of the 1930s and *BARBIE*® dolls of the 1960s are selling at prices higher than older bisque dolls of 1890 to 1920. So, in determining price, the age of the doll may or may not be significant.

Size

The size of a doll is usually taken into account when determining a price. Generally, the size and price for a certain doll are related: a smaller size is lower, a larger size is higher. However, there are a few exceptions. The 11in (28cm) *Shirley Temple* and tiny German dolly-faced dolls on fully-jointed bodies are examples of small dolls that bring higher prices than their larger counterparts.

Availability

In most cases, the price of a doll is directly related to its availability. The harder a particular doll is to find, the higher its price will be. As long as the demand for certain antique and collectible dolls remains high, prices will hold or rise. It is simply the old "supply and demand" axiom. This explains the higher prices of less common dolls, such as the early French *bébés*, Kämmer & Reinhardt and other German character children, early china head and papier-mâché dolls, and Alexander and *BARBIE®* dolls that were made for only a limited period of time. Dolls that are fairly common, primarily the German dolly faces and character babies and the later china head dolls made over a long period of production, sell for lower prices, as there is not as much demand for them.

Popularity

There are fads in dolls just as in clothes, food and other aspects of life. Dolls that have recently risen in price because of their popularity include the early French Brus, American cloth Columbians, German all-bisques, small bisque head dolls with fully-

20½in (52cm) long Averill *Bonnie Babe*. For additional information, see page 37. *H & J Foulke, Inc.*

jointed bodies, *Bleuettes*, early *Sashas*, *Blythe*, hard plastic dolls of the early 1950s, vinyl fashion dolls and *Nancy Ann Storybook* and *Style Show Dolls*. Some dolls are popular enough to tempt collectors to pay prices higher than the availability factor warrants. Although *Shirley Temples*, *Bye-Lo Babies* and *Hildas* are not rare, the higher prices they bring are due to their popularity. Some American cloth dolls, Gebrüder Heubach characters, closed-mouth shoulder head dolls, most common German dolly faces and character babies, *Tête Jumeaux* and *Patsy* family dolls are in a soft period, so many bargains can be found in these categories.

Desirability

Some very rare dolls do not bring a high price because they are not particularly desirable to collectors. There are not enough collectors looking for them to drive the prices up to what they should be considering the rarity. Examples are wax *Bye-Lo Babies,* American metal head and composition head dolls on fully-jointed composition or metal bodies, English slit-head wax dolls, Bartenstein multi-faced dolls and many German bisque dolly-faced dolls from obscure factories.

Uniqueness

Sometimes the uniqueness of a doll makes price determination very difficult. If you have never seen a doll exactly like it before, and it is not cited in a price guide or even shown in any books, deciding what to pay can be a problem. In this case, you have to use all available knowledge as a frame of reference for the unknown doll. Perhaps a doll marked "A.M. 2000" or "S & H 1289" has been found, and the asking price is 25 percent higher than for the more commonly found numbers by that maker. Or perhaps a black *Kamkins* is offered for twice the price of a white one, or a French fashion lady with original wardrobe is offered at 60 percent more than a re-dressed one. In cases such as these, you must use your own expertise and judgment to determine what the doll is worth.

Visual Appeal

Perhaps the most elusive aspect in pricing a doll is its visual appeal. Sometimes, particularly at auction, we have seen dolls bring well over their "book" value simply because of their look. Often this is nothing more than the handiwork of someone who had the ability to choose just the right wig, clothing and accessories to enhance the doll's visual appeal and make it look particularly cute, stunning, beautiful or otherwise especially outstanding.

Sometimes, though, the visual appeal comes from the face of the doll itself. It may be the way the teeth are put in, the placement of the eyes, the tinting on the face or the sharpness of the molding. Or it may not be any of these specific things; it may just be what some collectors refer to as the "presence" of the doll, an elusive indefinable quality which makes it the best example known!

11½in (29cm) *Caroline* and 9½in *John John* by Lita Wilson. For additional information, see page 227. *H & J Foulke, Inc.*

Selling A Doll

The doll question that we get asked most frequently is: "How do I go about selling a doll?" So it seems that a few paragraphs in answer would be helpful to readers.

First, you need to identify your doll and get an idea of its value. Look on the back of the doll's head and on the body for any marks, labels or stamps. With a little luck, you will find a name that you can check in the **Blue Book**. If not, page through the book with your doll in front of you, looking for a similar doll. After you have identified your doll, check out the prices and decide what you might ask for your doll. It is very difficult for a private person to get retail or "book" price for a doll.

Condition is very important in deciding on a price. Be realistic when evaluating your doll. If you have a

14in (36cm) Effanbee composition *Patsy* & Brother, all original. For additional information, see page 256. *H & J Foulke, Inc.*

marked 18in (46cm) *Shirley Temple* doll with combed hair, no clothing, faded face with crazing and a piece off of her nose, do not expect to get the "book" price of $1,000 for her because that would be a retail price for an excellent doll, all original, in pristine unplayed-with condition, if purchased from a dealer. Your very used doll is probably worth only $50 to $75 because it will have to be purchased by someone who wants to restore it.

If you have an antique doll with a perfect bisque head but no wig, no clothes and unstrung, but with all of its body parts, you can probably expect to get about half of its retail value depending upon how desirable the particular doll is. If your doll has a perfect bisque head with original wig, clothing and shoes, you can probably get up to 75 percent of its retail value.

As to actually selling the doll, there are several possibilities. Probably the easiest is to advertise in your local paper. You may not think there are any doll collectors in your area, but there likely are. You might also check your local paper to see if anyone is advertising to purchase dolls; many dealers and collectors do so. Check the paper to find out about antique shows in your area. If a dealer has dolls, ask if he would be interested in buying your doll. Also, you could inquire at antique shops in your area for dealers who specialize in dolls. You will probably get a higher price from a specialist than a general antique dealer because the former are more familiar with the market for specific dolls. A roster of doll specialists is available from The National Antique Doll Dealers Association, Inc., through their web site at www.nadda.org.

You could consign your doll to an auction. If it is a common doll, it will probably do quite well at a local sale. If it is a more rare doll, consider sending it to one of the auction houses that specialize in selling dolls; most of them will accept one doll if it is a good one, and they will probably get the best price for you.

If you are on-line, you can try selling your doll on one of the auction services, such as eBay™. You will need to have a digital camera or scanner to provide photographs, which are very important to on-line selling. You should decide on a reserve, a minimum price you will accept, just in case it is a slow auction week. Of course, you will have to ship the doll. If it has a bisque head with glass or sleep eyes, you will have to stuff the head to protect the eyes. Improper packing of the head is the most common cause of damage during shipping.

It would probably be worth your while to purchase a doll magazine from your local bookstore, doll shop or newsstand; most doll magazines include ads from auction houses, doll shows and leading dealers. You could advertise in doll magazines, but you might have to ship the doll and guarantee return privileges if the buyer does not like it.

If you cannot find your doll in the *Blue Book,* it might be a good idea to have it professionally appraised. This will involve your paying a fee to have the doll evaluated. We provide this service and can be contacted through the publisher. Many museums and auction houses also appraise dolls.

For more detailed information about collecting and selling dolls, consult my book *Doll Buying and Selling,* available from Hobby House Press, Inc.

Antique & Vintage Dolls

Dolls in this section are listed alphabetically by maker, by material or sometimes by trade name. Dolls are arranged in chronological order by date within a main entry.

Values given in this section are retail prices for clean dolls in very good overall condition with no cracks, chips or repairs in porcelain heads and with proper bodies and appropriate wigs and clothes. Exceptional dolls in all-original condition will be higher. Naked, wigless, dirty, unstrung "attic dolls" are worth 35 to 60 percent, depending upon the rarity of the doll.

25in (64cm) china with tinted complexion and wig. *Sheila Needle.*

Alabama

Early Alabama Indestructible Doll: All-cloth painted with oils, tab-jointed shoulders and hips, flat derrière for sitting; painted hair with circular seam on head, molded face with painted facial features; applied ears; painted stockings and shoes (a few with bare feet); appropriate clothes; all in very good condition, no repaint or touch up.

11-15in (28-38cm)	**$1,400-$1,600**
21-24in (53-61cm)	**$2,500-$3,000**
Black: 14-19in (36-48cm)	**$6,600****
Wigged: 24in (61cm)	
	$3,000-$3,500**

Later doll, molded ears, bobbed hair-do:

14-15in (36-38cm)	**$1,000-$1,200**
21-24in (53-61cm)	**$2,000-$2,500**
Black: 14-19in (36-48cm)	**$3,000****

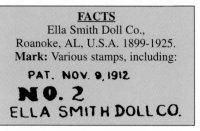

FACTS
Ella Smith Doll Co.,
Roanoke, AL, U.S.A. 1899-1925.
Mark: Various stamps, including:

PAT. NOV. 9, 1912
NO. 2
ELLA SMITH DOLL CO.

**Not enough price samples to compute a reliable range.

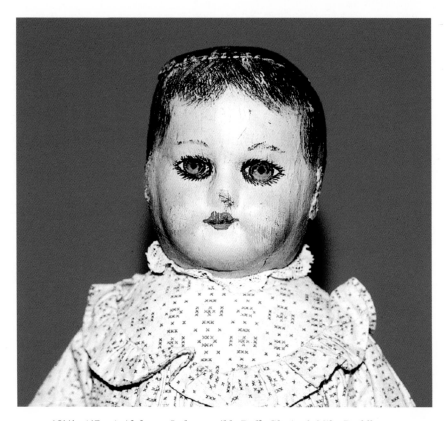

18½in (47cm) *Alabama Indestructible Doll. Gloria & Mike Duddlesten.*

Alexandre

All-Bisque
(So-called French)

FACTS
Henri Alexandre, Paris, France, 1888-1892; Tourrel, 1892-1895; Jules Steiner and successors, 1895-1901. **Designer:** Henri Alexandre. **Trademark:** Bébé Phénix.

FACTS
Various French and/or German firms. Ca. 1880-on. Smiling-faced dolls made by Simon & Halbig for the French trade. **Mark:** None, sometimes numbers.

H.A. Bébé: 1889-1891. Perfect bisque socket head, closed mouth, paper-weight eyes; jointed composition and wood body; lovely clothes; all in good condition.

Mark:

17-19in (43-48cm) **$5,800-$6,800****

Bébé Phénix: 1889-1900. As above; composition body sometimes with one-piece arms and legs.

Mark: Red Stamp: PHENIX

Incised: ★ 95

12-14in (31-36cm)	**$3,200-$3,500**
17-18in (43-46cm)	**$3,800-$4,000**
22-23in (56-58cm)	**$4,700-$5,000**
Open mouth:	
17-19in (43-48cm)	**$2,300-$2,500**

All-Bisque French Doll: Ca. 1880. Jointed at shoulders and hips, swivel neck, slender arms and legs; solid dome head, good wig, glass eyes, closed mouth; molded shoes or boots and stockings; appropriately dressed; all in good condition, with proper parts.

4¾-5¼in (11-13cm)	**$1,650-$1,850***
5¾in (15cm)	**$2,250-$2,500***
6½in (16cm)	**$3,000-$3,250**
7½in (19cm)	**$4,300**
8in (20cm)	**$5,000-$6,000****
9¼in (24cm) at auction	
	$8,800-$9,240

*Allow extra for original clothes.
**Not enough price samples to compute a reliable range.

14in (36cm) *Bébé Phenix* ★86. *Gloria & Mike Duddlesten.*

With bare feet:
  5in (13cm)   **$2,250-$2,500***
  6in (15cm)   **$2,800-$3,000***
  7in (18cm) F.G. style face **$5,000****
With jointed elbows and knees:
  5½in (14cm)   **$5,500-$6,500****
With jointed elbows:
  5½in (14cm)   **$5,250-$5,750***
Oriental: 5½in (14cm) **$1,800-$2,200***
Black: 5½in (14cm)   **$1,800-$2,200**
Painted eyes:
  4-4½in (10-12cm), all original
                                $1,000-$1,100
  2½in (6cm), blue boots, all
  original   **$225-$275**

Round face (German made for French trade): swivel neck, two-strap heeled shoes, pegged shoulders and hips; original French-style clothes.
  4½-5½in (11-14cm)   **$850-$950**

Later French Dolls: 1910-1920.
S.F.B.J., long tan stockings, swivel neck, glass eyes: 6in (15cm)   **$575-$675**
J.V., tall black boots, swivel neck, glass eyes: 6in (15cm)   **$450-$500**

*Allow extra for original clothes.
**Not enough price samples to compute a reliable range.

5½in (14cm) French all-bisque lady, all original. *H & J Foulke, Inc.*

4in (10cm) French-type all-bisque with round face. *H & J Foulke, Inc.*

All-Bisque Dolls (German)

All-Bisque with molded clothes: Ca: 1890-1910. Good quality work; all in good condition, with proper parts.

3½-4in (9-10cm)	**$115-$150**
5-6in (13-15cm)	**$200-$250**
7in (18cm)	**$275-$325**

All-Bisque Slender Dolls: Ca. 1900-on. Stationary neck, slender arms and legs; glass eyes; molded shoes or boots and stockings; many in regional costumes; all in good condition, with proper parts.

3¾-4in (9-10cm)

Folk costumes	**$165-$185**
School clothes	**$225**
Twins, pair	**$425-$450**
5-6in (13-15cm)	**$275-$300**

Swivel neck:

4in (10cm) 10a or 39/11	**$250-$300**
5½in (14cm) 13a	**$450-$500**

Black or Mulatto:

4-4½in (10-12cm)	**$350-$400**
Swivel neck: 5in (13cm)	**$550**

Round face: swivel neck, two-strap heeled shoes, pegged shoulders and hips:

4½-5½in (11-14cm)

Re-dressed	**$375-$425**
Original clothes	**$650-$750**

All-Bisque with painted eyes: Ca. 1880-1910. Stationary neck, painted eyes; molded and painted shoes and stockings; fine quality work; all in good condition, with proper parts.

1¼-1½in (3-4cm) original crocheted clothes	**$85-$125**
1½-2in (4-5cm)	**$75-$85**
4in (10cm)	**$200-$225**
5in (13cm)	**$225-$250**
6-7in (15-18cm)	**$300-$350**

Swivel neck:

4-5in (10-13cm)	**$300-$350**

Early style, bootines, yellow or blue boots or shirred hose:

4-5in (10-13cm)	**$300-$350**
6-6½in (15-16cm)	**$450-$500**
8in (20cm)	**$850-$950**

FACTS
Various firms including Hertwig & Co.; Alt, Beck & Gottschalck; Kestner; Kling; Simon & Halbig; Hertel, Schwab & Co.; Bähr & Pröschild; Limbach; Ca. 1880-on. **Mark:** Some with "Germany" and/or numbers; some with paper labels on stomachs.

6½in (17cm) Hertwig & Co. all-bisque boy with molded clothes. *H & J Foulke, Inc.*

Long black or brown stockings, tan slippers:

4¼in (11cm)	**$375**
5in (13cm)	**$425-$450**
6in (15cm)	**$500-$550**

All-Bisque with glass eyes: Ca. 1890-1910. Stationary neck, glass eyes, molded and painted shoes and stockings; all in good condition, with proper parts, fine quality.

3in (8cm)	**$275-325***
4½-5in (11-13cm)	**$275-$350***
6in (15cm)	**$375-$400***
7in (18cm)	**$450-$500***

4½ (11cm) early all-bisque with stiff hips, shirred hose and painted eyes. *H & J Foulke, Inc.*

8in (20cm)	**$600-$650***
9in (23cm)	**$800-$850***
10in (25cm)	**$900-$1,100***
12in (31cm)	**$1,200-$1,400***

Early style model, stiff hips, shirred hose or bootines:

3in (8cm)	**$325-$350**
4½in (11cm)	**$350-$400**
6in (15cm)	**$550-$575**
7in (18cm)	**$750-$850**
8-8½in (20-21cm)	**$1,200-$1,300**

Long black or white stockings, tan shoes:

5in (13cm)	**$575-$675**
7½in (19cm)	**$900-$950**

All-Bisque with swivel neck and glass eyes: Ca. 1880-1910. Swivel neck, glass eyes; molded and painted shoes or boots and stockings; all in good condition, with proper parts, fine quality.

3¼in (8cm)	**$350-$375****
4-5in (10-13cm)	**$450-$550****
6in (15cm)	**$650-$750****
7in (18cm)	**$750-$850****
8in (20cm)	**$1,100-$1,250****
9in (23cm)	**$1,400-$1,650****
10in (25cm)	**$1,800-$2,000**

Early Kestner or Simon & Halbig-type:

4½-5in (12-13cm)	**$1,850-$2,000**
6in (15cm)	**$1,850-$2,000**
7in (18cm)	**$2,150-$2,250**
8in (20cm)	**$2,500-$2,750**
10in (25cm)	**$3,200-$3,500**

With swivel waist:

8in (20cm) at auction	**$20,000**

With jointed knees:

6in (15cm) at auction	**$4,400**
8½in (22cm) at auction	**$8,225**

#102 (so-called *Wrestler*):

5½ (14cm)	**$2,000-$2,200**
8½-9in (22-23cm)	**$3,500-$4,000**

#120 (Bru-type face):

8½in (22cm)	**$4,500-$5,000***

*Allow $50 to $150 extra for yellow boots or unusual footwear and/or especially fine quality.
**Allow $100 to $150 extra for yellow boots or unusual footwear.
***Not enough sample prices to compute a reliable range.

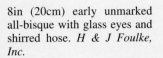

8in (20cm) early unmarked all-bisque with glass eyes and shirred hose. *H & J Foulke, Inc.*

8in (20cm) Kestner 40 all-bisque girl, with "30" limbs, a correct combination. *H & J Foulke, Inc.*

Bare feet:

5½-6in (14-15cm)	**$2,400-$2,600**
8in (20cm)	**$4,700-$5,200**
9½in (24cm) at auction	**$8,225**

Round face, bootines:

6in (15cm)	**$1,500-$1,650**
8in (20cm)	**$2,400-$2,500**

Long black stockings, tan slippers:

7½in (19cm)	**$1,250-$1,400**

Simon & Halbig **886** and **890**: See page 182.

All-Bisque Baby: Ca. 1900-on. Jointed at shoulders and hips, curved arms and legs; molded hair, painted features; all in good condition, with proper parts.

2½-3½in (6-9cm)	**$75-$95**
4-5in (10-13cm)	**$125-$175**

Fine early quality, blonde molded hair:

3½-4½in (9-11cm)	**$160-$185**
6-7in (15-18cm)	**$250-$300**
13in (33cm)	**$900-$1,000**

Immobile: 5-6in (13-15cm) **$160-$195**

All-Bisque Character Baby: Ca. 1910. Jointed at shoulders and hips, curved arms and legs; molded hair, painted eyes; all in good condition, with proper parts, very good quality.

3½in (9cm)	**$95-$110**
4½-5½in (11-14cm)	**$175-$225**
7in (18cm)	**$325-$375**
8in (20cm)	**$425-$475**

Molded white shift: 6in (15cm) **$300**

#830, #391 and others with glass eyes:

4-5in (10-13cm)	**$275-$325**
6in (15cm)	**$400-$450**
8in (20cm)	**$600-$650**
11in (28cm)	**$850-$950**

9in (23cm) early all-bisque Kestner 102, so-called *Wrestler*. *H & J Foulke, Inc.*

5in (13cm) all-bisque *Mildred the Prize Baby*. *H & J Foulke, Inc.*

Swivel neck, glass eyes:

6in (15cm)	**$625-$675**
8in (20cm)	**$800-$1,000**
10in (25cm)	**$1,000-$1,100**

Swivel neck, painted eyes:

5-6in (13-15cm)	**$325-$375**
8in (20cm)	**$575-$625**
11in (28cm)	**$800-$900**

Mildred, the Prize Baby:

5in (13cm)	**$5,000**

Baby Darling #497: 6in (15cm) **$850**

Limbach (clover mark):

4-5in (10-13cm)	**$55-$85**
7in (18cm)	**$110-$135**
11-12in (28-31cm) fine quality	
	$550-$650

All-Bisque Character Dolls with Glass Eyes: Ca. 1910. Excellent quality with proper parts.

#150, 155:

5-6in (13-15cm)	**$400-$500**
7in (18cm)	**$650**

#156:

5-6in (13-15cm)	**$400-$500**
7in (18cm)	**$850**

#602, swivel neck:

5½-6in (14-15cm)	**$550-$650**

#79, pierced nose:

4½in (12cm)	**$500-$550**

#609, 22: 4½in (12cm) **$425-$450**

Orsini girls, 5in (13cm):

Glass eyes	**$2,200-$2,500**
Painted eyes	**$1,200-$1,300**
7in (18cm) glass eyes	
	$4,000-$5,000**

#222 Our Fairy, glass eyes:

5in (13cm)	**$650-$700**
8½in (22cm)	**$875-$900**
11in (28cm)	**$1,800**

**Not enough sample prices to compute a reliable range.

5in (13cm) all-bisque Orsini *MiMi. H & J Foulke, Inc.*

4¼in (11cm) all-bisque 168 Kestner character girl. *H & J Foulke, Inc.*

4in (10cm) all-bisque *Happifats* girl. *H & J Foulke, Inc.*

All-Bisque Character Dolls: 1913-on. Painted eyes; all in good condition with proper parts.

Pink bisque:

2-3in (5-8cm)	**$55-$65**
5in (13cm)	**$100-$110**
Glass eyes, wig: 2¾in (7cm)	**$85-$95**

Girl with molded hair bow loop:

2½in (6cm)	**$75**

Thumbsucker: 3in (8cm)	**$225-$250**

Chubby:

4½in (11cm)	**$210-$240**
6in (15cm)	**$325-$375**

HEbee, SHEbee:

5in (13cm)	**$650**
7in (18cm)	**$850**
Boxed	**$950**

Peterkin: 5-6in (13-15cm)	**$275-$375**
Little Imp: 5in (13cm)	**$150**

Happifats: 4in (10cm) boy and girl

$500-$600 pair

Happifats Baby:

3¾in (10cm)	**$275-$300**

Wide Awake: 5in (13cm)	**$225**
Little Annie Rooney: 4in (10cm)	**$300**

September Morn, Grace Drayton:

4in (10cm)	**$2,500**
7in (18cm) at auction	**$4,000**

Max & Moritz:

3¾in (9cm)	**$2,000 pair**
4½in (11cm) molded clothes	**$2,500 pair**

Cupid or Sister: 5½in (14cm)	**$100**

Snowflake (Oscar Hitt):

2½in (6cm)	**$250**

#790, 791, 792:

5½-6in (14-15cm)	**$450-$500**

#150, 160, 165:

3¾in (10cm)	**$225**
5½-6in (14-15cm)	**$300-$350**

#168: 4¼in (11cm)	**$350**

Later All-Bisque with painted eyes: Ca. 1920. Many by Limbach (clover mark) and Hertwig & Co.; some of pretinted bisque; mohair wig or molded hair; molded and painted one-strap shoes and white stockings; all in good condition, with proper parts.

3½in (9cm)	**$75-$85**
4½-5in (12-13cm)	**$110-$125**
6in (15cm)	**$160-$185**
7-8in (18-20cm)	**$225-$250**

All-Bisque "Flapper" (tinted bisque): Ca. 1920. Molded bobbed hair with loop for bow, painted features; long yellow stockings, one-strap shoes with heels; all in good condition, with proper parts, very good quality.

5in (13cm)	**$325-$350**
6-7in (15-18cm)	**$450-$500**

Standard quality:

4-5in (10-13cm)	**$135-$165**

All-Bisque Baby: Ca. 1920. Pink bisque, curved arms and legs; all in good condition, with proper parts.

"Candy Baby," original factory clothes:

2½-3in (6-8cm)	**$95-$110**

Two-face, swivel neck:

4in (10cm)	**$150-$175**

All-Bisque "Flapper:" Ca. 1920. Pink bisque with molded bobbed hair; original factory clothes; all in good condition, with proper parts.

3in (8cm)	**$95-$125**
Molded hat	**$250**
Molded bunny ears cap	**$350**
Aviatrix	**$225-$250**
Swivel Waist, 3½in (9cm)	**$350**
Wigged, 3½in (9cm)	**$95-$125**
Adult, 5¾in (14cm)	**$300-$350**

All-Bisque Nodder Characters: Ca. 1920-on. Many made by Hertwig & Co. Nodding heads, elastic strung, molded clothes; all in good condition.

3-4in (8-10cm)	**$35-$50**
Comic characters	**$45 up***
Dressed Animals	**$150-$175**
Dressed Teddy Bears	**$200-$225**
Santa	**$200-$225**
Dutch Girl, 6in (15cm)	**$150-$165**

All-Bisque Immobiles: Ca. 1920. Molded clothes; in good condition.

Adults and children:

1½-2¼in (4-6cm)	**$35-$45**
Children: 3¼in (8cm)	**$55-$65**
Santa: 3in (8cm)	**$125-$135**

Children with animals on string:

3in (8cm)	**$165-$185**

Jointed Animals: Ca. 1910-on. All-bisque animals, wire-jointed shoulders and hips; original crocheted clothes; in good condition.

Rabbit: 2-2¾in (5-7cm)	**$475-$525**
Bear: 2-2½in (5-6cm)	**$450-$500**
Frog, Monkey, Pig	**$600-$700**

Bear on all fours:

3¼in (8cm)	**$225-$275**

*Depending on rarity.

3in (3cm) all-bisque immobile child with animal on string. *H & J Foulke, Inc.*

All-Bisque Dolls (Made in Japan)

Baby:
White: 4in (10cm) **$30-$33**
All-original elaborate outfit **$50-$65**
Two-face, crying and sleeping
$150-$175
Black: 4-5in (10-13cm) **$55-$65**
Bye-Lo Baby: 6in (15cm) **$125**
Betty Boop-type:
4-5in (10-13cm) **$25-$30**
6-7in (15-18cm) **$38-$42**
Black Character Girl:
Molded hair bow loop:
4½in (12cm) **$40-$50**
Bride & Groom: Boxed set,
4in (10cm) **$70-$75**
Buster Brown: 2¾in (7cm) **$40**
Child:
4-5in (10-13cm) **$32-$35**
6-7in (15-18cm) **$40-$50**
5½in (14cm) wigged "Nippon,"
excellent quality **$65-$75**
With animal on string:
4½in (12cm) **$38-$42**

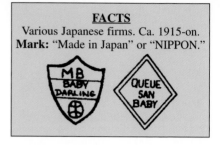

FACTS
Various Japanese firms. Ca. 1915-on.
Mark: "Made in Japan" or "NIPPON."

Stiff with molded clothes:
3-4in (8-10cm) **$10-$15**
Boxed set of five **$80**
6-7in (15-18cm) **$35-$40**
Cho-Cho San: 4½in (12cm) **$70-80**
Circus Set: Boxed, 11 pieces
$150-$175
Comic Characters:
3-4in (8-10cm) **$30 up***
Mickey Mouse **$175-$225**
"Nippon" Characters:
4-5in (10-13cm) **$85-$95**
JolliKids: 3½in (9cm) pair **$175**
Happifats: 3½in (9cm) pair **$275**
Girl with molded hat and shoes:
5¼in (13cm) **$95**
Kewpie: Rose O'Neill:
3½in (9cm) **$75**
Soldier: Molded clothes:
4½in (12cm) **$195**
Baby in Bath Tub:
2½in (6cm) **$55**
Nodders: 4in (10cm) **$25-$35**
Old Woman in Shoe: Boxed set
$225-$250
Orientals: 3-4in (8-10cm) **$20-$25**
Queue San: 4in (10cm) **$70-$80**
Shirley Temple: 5in (13cm) **$100-$125**
Skippy: 5½in (14cm) **$95-$110**
Snow White: Boxed set **$400-$600**
Teddy Bear: 3in (8cm) **$40-$50**
Three Bears: Boxed set **$250-$300**
Three Little Kittens: Boxed set,
at auction **$356**
Three Little Pigs: **$40-$50 each**
Wedding Set: Boxed, three pieces,
4½in (13cm) **$125-$135**

7in (18cm) "Made in Japan" all-bisque
Bye-Lo Baby. H & J Foulke, Inc.

*Depending upon rarity

Alt, Beck & Gottschalck

FACTS
Alt, Beck & Gottschalck, porcelain factory, Nauendorf near Ohrdruf, Thuringia, Germany. 1854-on.

China Shoulder Heads: Ca. 1880. Black or blonde-haired china head; old cloth body with china limbs; dressed; all in good condition. Mold numbers such as **784, 1000, 1008, 1028, 1046, 1142, 1210** and others.

Mark: *1 0 0 8 ✗ 9*

16-18in (41-46cm)	**$300-$350**
22-24in (56-61cm)	**$450-$500**
28in (71cm)	**$650-$750**

Bisque Shoulder Head: Ca. 1880. Molded hair, closed mouth; cloth body with bisque lower limbs; dressed; all in good condition. Mold numbers such as **890, 990, 1000, 1008, 1028, 1064, 1142, 1254, 1288, 1304.**
Painted eyes:

15-17in (38-43cm)	**$375-$425**
22-23in (56-58cm)	**$525-$575**

Glass eyes:

9-11in (23-28cm)	**$300-$350***
14-16in (36-41cm)	**$475-$575***
22in (56cm)	**$950***

#926, molded pink and white scarf on head: 16in (41cm)   **$2,000****
#990, pink mob cap; **#998,** white mob cap: 20in (51cm)   **$850-$950****
#894, blue scarf, glass eyes:
   21in (52cm)   **$1,650-$1,750****
#1024, molded orange bonnet:
   17½in (44cm)   **$2,100****
#1022, short blonde curly hair, molded blue hair band, molded necklace with orange pendant, glass eyes:
   22in (56cm)   **$1,650**
Blue hat with scarf and molded necklace: 5in (12cm), head only   **$1,050**

*Allow extra for unusual or elaborate hairdo or molded hat.
**Not enough sample prices to compute a reliable range.

19in (48cm) 1288 shoulder head. *H & J Foulke, Inc.*

25in (64cm) 1210 shoulder head. *H & J Foulke, Inc.*

15in (38cm) 1260 shoulder head. *H & J Foulke, Inc.*

23in (58cm) 1362 *Sweet Nell. H & J Foulke, Inc.*

Bisque Shoulder Head: Ca. 1885-on. Turned shoulder head, wig, glass eyes, closed mouth; kid or cloth body; dressed; all in good condition. Mold numbers, such as **639, 698, 870, 1032, 1123, 1235.**

Mark: 639 ₩ 6

with "DEP" after 1888

17-19in (43-48cm)	**$600-$700**
23-25in (58-64cm)	**$850-$950**
With open mouth:	
16-18in (41-46cm)	**$375-$425**
21-23in (53-58cm)	**$525-$575**
#911, 916, swivel neck, closed mouth:	
20-23in (51-58cm)	**$1,300-$1,400**
#912:	
21-23in (53-58cm)	**$1,200-$1,300**

Child Doll: Perfect bisque head, open mouth; ball-jointed body in good condition; appropriate clothes.

Mark: 2 ½
AB&G
Made in Germany

#1362 Sweet Nell:	
14-16in (36-41cm)	**$375-$425**
19-21in (43-53cm)	**$475-$525**
23-25in (58-64cm)	**$575-$625**
29-30in (74-76cm)	**$800-$900**
36in (91cm)	**$1,400**
#630, closed mouth:	
23in (58cm)	**$1,900-$2,200**
#911, closed mouth:	
16in (41cm)	**$1,500-$1,600**
#938, closed mouth:	
22in (56cm)	**$4,100****
#989, closed mouth:	
23in (58cm)	**$4,500****

All-Bisque Girl: 1911. Chubby body, molded white stockings, blue garters, black Mary Janes.

Mold #83 over #100, 125, 150 or **225:**	
5-6in (13-15cm)	**$225-$275***
7in (18cm)	**$325-$350***
8in (20cm)	**$475-$525***

*Allow extra for real eyelashes.
**Not enough price examples to compute a reliable range.

All-Bisque Baby:
  8½in (21cm) swivel neck, closed
  mouth **$900-$1,000****
#29-14, character baby, glass eyes,
swivel neck:
  6in (15cm) **$650-$700****

Character: Ca. 1910-on. Perfect
bisque head, good wig, sleep eyes, open
mouth; some with open nostrils; composition body; all in good condition;
suitable clothes.

Mark:

#1322, 1352, 1361:
  10-12in (25-31cm) **$300-$350***
  16-18in (41-46cm) **$475-$525***
  22-23in (56-58cm) **$675-$725***

Toddler:
  8-10in (20-25cm) five-piece body
  $750-$800
  14-16in (36-41cm) **$750-$850**
#1329, 1321: 17-18in (43-46cm)
toddler **$1,700-$1,800**
#1357:
  16-18in (41-46cm) **$1,100-$1,300**
#1407 Baby Bo Kaye:
  8in (20cm) **$1,350**
#1431 Orsini, earthenware baby:
  24in (61cm) **$900-$1,100****
#1450, smiling child:
  14in (36cm) **$16,000-$17,000****

*Allow $50 extra for flirty eyes.
**Not enough sample prices to compute a
reliable range.

13in (33cm) 1361 toddler. *H & J
Foulke, Inc.*

14in (36cm) 1450 character child.
Carmel Doll Shop.

Louis Amberg & Son

Newborn Babe, Bottle Babe, My Playmate: Ca. 1914-on. Perfect bisque head, painted hair, sleep eyes; soft cloth body; appropriate clothes; all in good condition. Mold **886** by Recknagel. Mold **371** with open mouth by Marseille.

Mark:
L·A·&·S·
371·3⁄0 D·R·G·M·
Germany

THE ORIGINAL
NEWBORN BABE
(C) Jan. 9th 1914 — No. G 45520
AMBERG DOLLS
The World Standard

Length:
9-10in (23-25cm)	**$275-$300**
13-14in (33-36cm)	**$400-$500**
17in (43cm)	**$600-$650**

Charlie Chaplin: 1915. Composition portrait head, molded mustache; straw-filled cloth body with composition hands; original clothes; all in good condition with wear.
Mark: cloth label on sleeve:
14in (36cm)	**$600-$650**

AmKid: 1918. Composition shoulder head, sleep eyes, wig; kidolene body, composition arms.
22in (56cm)	**$125-$150**

Mibs: 1921. Composition shoulder head designed by Hazel Drucker with wistful expression, molded blonde or reddish hair; cloth body with composition arms and legs with painted shoes and socks; appropriate old clothes; all in good condition.
Mark: None on doll; paper label only:
"Amberg Dolls
Please Love Me
I'm Mibs"

16in (41cm)	**$950-$1,050**

FACTS
Louis Amberg & Son,
New York, NY, U.S.A. 1907-on.

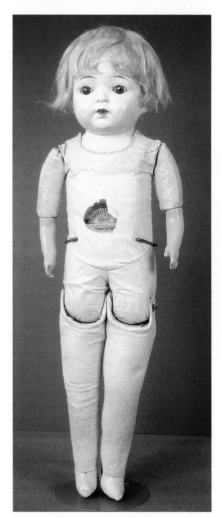

22in (56cm) *AmKid* with composition head. *H & J Foulke, Inc.*

Mibs: 1921. Bisque shoulder head only, at auction **$650**

Baby Peggy: 1923. Composition head, molded brown bobbed hair, smiling closed mouth; appropriately dressed; all in good condition.
    20in (51cm)   **$650-$750****

Baby Peggy: 1924. Perfect bisque head by Armand Marseille with character face, brown bobbed mohair wig, brown sleep eyes, closed mouth; composition or kid body, fully-jointed; dressed or undressed; all in very good condition.
Mark: "19 © 24
            LA & S NY
            Germany
            —50—
            982/2"

#982 or **983,** shoulder head:
    20in (51cm)   **$1,600-$1,800**
#972 or **973,** socket head:
    18-22in (46-56cm)   **$2,000-$2,200**

**Not enough price samples to compute a reliable range.

Below: 17in (43cm) composition *Mibs.* *H & J Foulke, Inc.*

7in (15cm) pink all-bisque girl with glass eyes and downward gaze. *H & J Foulke, Inc.*

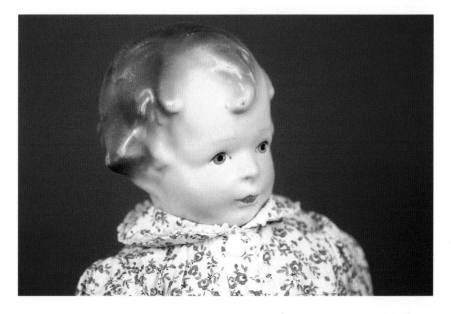

All-Bisque Character Children:
1920s. Made by a German porcelain factory, probably Hertwig & Co.; pink pretinted bisque.

4in (10cm)	**$125**
5-6in (13-15cm)	**$160-$185**

Girl with molded bow:

6in (15cm)	**$375-$425**

Girl with downward gaze, glass eyes, wig:

5½in (14cm)	**$475-$525**
7in (18cm)	**$600-$650**

Mibs:

3in (8cm)	**$250**
4¾in (12cm)	**$400-$425**
6in (15cm)	**$525-$550**

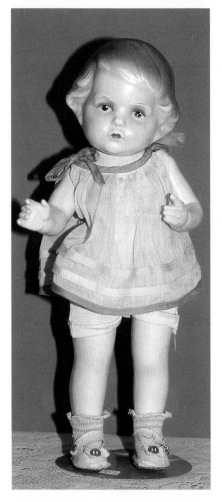

Baby Peggy:

3in (8cm)	**$325-$350**
5½in (14cm)	**$500-$550**
4½in (12cm) wigged	**$475-$525**

Mibs-type girl with molded flowers in hair: 4¾in (12cm)   **$225**

Vanta Baby: 1927. A tie-in with Vanta baby garments. Composition or bisque head with molded and painted hair, sleep eyes, open mouth with two teeth; suitably dressed; all in good condition.
Mark: Bisque Head

Vanta Baby
L ABS · ⅗₀ D.R.G.M.
Germany.

Bisque head:

10in (25cm)	**$550-$600**
20-22in (51-56cm)	**$1,000-$1,100**

Composition head, excellent condition:

18-20in (46-51cm)	**$325-$375**
All original in tagged clothes	**$450**

Sue, Edwina or It: 1928. All-composition with round ball joint at waist, appropriate clothes.

14in (36cm)	**$425-$475**

Tiny Tots Body Twists: 1928. All-composition with large round ball joint at the waist.

8in (20cm)	**$135-$165**
Little Amby, all original with paper label, at auction	**$300**

Sunny Orange Maid: 1924. Composition/cloth; molded "orange" hat; orange dress.

14in (36cm) at auction	**$1,100**

Peter Pan: 1928. All-composition with round ball joint at waist.

Original Peter Pan outfit	**$500**
Re-dressed	**$300-$350**

14in (36cm) *Edwina*, all original. *Kathy & Terri's Dolls.*

Georgene Averill
(Madame Hendren & Georgene Novelties, Inc.)

Bonnie Babe: 1926. Bisque heads by Alt, Beck & Gottschalck; cloth bodies by K & K Toy Co.; distributed by George Borgfeldt & Co., New York. Perfect bisque head with smiling face, open mouth with two lower teeth; cloth body with composition arms (sometimes celluloid) and legs often of poor quality; all in good condition. Mold #1386 or 1402.

Mark: *Copr. by Georgene Averill Germany 1005/3652 1386*

Length:
12-13in (31-33cm)	**$900-$1,000**
16-18in (41-46cm)	**$1,200-$1,400**
22-23in (56-58cm)	**$1,600-$1,700**

Composition body:
8in (20cm) tall	**$1,250****

Celluloid head:
16in (41cm) tall	**$550-$650****

All-Bisque Bonnie Babe: 1926.
5in (13cm)	**$1,000-$1,000**
7in (18cm)	**$1,500-$1,600**

Rag or Tag: All-bisque dog or cat with swivel neck, glass eyes; molded booties, crocheted yarn tail.
Mark: Incised "RAG TRADE MARK Copr. By Georgene Averill 890 Germany."
Tag is mold 891.
5in (13cm)	**$3,500****
Boxed, at auction	**$4,725**

Allie Dog: Bisque dog head by Alt, Beck & Gottschalck, glass eyes, smiling open mouth with teeth and tongue; cloth or fur body. **Mark:** "ALLIE DOG Copr. By Georgene Averill Germany 1405."
12-15in (31-38cm)	**$7,500-$8,000**

**Not enough price samples to compute a reliable range.

FACTS
Averill Mfg. Co. and Georgene Novelties, Inc., New York, NY, U.S.A. 1915-on.
Designer: Georgene Averill.
Trademarks: Madame Hendren, Georgene Novelties.

Sunny Boy and Girl: Ca. 1927. Celluloid "turtle" mark head; stuffed body with composition arms and legs; appropriate or original clothes; all in good condition.
15in (38cm)	**$350-$450**

Composition Dolls: All appropriately dressed in good condition.
Mme. Hendren Character: Ca. 1915-on. Original tagged felt costume, including Dutch children, Indians, cowboys, sailors:
10-14in (25-36cm)	**$150-$200**

7in (18cm) *Bonnie Babe. H & J Foulke, Inc.*

Mama and Baby Dolls: Ca. 1918-on. Composition with cloth bodies; names such as *Baby Hendren* and *Baby Georgene:*

    15-18in (38-46cm)   **$250-$300**
    22-24in (56-61cm)   **$400-$450**

Dolly Reckord: 1922. Record-playing mechanism in torso, with records:

    26in (66cm)   **$600-$700**

Grace G. Drayton: 1920s.

    Chocolate Drop with yarn pigtails:
    14in (36cm)   **$575**
    Bobby: 14in (36cm)   **$400-$425**

Whistling Doll: 1925-1929. Doll whistles when feet are pushed up or head is pushed down, 14-15in (36-38cm):

    Dan, sailor or cowboy: **$300-$350**
    Black Rufus or **Dolly Dingle**
                    $450-$475

Snookums: 1927.

    14in (36cm)   **$350-$375**

Body Twists: 1927. **Dimmie** and **Jimmie** with a large round ball joint at waist:

    14½in (37cm)   **$425-$475**

Patsy-type Girl, Peaches: 1928.

    14in (36cm)   **$325-$350**
    17-18in (43-46cm   )**$400-$450**

Lenci-type Girl: Ca. 1930. Lenci-style, composition face (some flocked); original felt and organdy clothes, may have **Val-Encia** tag:

    19in (48cm)   **$400-$500****

Little Cherub: 1937. Designed by Harriet Flanders; original clothes.

    16in (41cm)   **$300-$400**
    12in (31cm) painted eyes **$225-$250**

*Not enough price samples to compute a reliable range.

13in (33cm) whistling *Texas Centennial Cowboy,* all original. *H & J Foulke, Inc.*

14in *Peaches*, all original. *H & J Foulke, Inc.*

Cloth Dolls: Original clothes; all in excellent condition, clean with bright color.

Children or Babies:

12in (31cm)	**$135-$165**
24-26in (61-66cm)	**$225-$275**

International and Costume Dolls:

12in (31cm)	**$75-$100**
Mint-in-box with wrist tag	**$110-$135**

Girl Scout or Brownie:

13in (33cm) with complete outfit	**$225-$250**

Becassine:

8in (20cm)	**$400-$450**
13-15in (33-38cm)	**$700-$900**

Uncle Wiggily or Nurse Jane:

18-20in (46-51cm)	**$650-$750**

Comic Characters:

Little Lulu	**$400-$500**
Nancy, Sluggo, Tubby Tom:	
14in (36cm)	**$500-$600**

Topsy Turvy:

Topsy & Eva,	
10in (25cm)	**$175-$225**

Kris Kringle: vinyl face: 10in (25cm) boxed with tag   **$145**

Maud Tousey Fangel: 1938.

Snooks, Sweets, Peggy-Ann: Marked "M.T.F." Bright color, all original.

12-14in (31-36cm)	**$650-$750**
17in (43cm)	**$850-$900**
22in (56cm)	**$1,100-$1,250**

Grace G. Drayton: Good clean condition, some wear acceptable.

Chocolate Drop: 1923. Brown cloth with three yarn pigtails:

11in (28cm)	**$450-$500**
16in (41cm)	**$750-$850**

Dolly Dingle: 1923:

11in (28cm)	**$400-$450**
16in (41cm)	**$600-$650**
10in (25cm) double-faced	**$750**

Vinyl Dolls:

Baby Dawn: Ca. 1950. Vinyl and cloth, all original and excellent.

19in (48cm)	**$350**

13in (33cm) *Becassine*, all original. *Kay Jensen Antique Dolls.*

11in (28cm) *Holland Boy*, all original with tag. *H & J Foulke, Inc.*

Baby Bo Kaye

Baby Bo Kaye: Perfect bisque head with flange neck (marked as shown), molded hair, glass eyes, open mouth with two lower teeth; cloth torso with composition limbs; dressed; all in good condition.

16-19in (41-48cm)   **$2,400-$2,800**
Celluloid head: 16in (41cm)   **$750**
#1407 (ABG) bisque head; composition body: 7½in (19cm)   **$1,350**

All-Bisque Baby Bo Kaye: Molded hair, glass sleep eyes, open mouth with two teeth; swivel neck, jointed shoulders and hips; molded pink or blue shoes and socks; unmarked but may have sticker on torso:

5in (13cm)   **$1,500-$1,600**
6in (15cm)   **$2,000**

FACTS
Bisque heads made in Germany by Alt, Beck & Gottschalck; bodies by K & K Toy Co., New York, NY, U.S.A. 1925.
Designer: J.L. Kallus.
Distributor: George Borgfeldt & Co., New York, NY
Mark: "Copr. by J.L. Kallus Germany 1394/30"

5in (13cm) all-bisque *Baby Bo Kaye. H & J Foulke, Inc.*

Babyland Rag

Babyland Rag: Cloth face with hand-painted features, sometimes mohair wig; cloth body jointed at shoulders and hips; original clothes.
Mark: None

FACTS
E. I. Horsman, New York, NY, U.S.A.
Some dolls made for Horsman by
Albert Brückner. 1901-on.

Early face (hand-painted features):
  13-15in (33-38cm):
    Very good   **$750-$850**
    Fair   **$400-$500**
  22in (56cm):
    Very good   **$1,000-$1,200**
    Fair   **$550-$600**
  30in (76cm) Very good
                $2,000-$2,200
  Topsy Turvy: 13-15in (33-38cm)
    Very good   **$700-$800**
  Buster Brown: 30in (76cm)
    Very good   **$2,200**
  Black:
    15in (38cm) Fair   **$700-$800**
    20-22in (51-56cm) Very good
                $1,500-$1,600

Life-like face (printed features):
  13-15in (33-38cm) Very good
                $600-$650

Topsy Turvy: 14in (36cm) Good
                $700-$800

Babyland Rag-type (lesser quality):
  14in (36cm) White
    Good   **$375-$475**

Brückner Rag Doll: Stiffened mask face, cloth body, flexible shoulders and hips; appropriate clothes; all in good condition.
  12-14in (31-36cm)
    White   **$210-$235**
    Black   **$400-$450**
    Topsy Turvy   **$550-$600**
Dollypop and other dolls with printed faces: 12in (31cm)   **$250**
Mark:

PAT'D. JULY 8ᵀᴴ 1901

30in (76cm) *Babyland* Rag with hand-painted features. *H & J Foulke, Inc.*

Bähr & Pröschild

Marked Belton-type Child Doll: Ca. 1880. Perfect bisque head, solid dome with flat top having two or three small holes, paperweight eyes, closed mouth with pierced ears; wood and composition jointed body with straight wrists; dressed; all in good condition. Mold numbers in 200 series.

Mark: "204"

12-14in (30-36cm)	**$1,750-$2,000**
18-20in (46-51cm)	**$2,500-$2,800**
24in (61cm)	**$3,200-$3,500**

Marked Child Doll: Ca. 1888-on. Perfect bisque socket head, good human hair or mohair wig, set or sleep eyes, open mouth with four or six upper teeth; jointed composition body (many of French-type); dressed; all in good condition. Mold numbers in 200 and 300 series.

Mark: "224"

   dep

17in (43cm) 204 Belton-type child with closed mouth. *H & J Foulke, Inc.*

> **FACTS**
> Bähr & Pröschild, porcelain factory, Ohrdruf, Thuringia, Germany. Made heads for Bruno Schmidt, Heinrich Stier, Kley & Hahn and others. 1871-on.

#204, 239, 273, 275, 277, 289, 297, 300, 325, 340, 379, 394 and other socket heads:

12-13in (30-33cm)	**$500-$550**
16-18in (41-46cm)	**$600-$700**
22-24in (56-61cm)	**$850-$950**

#208, 209: 8-8½in (20-21cm) jointed body with molded shoes **$850-$950**

#224 (dimples):

14-16in (36-41cm)	**$750-$800**
22-24in (56-61cm)	**$1,100-$1,200**

#246, 309 and other shoulder heads on kid bodies:

16-18in (41-46cm)	**$400-$425**
22-24in (56-61cm)	**$525-$575**

#302, 325, swivel neck, kid body:

17in (43cm)	**$525-$550**
20in (51cm)	**$600-$650**

#513, possibly by B.P.:

22-26in (56-66cm)	**$650-$700**

All-Bisque Girl, yellow stockings (heart mark):

5in (13cm)	**$375-$425**
7in (18cm)	**$550-$600**

Marked B.P. Character Baby: Ca. 1910-on. Perfect bisque socket head, solid dome or good wig, sleep eyes, open mouth; composition bent-limb baby body; dressed; all in good condition. Mold **#585, 604, 624, 678, 619, 620** and **587.**

Mark: 585
5
8
B⨯P
o⚬
Germany

12-14in (31-36cm)	**$425-$475**
17-19in (43-48cm)	**$550-$600**
23-25in (58-64cm)	**$800-$900**
Toddler, fully-jointed body:	
12-13in (31-33cm)	**$750-$800**
22in (56cm)	**$1,200**
Toddler, five-piece body:	
10-12in (25-31cm)	**$550**
14in (36cm)	**$650**
#425, All-bisque baby:	
5½-6in (13-15cm)	**$300-$350**

23in (58cm) 289 child with open mouth. *H & J Foulke, Inc.*

11in (28cm) 585 character baby. *H & J Foulke, Inc.*

Belton-Type (So-called)

Belton-type Child Doll: Perfect bisque socket head, solid crown with one, two or three small holes for stringing or attaching wig, paperweight eyes, closed mouth, pierced ears; wood and composition ball-jointed body with straight wrists; dressed; all in good condition.

TR 809: 17in (43cm)   **$1,600-$1,650**

Bru-type face:
    12-14in (30-35cm)   **$2,500-$3,000**

French-type face, fine early quality (some mold **#137** or **#183**):
    13-15in (33-38cm)   **$1,900-$2,200**
    18-20in (46-51cm)   **$2,600-$2,900**
    22-24in (56-61cm)   **$3,200-$3,500**

German-type face, good quality:
    8-9in (20-23cm) five-piece body
                        $850-$950
    12in (31cm)   **$1,250-$1,450**
    15-17in (38-43cm)   **$1,600-$1,800**
    20in (51cm)   **$2,200-$2,400**

#200 Series, see Bähr & Pröschild, page 42.

FACTS
Various German firms, such as Bähr & Pröschild. 1875-on.
Mark:
None, except sometimes numbers.

Below: 15in (38cm) 177 Belton-type child. *H & J Foulke, Inc.*

12½in (32cm) 137 Belton-type child with "E.G." signed body. *H & J Foulke, Inc.*

C.M. Bergmann

FACTS
C. M. Bergmann
doll factory of
Waltershausen,
Thuringia, Germany;
heads manufactured
for this company by
Armand Marseille;
Simon & Halbig; Alt,
Beck & Gottschalck
and perhaps others.
1888-on.
Distributor: Louis
Wolfe & Co.,
New York, NY
Trademarks:
Cinderella Baby
(1897),
Columbia (1904),
My Gold Star (1926).
Mark:

CM BERGMANN
A-H½-M.
Made in Germany

C.M. Bergmann
Waftershausen
Germany
1916
6½a

20in (51cm) Bergmann child with head made by Simon & Halbig. *H & J Foulke, Inc.*

Bergmann Child Doll: Ca. 1889-on. Marked bisque head, good wig, sleep or set eyes, open mouth; composition ball-jointed body; dressed; all in nice condition.
#1916, heads by **A.M.** and unknown makers:

10in (25cm)	**$400**
14-16in (36-41cm)	**$350-$375**
20-22in (51-56cm)	**$450-$475**
25in (64cm)	**$525**
28-29in (71-74cm)	**$575-$625**
32-33in (81-84cm)	**$750-$850**
35-36in (89-91cm)	**$1,100-$1,200**
39-42in (99-111cm)	**$1,700-$2,000**

Heads marked **"Simon & Halbig":**

10in (25cm)	**$500-$600**
13-15in (33-38cm)	**$400-$450**
18-20in (46-51cm)	**$500-$525**
23-24in (58-61cm)	**$550-$575**
29-30in (81-91cm)	**$750-$850**
35-36in (81-91cm)	**$1,500-$1,650**
39in (99cm)	**$2,300-$2,500**
Eleonore: 25in (64cm)	**$700-$800**

#612 Character Baby, open-closed mouth:
14-16in (36-41cm) **$2,200-$2,400**
#134 Character Toddler:
12in (31cm) **$950**

Bisque, French
(Makers Not Listed Separately)

Marked A.L. Bébé: Ca. 1875. Possibly Alexander Lefebvre & Cie. Perfect pressed bisque socket head, closed mouth, paperweight eyes; French wood and composition jointed body; appropriate clothing; all in good condition.

22in (56cm) at auction **$35,000**

Marked B.M. Bébé: 1880-1895. Alexandre Mothereau. Perfect pressed bisque socket head, closed mouth, paperweight eyes; French wood and composition jointed body; appropriate clothing; all in good condition.

12-15in (31-38cm) **$11,000-$12,500**
33in (84cm) **$28,000**

Marked C.P. Bébé: Ca. 1875. Possibly Pannier. Perfect pressed bisque socket head, closed mouth, paperweight eyes; French wood and composition body; appropriate clothing; all in good condition.

20in (51cm) at auction **$58,500**

Marked F.R. Bébé: Ca. 1880s. Falck & Roussel. Perfect bisque socket head, closed mouth, paperweight eyes; French wood and composition body; appropriate clothing; all in good condition.

16-18in (41-46cm) **$14,000-$17,000**

Marked H. Bébé: Ca. late 1870s. Possibly by A. Halopeau. Perfect pressed bisque socket head of fine quality, cork pate, good wig, paperweight eyes, pierced ears, closed mouth; French wood and composition jointed body with straight wrists; appropriate clothing; all in excellent condition.

Mark:  2 • H

Size:	0 = 16½in (42cm)
	2 = 19in (48cm)
	3 = 21in (56cm)
	4 = 24in (61cm)

21-24in (53-61cm) **$65,000-$75,000**

18in (46cm)
F.R. Bébé.
Floyd Jones.

14in (36cm) J. Bébé.
*Kay Jensen Antique
Dolls.*

Huret Child: Ca. 1878. Maison Huret.
Perfect bisque head; appropriate cloth-
ing; all in excellent condition.
Gutta-percha body:
18in (46cm)   **$70,000-$80,000**
Wood body: 18in (46cm)   **$34,000**

Marked J. Bébé: Ca. 1880s. Joseph
Louis Joanny. Perfect pressed bisque
socket head, paperweight eyes, closed
mouth; French wood and composition
body; appropriate clothing; all in good
condition.
12in (31cm)   **$3,500**
17-18in (43-46cm)   **$5,000-$5,500**
27in (69cm) at auction   **$19,500**

Marked J.M. Bébé: Ca. 1880s. Perfect
pressed bisque socket head, good wig,
paperweight eyes, closed mouth,
pierced ears; French composition and
wood body; appropriate clothing; all in
good condition.
Mark:

23in (58cm)   **$18,500**

Marked M. Bébé: Mid 1890s. Perfect
bisque socket head, good wig, closed
mouth, paperweight eyes, pierced ears;
French jointed composition and wood
body; appropriate clothing; all in good
condition. Some dolls with this mark
may be **Bébé Mascottes.**
Mark: M
4
19-23in (48-58cm)   **$3,100-$3,500**

24in (61cm) M. Bébé.
Private Collection.

Marked Bébé Mascotte: 1890-1897, May Freres Cie; 1898-on. Jules Nicholas Steiner. Perfect bisque socket head, closed mouth, paperweight eyes; pierced ears; jointed composition and wood body; appropriate clothing; all in good condition.

10-12in (25-31cm)	**$2,250-$2,500**
19-20in (48-51cm)	**$3,600-$3,700**
24in (61cm)	**$4,500**

Marked P.D. Bébé: 1878-1890. Petit & Dumontier, Paris. Perfect bisque head with good wig, paperweight eyes, closed mouth, pierced ears; jointed composition body (some with metal hands); appropriate clothes; all in good condition.

16in (41cm)	**$10,500**
19-23in (48-58cm)	**$13,500-$15,500**

Mark: P.2.D

Marked P.G. Bébé: Ca. 1880-1899. Pintel & Godchaux, Montreuil, France. Perfect bisque socket head, good wig, paperweight eyes, closed mouth; jointed French composition and wood body; appropriate clothing; all in good condition.

Trademark: Bébé Charmant
Mark: B   A
           P9G   P7G

20-22in (51-56cm)	**$3,000-$3,200**

Open mouth:

18-20in (46-51cm)	**$1,600-$1,800**

Marked PAN Bébé: Ca. 1887. Henri Delcroix, Paris and Montreuil-sous-Bois (porcelain factory). Perfect bisque socket head, good wig, paperweight eyes, closed mouth, pierced ears; French composition and wood body; appropriate clothes; all in good condition.

Mark: PAN
          2

Size:	2 = 12in (31cm)
	10 = 27in (68cm)
	11 = 28½in (72cm)

12in (31cm)	**$6,000-$7,000****

Marked Van Rozen: Ca, 1912. Character dolls made from a bisque-like material; glass eyes, wig.

17-19in (43-48cm)	**$9,000-$10,000****

For lady and fashion dolls *(poupées)* see pages 82-83.
**Not enough price samples to compute a reliable range.

19in (58cm) Van Rozen lady. *Private Collection.*

Bisque, German
Unmarked or Makers Not Listed Separately

Shoulder head with molded hair: Ca. 1880. Tinted bisque shoulder head with beautifully molded hair (usually blonde), closed mouth; original kid or cloth body, bisque lower arms; appropriate clothes; all in good condition.

American Schoolboy:

12-14in (31-36cm)	**$475-$550**
17-20in (43-51cm)	**$650-$750**

Composition body, socket head:

11-12in (28-31cm)	**$650-$750**

Boy or girl, painted eyes:

14-16in (36-41cm)	**$300-$400**

Boy or girl, glass eyes:

16in (41cm)	**$600-$650**

Lady, painted eyes:

12-14in (31-36cm)	**$300-$350**

Hatted or Bonnet Doll: Ca. 1880-1920. Bisque shoulder head, molded bonnet; original cloth body with bisque arms and legs; good old clothes or nicely dressed; all in good condition.

Standard quality:

8-9in (20-23cm)	**$210-$265**
11-13in (28-33cm)	**$325-$375**
15in (38cm)	**$450-$500**
18in (46cm)	**$600**

Fine quality:

18-22in (46-56cm)	**$1,000 up***

All-bisque:

4½in (12cm)	**$175-$195***
7in (18cm)	**$250-$300***

*Allow extra for unusual style.

FACTS
Various German firms. 1860s-on.
Mark: Some numbered, some "Germany," some both.

12in (31cm) bonnet bisque lady. *H & J Foulke, Inc.*

9in (23cm) so-called "American Schoolboy." *H & J Foulke, Inc.*

Dolls' House Doll: Ca. 1890-1920. Man or lady bisque shoulder head; cloth body, bisque lower limbs; original clothes or suitably dressed; all in nice condition.

4½-7in (12-18cm):

Molded hair, glass eyes, ca. 1870
$450-$500

Girl with bangs, ca. 1880, all original
$210

Victorian man with mustache
$200-$225

Victorian lady, all original   **$200**

Lady with glass eyes and wig
$350-$400

Man with mustache, original military uniform   **$1,200-$1,500**

Chauffeur with molded cap
$350-$400

Black man   **$650-$700**

Maid, all original   **$110-$135**

1920s man or lady   **$100-$125**

1920s man with molded hat, all original   **$225**

Child Doll with closed mouth: Ca. 1880-1890. Perfect bisque head, good wig, glass eyes; nicely dressed; all in good condition, excellent quality.

Kid or cloth body:

17-19in (43-48cm)   **$600-$700***

23-25in (58-64cm)   **$850-$950***

#50 shoulder head:

14-16in (35-41cm)   **$800-$900**

22in (56cm)   **$1,250-$1,300**

#132, 120, 126 Bru-type face:

13-14in (33-36cm)   **$2,500-$2,800**

19-21in (48-53cm)   **$3,800-$4,000**

#51, swivel neck shoulder head:

17-19in (43-48cm)   **$1,200-$1,500**

#86, Bru-type Nurser:

13in (33cm) at auction   **$1,000**

*Allow 30 percent extra for swivel neck fashion-type model.

6in (15cm) dolls' house lady with glass eyes and original wig. *H & J Foulke, Inc.*

18in (46cm) shoulder head with closed mouth. *H & J Foulke, Inc.*

Composition body (German look):
11-13in (28-33cm) **$1,250-$1,350**
16-19in (41-48cm) **$1,650-$1,850**
#136 (French look):
12-15in (31-38cm) **$1,900-$2,100**
19-21in (48-53cm) **$2,500-$2,800**
E. G. (Ernst Grossman):
16in (41cm) **$2,600**

Child Doll with open mouth "Dolly Face": 1888-on. Perfect bisque head, good wig, glass eyes, open mouth; ball-jointed composition body or kid body with bisque lower arms; dressed; all in good condition. Very good quality; including dolls marked "G.B.," and "K" inside "H," "L.H.K.," "P.Sch.," "D&K."
12-14in (31-35cm) **$375-$425**
18-20in (46-51cm) **$500-$550**
23-25in (58-64cm) **$600-$700**
30-32in (76-81cm) **$1,000-$1,200**
#50, 51, square teeth:
14-16in (36-41cm) **$950-$1,050**
#444, 478, 422, 457:
17in (43cm) **$600-$650**
23-25in (58-64cm) **$800-$900**
35in (81cm) **$1,600-$1,800**
Standard quality; including **My Sweetheart, Princess, My Girlie, My Dearie, Pansy, Viola, G & S, MOA** and **A.W.**:
18-20in (46-51cm) **$250-$300**
24-26in (61-66cm) **$375-$425**
32-33in (81-84cm) **$600-$700**

Small Child Doll: 1890 to World War I. Perfect bisque socket head, set or sleep eyes; five-piece composition body; cute clothes; all in good condition.
Very good quality (Simon & Halbig-type):
5-6in (13-15cm) **$350**
8-10in (20-25cm) **$400-$450**
Fully-jointed body:
7-8in (18-20cm) **$600-$650**
Closed mouth:
4½-5½in (12-14cm) all original **$500**
8in (20cm) **$750-$850**

Standard quality:
5-6in (13-15cm) **$100-$125**
8-10in (20-25cm) **$175-$200**
#39-13, five-piece mediocre body, original clothes:
5in (13cm) glass eyes **$175-$200**
Painted eyes **$90-$100**
#13a Georg Bruchlos: glass eyes; mediocre body; original clothes.
5in (13cm) **$175-$200**

Globe Baby: 1898. Carl Hartmann.
8in (20cm) **$325**
8in (20cm) all-original clothes and wig **$400-$450**
12in (31cm) **$450-$550**

14in (36cm) child, incised "23 3x DEP."
H & J Foulke, Inc.

Character Baby: Ca. 1910-on. Perfect bisque head, good wig or solid dome with painted hair, sleep eyes, open mouth; composition bent-limb baby body; suitably dressed; all in good condition. Including dolls marked "G.B.," "S&Q," "P.M." and "F.B."

9-10in (23-25cm)	**$200-$250**
14-16in (35-41cm)	**$300-$350**
19-21in (48-53cm)	**$400-$450**
23-24in (58-61cm)	**$550-$650**

My Sweet Baby:
23in (58cm) toddler   **$1,000-$1,200**
#110, A. Wislizenus toddler:
15in (38cm)   **$1,100-$1,200**

Character Doll: Ca. 1910-on. Perfect bisque head, jointed composition body; dressed; all in good condition.

#111: 18-20in (46-51cm)	**$20,000****
#125, smiling:	
13in (33cm) at auction	**$6,380**
#128: 18-20in (46-51cm)	**$25,000****
#159: 23in (58cm)	**$1,150**
#163: 14in (36cm)	**$550-$600**
#213, Bawo & Dotter:	
12in (31cm) at auction	**$7,250**
#214, Bawo & Dotter:	
14in (36cm)	**$4,800-$5,200**
#221, toddler: 16in (41cm)	**$2,500****
#411, lady shoulder head:	
14in (36cm)	**$3,500****
#838, P.M. "Coquette":	
11-12in (28-31cm)	**$550-$600**

11in (28cm) P.M. 828 "Coquette." *H & J Foulke, Inc.*

Infant, unmarked or unidentified maker: Ca. 1924-on. Perfect bisque head; cloth body; dressed; all in good condition. **Baby Weygh, IV** and others.

10-12in (25-31cm) long	**$225-$275**
15-18in (38-46cm) long	**$400-$425**
#1924, composition body:	
9in (23cm)	**$235**
HvB: 15in (38cm) long	**$450**
Gerling Baby:	
17in (43cm) long	**$550-$600**

**Not enough price samples to compute a reliable range.

16in (41cm) 221 character toddler. *Linda Kellermann.*

Bisque, Japanese
(Caucasian Dolls)

Character Baby: Perfect bisque socket head with solid dome or wig, glass eyes, open mouth with teeth, dimples; composition bent-limb baby body; dressed; all in good condition.

9-10in (23-25cm)	**$110-$125***
13-15in (33-38cm)	**$150-$200***
19-21in (48-53cm)	**$275***
24in (61cm)	**$350-$450***

Hilda look-alike, RE Nippon:

19in (48cm)	**$750-$850***

Heubach Pouty look-alike, F.Y. Nippon 300 Series:

17-18in (43-46cm)	**$800-$900***

Child Doll: Perfect bisque head, mohair wig, glass sleep eyes, open mouth; jointed composition or kid body; dressed; all in good condition.

14-16in (36-41cm)	**$200-$250**
20-22in (51-56cm)	**$300-$350**
26-28in (66-71cm)	**$450-$500**

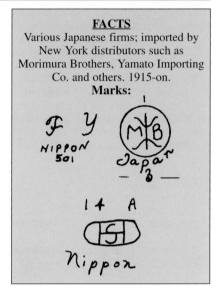

FACTS
Various Japanese firms; imported by New York distributors such as Morimura Brothers, Yamato Importing Co. and others. 1915-on.
Marks:

*Do not pay as much for doll with inferior bisque head.

All-Bisque Dolls: See page 30.

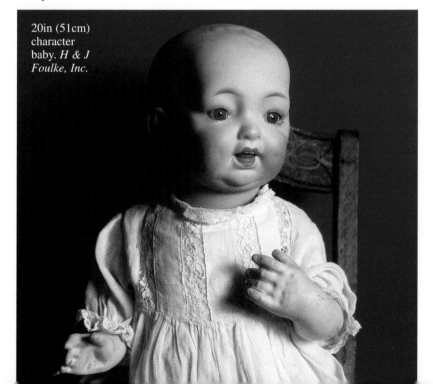

20in (51cm) character baby. *H & J Foulke, Inc.*

Black Bisque Doll: Ca. 1880-on. Various French and German manufacturers from their regular molds or specially designed ones with Negroid features. Perfect bisque socket head either painted dark or with dark coloring mixed in the slip, running from light brown to very dark; composition or sometimes kid body in a matching color; cloth bodies on some baby dolls; appropriate clothing; all in good condition.

French Makers:
B.M., closed mouth:
15in (38cm) Portrait doll, all original, at auction   **$24,000**
Bru:
Circle Dot: 17in (43cm)   **$30,000**
Poupée Peau: 17in (43cm) original Eastern costume   **$9,800**
E.D., open mouth: 16in (41cm) **$2,200**
Eden Bébé, open mouth:
15in (38cm)   **$2,400**

*Also see entry for specific maker of doll or for material of doll.

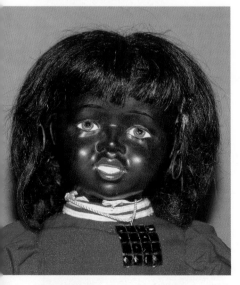

21in (53cm) rare R.A. character child. *Laraine & Gangolf Freisberg.*

Jumeau:
Bébé, open mouth:
10in (25cm)   **$1,650**
13in (33cm)   **$2,200-$2,300**
20in (51cm)   **$3,100-$3,300**
DEP, open mouth:
16in (41cm)   **$2,500**
Poupée Peau: 15in (38cm) original Eastern costume   **$9,000**
Lanternier:
18-20in (46-51cm)   **$950-$1,250**
Paris Bébé, closed mouth:
13in (33cm)   **$3,800-$4,200**
S.F.B.J. #301, fully-jointed body:
10in (25cm)   **$1,100-$1,200**
16in (41cm) original Eastern costume   **$1,500-$1,600**
Steiner, Figure A:
15-16in (38-41cm) open mouth   **$3,000-$3,500**
22in (56cm) original operatic costume, at auction   **$36,000**

German Makers:
#120, Bru-type mulatto, closed mouth:
9½in (24cm) at auction   **$2,750**
Bähr & Pröschild #277:
12in (30cm)   **$1,000**
Belton-type 179:
14in (36cm)   **$3,000-$4,000**
Gebrüder Heubach #7657:
Shoulder head only   **$625**
H. Handwerck:
18-21in (46-53cm)   **$1,600-$1,800**

E. Heubach, #399, 414, 452:
7½in (19cm) toddler   **$425-$450**
10-12in (25-30cm)   **$500-$550**
#444, 13in (33cm)   **$650**
#463, 10-12in (25-30cm)   **$750**
#300, 6in (15cm)   **$450-$500**
#316, 18in (46cm)   **$1,925**
#418, 14in (38cm)   **$1,100**
Kämmer & Reinhardt:
Child, 16in (41cm)   **$1,500-$1,700**
#100 Baby:
11in (28cm)   **$800-$900**
19in (48cm)   **$1,800**
#101:
13-14in (33-36cm)   **$4,000-$4,500**

Right: 17in (43cm) Simon & Halbig
1358 character. *Connie & Jay Lowe.*

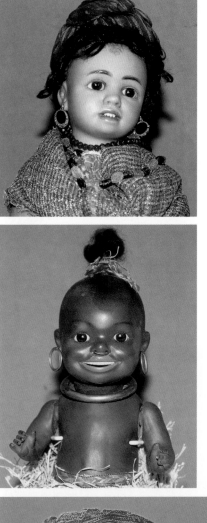

#126, toddler:
   8-9in (20-23cm)   **$1,250**
   #192: 21in (53cm)   **$2,500-$2,650**
J. D. Kestner:
   Child, 16in (41cm)   **$1,600-$1,800**
   Hilda, 18in (46cm)   **$4,000-$4,500**
Kuhnlenz #34:
   7-9in (18-23cm) fully-jointed
                  $850-$950
   8½in (21cm) five-piece body, all-
   original Mammy with baby   **$750**
   19-20in (48-53cm)   **$6,500**
Armand Marseille:
   #341, cloth body:
      10-12in (25-31cm)   **$400-$425**
   #351, composition body:
      8-12in (20-31cm)   **$500-$600**
      14-16in (38-41cm)   **$650-$750**
      21in (53cm)   **$1,000**
   #362, composition body:
      15in (38cm)   **$900**
   #1894:
      10in (25cm) fully-jointed   **$600**
Recknagel:
   #126 infant, 10½in (26cm)   **$400**
S P B H:
   Hanna, 7-8in (18-20cm) **$375-$425**
   #1923 child,
      19-20in (48-51cm)   **$900-$1,000**
Simon & Halbig:
   #949, open mouth:
      16in (41cm)   **$2,200-$2,500**
   #1009:
      15in (38cm)   **$1,500**
      19-21in (48-53cm)
               $2,200-$2,500
   #1069: 15in (38cm)   **$2,700**
   #1078, 1079:
      15in (38cm)   **$1,400-$1.600**
   #1159 lady:
      19in (48cm) at auction   **$3,300**
   #1301 character:
      20in (51cm)   **$33,000**
   #1358: 19-20in (48-51cm)**$11,000**
   #1368: 14in (36cm)   **$4,000**

Middle: 12in (31cm) Heubach Köppelsdorf
463 character. *Bart Boeckmans.*

Right: 19in (48cm) Simon & Halbig
1009 child. *Gloria & Mike Duddlesten.*

Unmarked Shoulder Head Character:
13in (33cm) "Mammy," glass eyes,
wig, at auction   **$1,500**

Unmarked Child:
Simon & Halbig quality, five-piece
body:

3in (8cm)	**$350**
4-5in (10-14cm)	**$450-$500**

Ordinary quality:
8-9in (20-23cm) five-piece body
    $300-$350
10-13in (25-33cm) jointed body
    $400-$500

All-Bisque:
Glass eyes, wig:

3¾in (9cm)	**$425**
5in (14cm)	**$550-$575**

Kestner, swivel neck, bare feet:
6in (15cm)	**$1,850**

Simon & Halbig 886:
4½in (11cm)	**$600**
7in (18cm)	**$1,200-$1,350**

G.K. 61, swivel neck:
3½in (9cm)	**$575**
5in (13cm)	**$900**

5½in (13cm) mulatto	**$1,300**
7in (18cm) mulatto	**$2,200**

Molded shorts:
5-6in (13-15cm)	**$500-$600**

Hertwig character: 2¾in (6cm)   **$95**

Cloth Black Doll*: Ca. 1880-on. American-made cloth doll with black face, painted, printed or embroidered features; jointed arms and legs; original clothes; all in good condition.

Primitive: Painted or embroidered face
    $1,000-$2,000+

Stockinette (so-called Beecher-type):
20in (51cm)	**$3,200**

1930s Mammy:
18-20in (46-51cm)	**$500-$600+**

WPA: Molded cloth face,
22in (56cm)	**$1,200-$1,500**

Alabama-type:
24in (61cm)	**$2,500-$3,500**

Chase Mammy:
26in (66cm)	**$10,000****

Golliwogg: Ca. 1925-1930. English cloth character; all original; very good condition.
18in (46cm)	**$425-$525**

16-18in (41-46cm), ca. 1950
    $225-$325

Black Papier-mâché Doll: Ca. 1890. By various German manufacturers. Papier-mâché character face, arms and legs, cloth body; glass eyes; original or appropriate clothes; all in good condition.
12-14in (31-36cm)	**$350-$450**

18-20in (46-51cm) character with
broad smile   **$1,200-$1,500**

Black Low-Fired Pottery: Ca. 1930. English and German. Molded curly hair.
16in (41cm)	**$850**

Walnut Head Folk Doll: Ca. 1940s. Loveleigh Novelty Doll, Grantville, GA.
8-11in (20-28cm) caricature faces
    $250-$275

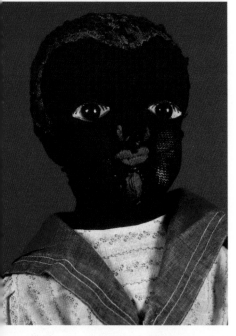

20in (51cm) stockinette boy (so-called *Beecher-type*). *Private Collection.*

*Also check under manufacturer, if known.
**Not enough price samples to compute a reliable range.
+Greatly depending on appeal.

Bru

Poupée (Fashion Lady): Ca. 1866-on. Perfect bisque swivel head on shoulder plate, cork pate, appropriate old wig, closed mouth, paperweight eyes, pierced ears; gusseted kid lady body; original or appropriate clothes; all in good condition.

Smiling face, sizes **A** (11in [8cm]) to **O** (36in [91cm]):

14-16in (35-41cm)	**$3,500-$4,000***
14in (35cm) with four extra dresses and hats	**$6,600**
20-21in (51-53cm)	**$5,500-$6,000***

Wood arms:

16in (41cm)	**$4,900-$5,100***

Wood body, naked:

15-17in (38-43cm)	**$6,000-$6,800***
21in (53cm)	**$9,000**

FACTS
Bru Jne. & Cie, Paris, and Montreuil-sous-Bois, France. 1866-1899.

Oval face, incised with numbers only; shoulder plate sometimes marked "B. Jne & Cie."

12-13in (31-33cm)	**$2,800-$3,000***
15-17in (38-43cm)	**$3,500-$3,800***
20-21in (51-53cm)	**$4,400-$4,900***

Wood body, naked: 16in (41cm) **$5,500**

Surprise Doll: Two faces:

13in (33cm) at auction	**$8,750***

*Allow extra for original clothes.
**Not enough samples to compute a reliable range.

Bèbè Brevetè. Carmel Doll Shop.

Marked Breveté Bébé: Ca. 1879-1880. Perfect bisque swivel head on shoulder plate, cork pate, skin wig, paperweight eyes with shading on upper lid, closed mouth with white space between lips, full cheeks, pierced ears; gusseted kid body pulled high on shoulder plate and straight cut with bisque lower arms (no rivet joints); appropriate old clothes; all in good condition.

Mark: Size number only on head.

Oval sticker on body: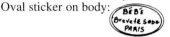

or rectangular sticker like Bébé Bru one, but with words **"Bébé Breveté."**

Size 5/0	= 10½in (27cm)
Size 2/0	= 14in (36cm)
Size 1	= 16in (41cm)
Size 2	= 18in (46cm)
Size 3	= 19in (48cm)

11in (28cm)	**$12,000-$14,000**
14-16in (35-41cm)	**$16,000-$18,000**
19-22in (48-56cm)	**$22,000-$23,000**

Bébé Modèle: Ca. 1880. Breveté face, wood body:

23in (58cm)	**$30,000** **

Marked Crescent or Circle Dot Bébé: 1879-1884. Perfect bisque swivel head on a deep shoulder plate with molded breasts, cork pate, attractive wig, paperweight eyes, closed mouth with slightly parted lips, molded and painted teeth, plump cheeks, pierced ears; gusseted kid body with bisque lower arms (no rivet joints); appropriate old clothes; all in good condition.

Mark:

Sometimes with "BRU Jne"

Approximate size chart for Circle Dot and Bru Jne Bébés:

0	= 11in (28cm)
1	= 12in (31cm)
2	= 13in (33cm)
5	= 17in (43cm)
8	= 22in (56cm)
10	= 26in (66cm)
12	= 30in (76cm)
14	= 35in (89cm)

**Not enough price samples to compute a reliable range.

21in (53cm) *Bébé Bru* with circle dot mark.

10½in (26cm)	**$12,000-$14,000**	
13-14in (33-35cm)	**$15,000-$17,000**	
18-19in (46-48cm)	**$20,000-$22,500**	
24in (61cm)	**$26,500-$28,500**	
31in (79cm)	**$32,000-$35,000**	
19in (48cm) two hairlines on plate, at auction	**$9,500**	

Marked Nursing Bru (Bébé Têteur):
Ca. 1878-1898. Perfect bisque head, shoulder plate, open mouth with hole for nipple, mechanism in head sucks up liquid, operates by turning key; nicely clothed; all in good condition.

Early model:
   13-15in (33-38cm)   **$8,500-$9,500**
Later model:
   13-15in (33-38cm)   **$5,500-$6,500**

Bébé Gourmand:
   18in (46cm)   **$26,500****

Bébé Musique:
   17in (43cm) with trunk and trousseau, at auction   **$56,000**

**Not enough price samples to compute a reliable range.

15in (38cm) *Bébé Têteur.* *Private Collection.*

16in (41cm) *Bébé Bru* with "Bru Jne" mark.

Marked Bru Jne Bébé: Ca. 1884-1889. Perfect bisque swivel head on deep shoulder plate with molded breasts, cork pate, attractive wig, paperweight eyes, closed mouth, molded tongue, pierced ears; gusseted kid body with scalloped edge at shoulder plate, bisque lower arms with lovely hands, kid over wood upper arms, hinged elbow, all kid or wood lower legs (sometimes on a jointed wood body); appropriate old clothes; all in good condition (for photograph, see *6th Blue Book,* page 79).
Mark: "BRU Jne"
Body Label:

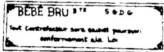

10in (25cm)	**$21,000**
12-13in (31-33cm)	
	$16,500-$18,500*
15-17in (38-43cm)	
	$22,000-$25,000*
23-24in (58-61cm)	**$25,000-$27,000**
27in (69cm)	**$27,500-$30,000***

Late model, no molded tongue:

14in (36cm)	**$10,000**
18-20in (46-51cm)	**$12,500-$13,500**

Marked Bru Shoes	**$800-$900**

Bru factory dress and hat	
	$1,700-$2,000

Marked Bru Jne R Bébé: Ca. 1889-1899. Perfect bisque head on a jointed composition body.
Mark: BRU Jⁿᴱ R
11

Body Stamp: "Bebe Bru" with size number.

Closed mouth:

11-13in (28-33cm)	**$2,200-$2,600**
19-21in (48-53cm)	**$6,000-$7,000**
27in (69cm)	**$9,000**

Open mouth:

12in (31cm)	**$1,500-$1,800**
20-21in (51-53cm)	**$3,000-$4,000**

*Allow extra for original clothes.

Bucherer

FACTS
A. Bucherer, Amriswil, Switzerland. 1921.
Mark: "MADE IN SWITZERLAND PATENTS APPLIED FOR"

Saba Figures: Composition character head sometimes with molded hat; metal ball-jointed body with large composition hands and composition molded shoes; original clothes, often felt; all in good condition.
8in (20cm) average:

Man and woman in provincial costumes **$200 each**
Fireman, clown, black man, aviator, military, baseball player, **Pinocchio, Mr. & Mrs. Peter Rabbit** and others
$275-$325

Becassine	**$400**

Characters: *Mutt, Jeff, Maggie, Jiggs, Katzenjammers, Happy Hooligan, Charlie Chaplin, Aggie, Jimmy Dugan, Puddin' head* and others
$400-$500

Bucherer *Aggie. H & J Foulke, Inc.*

Bye-Lo Baby

Bisque Head Bye-Lo Baby: Ca. 1923. Perfect bisque head, sleep eyes; cloth body with curved legs (sometimes with straight legs), composition or celluloid hands; dressed. Made in seven sizes, 9-20in (23-51cm). "Bye-Lo Baby" stamp on front of body. Sometimes Mold #1373 (ABG).

Mark: © 1923 *by*
Grace S. Putnam
MADE IN GERMANY

Head circumference:

7½-8in (19-20cm)	**$500-$525***
9-10in (23-25cm)	**$400-$450***
12-13in (31-33cm)	**$500***
15in (38cm)	**$700-$750***
17in (43cm)	**$900-$1,000***
18in (46cm)	**$1,200-$1,300***
Tagged **Bye-Lo** gown	**$50**
Bye-Lo pin	**$95**
Bye-Lo blanket	**$40-$50**

#1369 (ABG) socket head on composition body, some marked "K&W":
12-13in (30-33cm) long **$700-$900**
Painted eyes:
12-13in (30-33cm) long **$800**
#1415, smiling with painted eyes:
13-1/2in (34cm) head circumference
$4,000**
Composition head: 1924.
12-13in (31-33cm) head circumference:
All original with tag **$350-$400**
Re-dressed **$175-$225**
Celluloid head: 10in (25cm) head circumference **$350-$375**
Painted bisque head: Late 1920s.
12-13in (31-33cm) head circumference
$325-$350
Wooden head: (Schoenhut), 1925.
$1,700-$2,000**
Vinyl head: 1948. 16in (41cm) **$150**
Wax head: 1922.
16in (41cm) **$700-$900**

*Allow extra for original tagged gown and button.
**Not enough price samples to compute a reliable range.

FACTS

Bisque heads — J.D. Kestner; Alt, Beck & Gottschalck; Kling & Co.; Hertel, Schwab & Co.; all of Thuringia, Germany.
Composition heads – Cameo Doll Company, New York, NY, U.S.A.
Celluloid heads – Karl Standfuss, Saxony, Germany.
Wooden heads (unauthorized) – Schoenhut of Philadelphia, PA, U.S.A.
All-Bisque Baby – D. Kestner.
Cloth Bodies and Assembly – K & K Toy Co., New York, NY, U.S.A.
Composition Bodies – König & Wernicke, 1922-on.
Designer: Grace Storey Putnam.
Distributor: George Borgfeldt & Co., New York, NY, U.S.A.

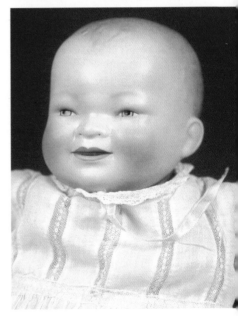

13½in (35cm) head circumference smiling *Bye-Lo Baby. Richard Wright Antiques.*

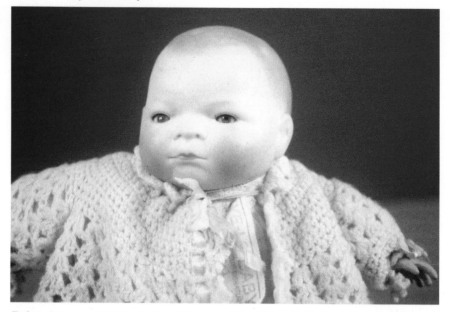

Baby Aero or Fly-Lo Baby, bisque head:

#1418: 11in (28cm)   **$3,800-$4,200****

Composition head, original costume:
   12in (31cm)   **$800-$900**

Marked All-Bisque Bye-Lo Baby: Ca. 1925-on. Solid head with molded hair and painted eyes; jointed shoulders and hips, some with pink or blue shoes:
   4-5in (10-13cm)   **$325-$425***
   6in (15cm)   **$475-$525***
   8in (20cm)   **$675-$725***
Solid head with swivel neck, glass eyes, jointed shoulders and hips:
   4-5in (10-13cm)   **$550-$650***
   6in (15cm)   **$750-$850***
   8in (20cm)   **$1,200-$1,300***
Head with wig, glass eyes; jointed shoulders and hips:
   4-5in (10-13cm)   **$700-$800**
   6in (15cm)   **$900-$1,000**
   8in (20cm)   **$1,450**
Action Bye-Lo Baby, immobile, in various positions, painted features:
   3in (8cm)   **$350-$400**
All-Celluloid: 4in (10cm)   **$250-$300**

*Allow extra for original clothes.
**Not enough price samples to compute a reliable range.

10in (25cm) head circumference *Bye-Lo Baby. H. & J. Foulke, Inc.*

8in (20cm) all-bisque *Bye-Lo Baby* with painted eyes. *H & J Foulke, Inc.*

Catterfelder Puppenfabrik

C.P. Child Doll: Ca. 1902-on. Perfect bisque head, good wig, sleep eyes, open mouth with teeth; composition jointed body; dressed; all in good condition.
#264 (made by Kestner):

14-17in (36-43cm)	**$500-$600**
25in (64cm)	**$825**

C.P. Character Child: Ca. 1910-on. Perfect bisque character face with wig, painted eyes; composition jointed body; dressed; all in good condition.
#207, 219:

15-16in (38-41cm)	**$3,000-$4,000****
#217: 18in (46cm)	**$9,750****
#220: 14in (36cm) glass eyes	**$7,500****
#210: 14in (36cm) at auction	**$8,250**
#215: 15in (38cm) at auction	**$9,000**

C.P. Character Baby: Ca. 1910-on. Perfect bisque character face with wig or molded hair, painted or glass eyes; jointed baby body; dressed; all in good condition.
#200, 201, 208:

14-16in (36-41cm)	**$375-$425**
19-21in (48-53cm)	**$575-$650**

#201, toddler:

8-10in (20-25cm)	**$600-$700**

#262, 263 (made by Kestner):

15-17in (38-43cm)	**$425-$475**
20-22in (51-56cm)	**$625-$675**

#262, toddler, five-piece body:

18in (46cm)	**$800**

**Not enough price samples to computer a reliable range.

FACTS
Catterfelder
Puppenfabrik,
Catterfeld,
Thuringia,
Germany.
Heads by J.D.
Kestner and other
porcelain makers.
1902-on.
Trademark:
My Sunshine.
Mark:

C. P.
208
45
N

16½in (42cm) 262 toddler with head made by J.D. Kestner. *H & J Foulke, Inc.*

Celluloid Dolls

Celluloid Shoulder Head Child Doll:
Ca. 1900-on. Cloth or kid body, celluloid or composition arms; dressed; all in good condition.
Painted eyes:

16-18in (41-46cm)	**$125-$135**

Glass eyes:

19-22in (48-56cm)	**$175-$225**

Original provincial costume:

12-14in (30-36cm)	**$210-$235**
Boy/girl pair	**$525-$550**

All-Celluloid Child Doll: Ca. 1900-on. Jointed at neck, shoulders and hips; all in good condition.
Painted eyes:

4in (10cm)	**$35-$45***
7-8in (18-20cm)	**$65-$85***
10-12in (25-31cm)	**$100-$125***
14-15in (36-38cm)	**$150-$165***
Googly: 5in (12cm)	**$175-$200**

Tommy Tucker-type character:

12-14in (31-36cm)	**$165-$185**

French with original provincial costume by **LeMinor, Poupées Magali** and others:

8in (20cm)	**$55-$65**
12-14in (31-36cm)	**$135-$160**
19in (48cm)	**$225-$250**

SNF pair with molded provincial costumes: 9in (23cm)   **$250**

Glass eyes:

12-13in (31-33cm)	**$165-$185**
15-16in (38-41cm)	**$200-$225**
18in (46cm)	**$275**
21in (53cm)	**$350-$375**

Turtle Mark Black Toddler:

16in (41cm)	**$450-$500**

Marie-France, by Petitcolin, smiling character, all original:

18in (46cm)	**$350-$400**
Boxed, in child's dress	**$565**

K ★ R 717 or **728:**

14-16in (36-41cm)	**$550-$600**

*Allow extra for unusual dolls or provincial clothing.

FACTS
Germany: Rheinische Gummi und Celluloid Fabrik Co. (Turtle symbol); Buschow & Beck, *Minerva* trademark (Helmet symbol); E. Maar & Sohn, *Emasco* trademark (3 M symbol); Cellba (Mermaid symbol).
Poland: P.R. Zask ("ASK" in triangle).
France: Petitcolin (Eagle symbol); Société Nobel Française ("SNF" in diamond); Neumann & Mars (Dragon symbol); Société Industrielle de Celluloid (Sicoine).
United States: Parsons-Jackson Co., Cleveland, OH, and other companies
England: Cascelloid Ltd. (Palitoy). 1895-1940s.
Marks: Various as indicated above; may also be in combination with the marks of J.D. Kestner, Kämmer & Reinhardt, Bruno Schmidt, Käthe Kruse and König & Wernicke.

12in (31cm) French celluloid baby, original Brittany costume. *H & J Foulke, Inc.*

All-Celluloid Baby: Ca. 1910-on. All in good condition.

6-8in (15-20cm)	**$65-$85**
10-12in (25-31cm)	**$110-$135**
15in (38cm)	**$150-$175**
21in (53cm)	**$225-$250**

SNF black baby:

16-18in (41-46cm)	**$450-$500**

All-Celluloid, Made in Japan: Ca. 1920s. Molded clothes:

4-5in (10-12cm)	**$50-$60**
8-9in (20-23cm)	**$125-$150**

Child with pedestal legs, jointed arms:

3-4in (8-10cm)	**$15**
6-7in (15-18cm)	**$25**

Baby:

4-5in (10-13cm)	**$15-$20**
8-10in (20-25cm)	**$65-$85**
13in (33cm)	**$125-$150**
24in (61cm)	**$250-$275**

Occupied Japan:

Chubby toddler character:

6½in (17cm)	**$85-$95**
Baby, 24in (61cm)	**$175**

Bride & Groom:

3in (8cm) molded clothes	**$50**

Parsons-Jackson, Stork Mark:

11½in (29cm) baby	**$165-$185***
14in (36cm) toddler	**$350***

Celluloid Head Infant: Ca. 1920s-on. Baby head with glass eyes; cloth body, appropriate clothes; all in good condition.

12-15in (31-38cm)	**$150-$175**

Celluloid Socket Head Doll: Ca. 1910-on. Wig, glass eyes, sometimes flirty, open mouth with teeth; ball-jointed or bent-limb composition body; dressed; all in good condition.

K ★ R 701, child:

12-13in (31-33cm)	**$900-$1,100****

K ★ R 717, child, flapper body:

16-18in (41-46cm)	**$700-$750**

K ★ R 700, baby:

14-15in (36-38cm)	**$325-$375**

K ★ R 728:

12-13in (31-33cm) baby	**$300**
23in (38cm) baby	**$650**
14-15in (36-38cm) toddler	
	$450-$500
18in (46cm) flapper	**$700-$750**

F.S. & Co. 1276:

20in (51cm) baby	**$500-$550**

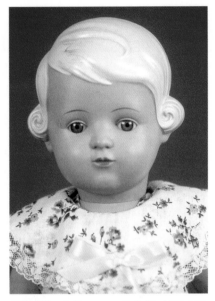

16in (41cm) German celluloid child with turtle trademark. *H & J Foulke, Inc.*

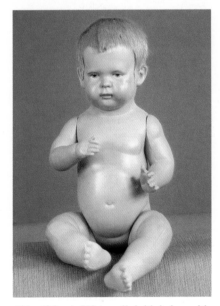

10in (25cm) USA celluloid baby with skin wig. *H & J Foulke, Inc.*

*Allow extra for molded shoes and socks.
**Not enough price samples to compute a reliable range.

Chad Valley

Chad Valley Doll: All-cloth, usually felt face and velvet body, jointed neck, shoulders and hips; mohair wig, glass or painted eyes; original clothes; all in excellent condition, clean with good color.

Characters, painted eyes:
10-12in (25-31cm) **$85-$115**

Characters, glass eyes:
10-12in (25-31cm) **$225-$250**
17-20in (43-51cm) **$1,000-$2,000***

Children, painted eyes:
9in (23cm) **$135**
13-14in (33-36cm) **$375-$400**
16-18in (41-46cm) **$550-$575**

Smiling face:
14-15in (36-38cm) **$425-$475**

Children, glass eyes:
16-18in (41-46cm) **$650-$700**

Royal Children, glass eyes:
16-18in (41-46cm) **$1,250-$1,350**

Mabel Lucie Attwell, glass inset side-glancing eyes, smiling watermelon mouth:
15-17in (38-43cm) **$750-$850**

Snow White Set:
Dwarfs, 10in (25cm) **$250-$275 each**

Snow White:
16in (41cm) **$500-$600**
Complete set **$2,500-$3,000**

*Depending on rarity.

FACTS
Chad Valley Co. (formerly Johnson Bros., Ltd.), Birmingham, England. 1917-on. **Mark:** Cloth label usually on foot: "HYGIENIC TOYS Made in England by CHAD VALLEY CO. LTD."

17in (43cm) *Bambino,* by Mabel Lucie Attwell. *H & J Foulke, Inc.*

Martha Chase

Chase Doll: Head and limbs of stockinette, treated and painted with oils, large painted eyes with thick upper eyelashes, rough-stroked hair to provide texture; cloth bodies jointed at shoulders, hips, elbows and knees, later ones only at shoulders and hips; some bodies completely treated; appropriate clothing; showing wear, but no repaint.

Baby:

9in (23cm) at auction	**$8,225**
13-15in (33-38cm)	**$525-$575***
17-20in (43-51cm)	**$650-$750***
24-26in (61-66cm)	**$850***

Hospital Baby:

19-20in (49-51cm)	**$650-$750**

Child, molded bobbed hair:

12-15in (31-38cm)	**$1,000-$1,200**
20in (51cm)	**$1,500-$1,600**

Boy with side part and side curl:

15-16in (38-41cm)	**$3,000**

Lady:

13-15in (33-38cm)	**$1,300-$1,500**
Man: 15-16in (38-41cm)	**$3,000****
Black, Mammy or **child:**	**$10,000**

Hospital Lady:

64in (163cm)	**$900-$1,200**

FACTS
Martha Jenks Chase,
Pawtucket, RI, U.S.A. 1889-on.
Designer: Martha Jenks Chase.
Mark: "Chase Stockinet Doll" stamp on left leg or under left arm, paper label on back (usually gone).

Alice in Wonderland character set: Six dolls   **$67,000**

George Washington:
24in (61cm) all original
$5,500-$6,500

*Allow extra for a doll in excellent condition or with original clothes.
**Not enough price samples to compute a reliable range.

13in (33cm) child with molded bobbed hair. *H & J Foulke, Inc.*

China Heads, French

French China Head Fashion-type Doll: China shoulder head, open crown, cork pate, good wig, glass or beautifully painted eyes, painted eyelashes, feathered eyebrows, closed mouth; shapely kid fashion body (may have china arms curved to above elbow); appropriately dressed; all in good condition.

12-14in (31-36cm)	**$2,800-$3,300**
16-17in (41-43cm), naked	
	$3,600-$4,000

Child, 28in (71cm), with lever eyes, at auction **$5,830**

Rohmer *poupée:* See page 83.
Huret *poupée:* See page 83.

Painted black hair:

12in (31cm)	**$1,100**
16in (41cm)	**$2,500**

Jacob Petit, flesh tint, black painted pate:

22in (56cm) at auction	**$3,300**

FACTS
Various French doll firms; some heads sold through French firms may have been made in Germany. 1850s on.
Mark: None.

English

English China Doll: Possibly Rockingham area. Ca. 1840-1860. Flesh-tinted shoulder head with bald head (some with molded slit for inserting wig), human hair wig, painted features, closed mouth; cloth torso and upper arms and legs, china lower limbs with holes to attach them to cloth, bare feet; appropriately dressed; all in good condition.

19-22in (48-56cm)	**$2,500-$3,000**
Without china limbs	**$1,200**

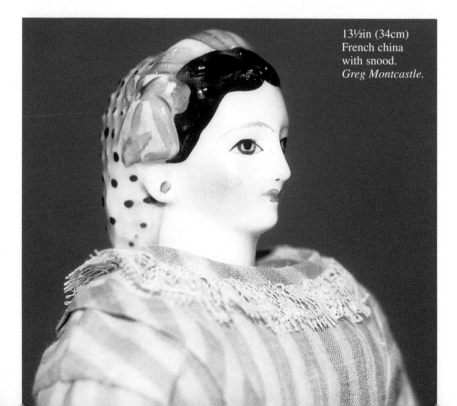

13½in (34cm) French china with snood. *Greg Montcastle.*

China Heads, German

1840s Hairstyles: China shoulder head with black molded hair; may have pink tint complexion; old cloth body; (may have china arms); appropriate old clothes; all in good condition.
Hair swept back into bun:

5in (13cm)	**$600**
13-15in (33-38cm)	**$2,000-$2,600**
18-21in (46-53cm)	**$3,200-$4,200**

Fancy braided bun:

22-24in (56-61cm)	**$5,000-$6,000**

Long curls, early face:

21in (53cm)	**$3,400**

K.P.M.:
Brown hair with bun:

16-18in (41-46cm)	**$6,500-$7,000**

Brown hair with side curls:

14in (36cm) at auction	**$5,100**

Young man, brown hair:

16-18in (41-46cm)	**$4,500**
22-23in (56-58cm)	**$7,000-$8,000**

Kinderkopf (child head):

10½in (27cm)	**$800-$900**
18-22in (46-56cm)	**$2,200-$2,800**

Wood jointed body, china lower limbs:

5-6in (13-15cm)	**$1,800-$2,200**
11in (28cm)	**$5,000**

Molded Bonnet:

11½in (30cm) at auction	**$8,225**

1850s Hairstyles: China shoulder head (some with pink tint), molded black hair (except bald), painted eyes; old cloth body with leather or china arms; appropriate old clothes; all in good condition.
Morning Glory, brown hair with molded flowers:

21in (53cm)	**$6,500-$7,500**
27in (69cm)	**$9,500**

Brown hair in bun with entwined blue ribbon:

33in (84cm) at auction	**$12,100**

Bald head, some with black areas on top, proper wig. Allow extra for original human hair wig in fancy style.
Fine quality:

12in (31cm)	**$700-$750**
15-17in (38-43cm)	**$1,000-$1,200**
22-24in (56-61cm)	**$1,700-$1,900**

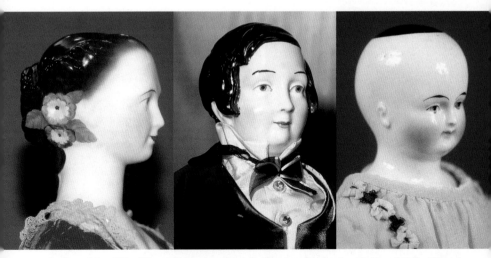

Left to right: 27in (69cm) "Morning Glory" china head lady. *Sue Kallen;* 16½in (42cm) K.P.M. young man with brown hair. *Private Collection;* 19in (48cm) "black spot," meant to have a human hair wig. *H & J Foulke, Inc.*

22in (56cm) child with rare blue glass eyes. *Sue Kallen.*

Standard quality:
13in (33cm)	**$500-$550**
16-17in (41-43cm)	**$750-$800**
20-22in (51-56cm)	**$900-$1,000**
17in (43cm) glass eyes, at auction	**$1,400**

Covered wagon with blue eyes:
5-7in (13-18cm)	**$325-$350**
17-20in (43-51cm)	**$800-$900**
24-26in (61-66cm)	**$1,250-$1,350**
6in (15cm) wood body	**$1,300-$1,400**

Covered wagon with brown eyes:
20-22in (51-56cm)	**$1,400-$1,500**

Greiner-style with brown eyes:
14-15in (36-38cm)	**$1,000-$1,200**
19-22in (48-56cm)	**$1,700-$2,000**

Greiner-style with glass eyes:
15-16in (38-41cm)	**$3,850****
22in (56cm)	**$4,800****

Waves, framing face, brown eyes:
20-21in (51-53cm)	**$2,000-$2,200**
With glass eyes: 18-21in (46-53cm)	**$3,000-$3,500**

Alice Hairdo, with molded headband:
22-24in (56-61cm)	**$950-$1,150**

Molded white cap, pink ribbon:
12in (33cm) at auction	**$3,190**

Sophia Smith, long curls, brown eyes:
18-22in (46-56cm)	**$2,100-$2,500**

Lydia: 28in (71cm) at auction   **$7,637**
Molded Hat: 19in (48cm) hairline, at auction   **$15,000**
Young Victoria: 18in (46cm)   **$2,500**

Child or Baby, flange swivel neck; taüfling body with china or papiermâché shoulder plate and hips, china lower limbs; cloth midsection (may have voice box) and upper limbs.
10in (25cm)	**$3,000-$4,000**

Child with Alice Hairstyle:
12in (31cm)	**$5,000**

**Not enough price samples to compute a reliable range.

18in (46cm) *Young Victoria* china head. *Sue Kallen.*

22in (56cm) 1860s china lady with "high brow" hairdo.
H & J Foulke, Inc.

20in (51cm) 1860s china lady with "flat top" hairdo.
H & J Foulke, Inc.

19½ (49cm) china lady with fancy hairdo. *Private Collection.*

1860s and 1870s Hairstyles: China shoulder head with black molded hair (a few blondes); old cloth body may have leather arms or china lower arms and legs; appropriate old clothes; all in good condition.

Plain style with center part (so-called flat top and high brow):

4½in (11cm)	**$150-$175***
6-7in (15-18cm)	**$165-$185***
14-16in (36-41cm)	**$275-$325***
19-22in (48-56cm)	**$400-$450***
24-26in (61-66cm)	**$450-$550***
28in (71cm)	**$750-$850***
34-35in (86-89cm)	**$1,000-$1,100**

Molded necklace:

22-24in (56-61cm)	**$700-$800**
Blonde hair: 18in (46cm)	**$475-$525**

Brown eyes:

20-22in (51-56cm)	**$600-$700**
Swivel neck: 15½in (40cm)	**$1,500**
Child face, 22in (56cm)	**$600-$650**

Youthful face:

20-23in (51-58cm)	**$550-$600**

All-china Child, jointed shoulders and hips: 9in (23cm)   **$3,800-$4,000**

Mary Todd Lincoln, with snood:

14-15in (36-38cm)	**$850**
18-21in (46-53cm)	**$1,000-$1,100**

Blonde hair, fancy snood:

20-21in (51-53cm)	**$1,500**

Conta and Boehme:

19in (48cm)	**$700-$800**

Molded bonnet, applied flowers, poor quality: 20in (51cm)   **$500**

Young Man:

21in (53cm)	**$1,300-$1,500**

Dolley Madison, with molded bow:

14-16in (36-41cm)	**$425-$475**
21-24in (53-61cm)	**$625-$700**

Blonde hair, pierced ears:

22in (56cm)	**$750-$800**

Adelina Patti:

13-15in (33-38cm)	**$425-$475**
19-22in (48-56cm)	**$650-$725**

14in (36cm) original body and limbs   **$600**

Dagmar-type: 18in (46cm)   **$800**

Jenny Lind:

12in (31cm)	**$850**
21-24in (53-61cm)	**$1,600-$1,800**

*Allow more for all-original body and clothes.

Currier & Ives, long hair on shoulders: 15in (38cm)   **$600**
Curly Top:
  14in (36cm) black hair   **$600**
  19in (48cm) tan hair   **$900**
Grape Lady:
  18in (46cm)   **$2,200-$2,500**
Youth and Old Age, two faces:
  11in (28cm)   **$2,300**
Spill Curl:
  19-22in (48-56cm)   **$900-$1,100**
  Café-au-lait color with black hair
  band, 24in (61cm)   **$1,430**
Fancy Hair Styles:
  Black hair with bun and pouf curls
  at back, two long ringlets onto
  shoulders:
    22in (56cm) at auction   **$5,100**
  Black hair with three large horizontal
  rolls in back, molded gold comb:
    20in (51cm) at auction   **$3,190**
  Blonde hair with small overall curls,
  molded black hair band:
    15in (38cm) at auction   **$1,760**
  Black hair with braided cornet,
  molded hair band, pierced ears:
    20in (51cm)   **$2,200**

1880s Hairstyles: China shoulder head with black or blonde molded hair; appropriate old clothes; all in good condition. Many made by Alt, Beck & Gottschalck or Kling & Co.

10in (25cm) china head with molded bonnet. *H & J Foulke, Inc.*

14-16in (36-41cm)   **$275-$325**
21-23in (53-58cm)   **$450-$500**
28in (71cm)   **$600-$650**
Head only, 5in (13cm)   **$150-$200**

Bawo and Dotter, "Pat. Dec. 7/80":
  18-20in (46-51cm)   **$400-$450**

Dressel & Kister: Ca. 1890-1920. China shoulder head with varying hair-dos and brush-stroked hair; delicately painted features; cloth body with china arms having beautifully molded fingers. Often used as ornamental dolls in only half form as for a boudoir lamp or candy box.
  13in (33cm)   **$1,500 up**
  Heads only   **$675-$750**

1890s Hairstyles: China shoulder head with black or blonde molded wavy hair; appropriate clothes; all in good condition.
  4½in (11cm)   **$55-$60**
  8-10in (20-25cm)   **$110-$135***
  13-15in (33-38cm)   **$165-$195***
  19-21in (48-53cm)   **$235-$285***
  24in (61cm)   **$350**
  Open mouth, 10in (25cm) **$175-$200**
Molded bonnet:
  8-10in (20-25cm)   **$165-$185**
Molded "Jewel" necklace:
  22in (56cm)   **$400-$425**
  8½in (21cm)   **$150-$165**
Black Man:
  12in (31cm) at auction   **$1,050**
Jester, molded hat:
  14-17in (36-43cm)   **$650-$750**

Pet Name: Ca. 1905. Made by Hertwig & Co. for Butler Bros., New York. China shoulder head, molded yoke with name in gold; black or blonde painted hair (one-third were blonde). Used names such as **Agnes, Bertha, Daisy, Dorothy, Edith, Esther, Ethel, Florence, Helen, Mabel, Marion** and **Pauline.**
  12-14in (30-36cm)   **$200-$250**
  18-21in (46-53cm)   **$350-$400**
  24in (61cm)   **$450**

*Allow $50 to $100 for lithographed body.

Dolls Printed on Cloth: To be cut out and sewn. Very good condition with bright color. **Dolly Dear, Merry Marie, Improved Foot Doll, Standish No Break Doll** and others with printed underwear:

7-9in (18-23cm)	**$65-$85**
16-18in (41-46cm)	**$125-$135**
22-24in (56-61cm)	**$165-$185**

Uncut sheet:

13in (33cm) doll	**$110-$125**
20in (51cm) doll	**$135-$165**

Black Child, Art Fabric:

18in (46cm)	**$250**

Boys and Girls with printed outer clothes. Ca. 1903:

12-13in (31-33cm)	**$100-$125**
17in (43cm)	**$150-$175**

Aunt Jemima Family: Four dolls
$65-$75 each

Ball, uncut **$250-$275**

Brownies: Ca. 1892. Designed by Palmer Cox; marked on foot:

8in (20cm)	**$75-$85**
Uncut sheet of six	**$250**
Buster Brown and Tige	**$325**
Cream of Wheat Rastus	**$90-$110**

Darkey Doll: Cocheco, made up.

16in (41cm)	**$225-$250**

E.T. Gibson: Ca. 1912.

Red bathing suit	**$200-$225**

George & Martha Washington
$350/pair

Hen and Chicks: uncut sheet **$65**

Hug-Me-Tight: Ca. 1916. Grace G. Drayton Mother Goose Characters:

11in (28cm)	**$225-$250**

Pitti Sing: uncut **$65**

Punch & Judy	**$350 pair**
Red Riding Hood	**$150**
Santa: Peck, 1886.	**$225**
Tabby Cat	**$70-$80**
Tabby's Kittens	**$45-$55**

Topsy: uncut,
8½in (22cm) two dolls on sheet **$195**
Pillow-type, printed and hand-embroidered, 1920s-1930s:

16in (41cm)	**$65-$85**

Oilcloth:

Orphan Annie: 17in (43cm)	**$185**
Sandy	**$75-$85**
Smitty	**$60-$70**
Skeezix	**$60-$70**

Mothers' Congress: 1900.

17in (43cm) faded	**$650**
Gerber Baby: 8in (20cm) pair	**$220**

27in (69cm) Art Fabric Mills printed cloth girl. *Private Collection.*

Cloth, Russian

FACTS
Unknown craftsmen. Ca. 1930.
Mark: "Made in Soviet Union"
sometimes with identification of doll,
such as "Ukrainian Woman," "Village
Boy," "Smolensk District Woman."

Russian Cloth Doll: All-cloth with
stockinette head and hands, molded
face with hand-painted features;
authentic regional clothes; all in very
good condition.

6½in (16cm) child	**$40-$45**
11in (28cm) child	**$90-$110**
15in (38cm)	**$175-$200**
Tea Cosy: 20in (51cm)	**$200-$225**

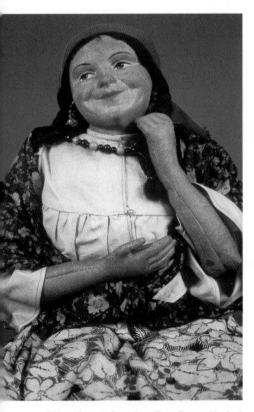

20in (51cm) Russian Tea Cosy. *H & J Foulke, Inc.*

Columbian Doll

FACTS
Emma and Marietta Adams.
1891-1910 or later.
Mark: Stamped on back of body.
Before 1900: "COLUMBIAN DOLL
EMMA E. ADAMS OSWEGO
CENTRE N.Y."
After 1906: "THE COLUMBIAN
DOLL MANUFACTURED BY
MARIETTA ADAMS RUTTAN
OSWEGO, N.Y."

Columbian Doll: All-cloth with hair
and features hand-painted on a flat
face; treated limbs; appropriate
clothes; all in very good condition, no
repaint or touch up.

15in (38cm)	**$6,000-$7,000**
19-23in (48-58cm)	**$8,000-$10,000**
Some wear: 23in (58cm)	**$4,000-$4,200**
Worn: 20in (51cm)	**$2,200**

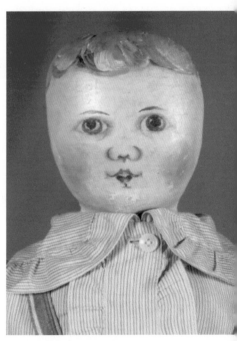

Columbian, original paint. *McMasters Harris Premier Doll Auctions.*

Danel, Later Jumeau

Marked Paris Bébé: Ca. 1889-1892. Perfect bisque socket head, good wig, paperweight eyes, closed mouth, pierced ears; composition jointed body; appropriately dressed; all in good condition. This doll was a copy of a Jumeau.

Mark: On Head

TÊTE DÉPOSÉ
PARIS BEBE

On Body

PARIS·BEBE
Breveté

11in (28cm)	$2,500
18-20in (46-51cm)	$3,500-$3,800
24-26in (61-66cm)	$4,200-$4,500

Marked Paris Bébé: Ca. 1892-on. Character face developed by Jumeau for use with this trademark after he won a lawsuit against Danel. (For photograph, see *11th Blue Book,* page 144.)

18-19in (46-48cm)	$4,500-$5,000
26-28in (66-71cm)	$6,000-$6,500

Marked B.F.: Ca. 1891. Bébé Française was used by Jumeau after 1892. Perfect bisque head, appropriate wig, paperweight eyes, closed mouth, pierced ears; jointed composition body; appropriate clothes; all in good condition.

Mark: B9F

14-16in (36-41cm)	$3,500-$3,800
23-25in (58-64cm)	$5,200-$5,700

FACTS

Danel & Cie., Paris & Montreuil-sous-Bois, France. 1889-1895.
Trademarks: Paris Bébé, Bébé Française. Both used by Jumeau after winning an 1892 lawsuit.

24in (61cm)
Bébé Française.
Gloria & Mike
Duddlesten.

DEP

DEP Closed Mouth: Ca. 1890. Perfect bisque socket head, lovely wig, set paperweight eyes, upper and lower painted eyelashes, closed mouth, pierced ears; jointed French composition and wood body (may be stamped "Jumeau"); pretty clothes; all in good condition.

Mark: "DEP
[size number]"

12in (31cm)	$1,500-$1,600
15in (38cm)	$2,000-$2,100
18-20in (46-51cm)	$2,500-$2,800
25-27in (63-68cm)	$3,800-$4,200

Jumeau DEP: Ca. 1899-on. Heads possibly by Simon & Halbig. Perfect bisque socket head (sometimes with "Tête Jumeau" stamp), human hair wig, deeply molded eye socket, sleep eyes, painted lower eyelashes, upper hair eyelashes (sometimes gone), pierced ears; jointed French composition and wood body (sometimes with Jumeau label or stamp); lovely clothes; all in good condition.

Mark: "DEP
8"

9½-10in (24-25cm)	$1,000-$1,200*
11-1/2in (29cm)	$850*
13-15in (33-38cm)	$900-$950*
18-20in (46-51cm)	$1,050-$1,200*
23-25in (58-64cm)	$1,300-$1,500*
29-30in (74-76cm)	$1,800-$2,000*
35in (89cm)	$2,500-$2,600*

*Allow extra for Jumeau flowered shift.

9½in (24cm)
DEP Jumeau.
*H & J Foulke,
Inc.*

Door of Hope

Dressel

Door of Hope: Carved wooden head
with painted and/or carved hair; cloth
body, some with stubby arms, some
with carved hands; original handmade
clothes, exact costuming for different
classes of Chinese people; all in excellent condition. 25 dolls in the series.

Adult: 11-13in (28-33cm)	**$900-$1,500**
Child: 7-8in (18-20cm)	**$1,200-$1,700**
Amah and **Baby**	**$1,100**
Manchu Lady:	
Carved headdress	**$2,000**
Bride:	
Old style, with face veil	**$1,500**
New style	**$1,200**
Women or **Girls** with special carving	
in the hair	**$1,500**

Marked Holz-Masse: Ca. 1875-on.
Papier-mâché or composition shoulder
head; cloth/composition body. See
page 159.

Child Doll: Ca. 1893-on. Perfect
bisque head, good wig, glass eyes, open
mouth; suitable clothes; all in good
condition.
Mark:

Composition body:

16-18in (41-46cm)	**$325-$375**
22-24in (56-61cm)	**$425-$475**
32in (81cm)	**$750**
38in (96cm)	**$1,600**
#93, 1896, kid body:	
15-16in (38-41cm)	**$235-$265**
19-22in (48-56cm)	**$350-$400**

Character-type face, similar to **K ★ R**
117n. (For photograph, see *12th Blue
Book,* page 151.):

16in (41cm)	**$1,100**
20-22in (51-56cm)	**$1,400-$1,500**
34in (86cm)	**$2,200-$2,400**

Door of Hope young girl with side part.
Private Collection.

Portrait Series: 1896. Perfect bisque heads with portrait faces, glass eyes, some with molded mustaches and goatees; composition body; original clothes; all in good condition. Some marked "S" or "D" with a number.

Uncle Sam:
   12-14in (31-36cm) **$1,500-$1,800**
Admiral Dewey and Officers:
   8in (20cm) **$850**
   15in (38cm) **$1,600-$1,800**
Old Rip: 11in (28cm) **$1,200-$1,300**
Farmer: 13in (33cm) **$1,500**
Buffalo Bill: 10in (23cm) **$750**

Marked Jutta Child: Ca. 1906-1921. Perfect bisque socket head, good wig, sleep eyes, open mouth, pierced ears; ball-jointed composition body; dressed; all in good condition. Head made by Simon & Halbig.
Mold **1348** or **1349**

Mark:

   14-16in (36-41cm) **$575-$625***
   19-21in (43-53cm) **$650-$700***
   24-26in (61-66cm) **$800-$900***
   30-32in (76-81cm) **$1,200-$1,500**
   38-39in (96-99cm) **$3,000-$3,250**

Character Child: Ca. 1909-on. Perfect bisque socket head, mohair wig, painted eyes, closed mouth; ball-jointed composition body; suitable clothes; all in good condition. Glazed inside of head. (For photograph, see *10th Blue Book,* page 179.)

Mark:

   10-12in (25-31cm) **$1,500-$1,800****
   16-18in (41-46cm) **$3,000**
Limbach 8679 pouty, glass eyes (For photograph, see *14th Blue Book*, page 84.):
   14in (36cm) **$1,800-$2,000****

*Allow $100 extra for flapper body with high knee joint.
**Not enough price samples to compute a reliable range.

23in (58cm) Dressel 1896 shoulder head child. *H & J Foulke, Inc.*

21in (53cm) 1349 *Jutta* child. *H & J Foulke, Inc.*

11in (28cm) 1914 *Jutta* character baby. *H & J Foulke, Inc.*

Composition head:
   19in (48cm)   **$2,600-$3,000****
   13in (33cm) wear on nose and lips
                     $1,300

Marked C.O.D. Character Baby: Ca. 1910-on. Perfect bisque character face with marked wig or molded hair, painted or glass eyes; jointed baby body; dressed; all in good condition.
   12-14in (31-36cm)   **$300-$350**
   17-19in (43-48cm)   **$400-$450**
   23-24in (58-61cm)   **$600-$650**

Marked Jutta Character Baby: Ca. 1910-1922. Perfect bisque socket head, good wig, sleep eyes, open mouth; bent-limb composition baby body; dressed; all in good condition.
Simon & Halbig:
   16-18in (41-46cm)   **$550-$650**
   23-24in (58-61cm)   **$1,000-$1,200**
   Toddler, fully-jointed body:
     18-20in (46-51cm) **$1,400-$1,600**
Other Makers: (Armand Marseille, E. Heubach):
   16-18in (41-46cm)   **$400-$450**
   23-24in (58-61cm)   **$600-$650**
Marks:

Heubach 6½ Koppelsdorf
Jutta Baby
Dressel
Germany
1922
10½

Jutta
1914
8

Lady Doll: Ca. 1920s. Bisque socket head with young lady face, good wig, sleep eyes, closed mouth; jointed composition body in adult form with molded bust, slim waist and long arms and legs, feet modeled to wear high-heeled shoes; all in good condition.
Mark: 1469

C O. Dressel
Germany
2

#1469:
   14in (36cm) naked   **$2,500**
   14in (36cm) original clothes **$3,500**

**Not enough price samples to compute a reliable range.

14in (36cm) COD 1469 lady. *H & J Foulke, Inc.*

E.D. Bébé

FACTS
Etienne Denamur of Paris, France.
1889-on.
Mark:

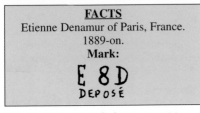

DEPOSÉ

Marked E. D. Bébé: Perfect bisque head, good wig, beautiful blown glass eyes, pierced ears; wood and composition jointed body; nicely dressed; good condition.

Closed mouth:

15-17in (38-48cm)	**$2,400-$2,500**
22-24in (56-61cm)	**$3,200-$3,500**
28in (71cm)	**$3,800**

Open mouth:

18-20in (35-51cm)	**$1,700-$1,900**
25-27in (64-69cm)	**$2,250-$2,350**

Note: Dolls with Jumeau look but signed "E. D." are Jumeau factory dolls produced when Emile Douillet was director of the Jumeau firm, 1892-1899. They do not have the word "Déposé" under the "E. D." They should be priced as Jumeau dolls. (For photograph, see *10th Blue Book,* page 181.)

20in (51cm) E.D. *Bébé. Gloria & Mike Duddlesten.*

Eden Bébé

FACTS
Fleischmann & Bloedel doll factory,
Paris, France. 1890,
then into S.F.B.J. in 1899.
Trademark: Eden Bébé (1890),
Bébé Triomphe (1898).
Mark: "EDEN BEBE, PARIS"

Marked Eden Bébé: Ca. 1890. Perfect bisque head, beautiful wig, large set paperweight eyes, closed or open/closed mouth, pierced ears; fully-jointed or five-piece composition jointed body; lovely clothes; all in nice condition.

Closed mouth:

14-16in (36-41cm)	**$1,800-$2,000**
21-23in (53-58cm)	**$2,300-$2,600**

Five-piece body:

12in (31cm)	**$1,000-$1,100**

Open mouth:

19-20in (48-51cm)	**$1,500-$1,700**

16½in (42cm) *Eden Bébé. H & J Foulke, Inc.*

French Fashion-Type
(Poupée)

French Fashion Lady (Poupée): Perfect unmarked bisque shoulder head, swivel or stationary neck, original or old wig, lovely blown glass eyes, closed mouth, earrings; kid body *(poupée peau)* or cloth body with kid arms – some with wired fingers; appropriate old clothes; all in good condition. Fine quality bisque.

12-13in (31-33cm)	**$1,800-$2,000***
15-16in (38-41cm)	**$2,500-$2,800***
18-19in (46-48cm)	**$3,200-$3,500***
21in (53cm)	**$4,000-$4,200***
33in (84cm)	**$6,750**

Bisque arms and lower legs:

16in (41cm)	**$6,500**

FACTS
Various French firms. Ca. 1860-1930.
(See also **Bru, Jumeau, Gaultier, Gesland** and **China Heads, French.**)

Painted eyes, stiff neck:

16-17in (41-43cm)	**$1,800-$2,200**

Fully-jointed wood body *(poupée bois):*

16-18in (41-46cm)	**$6,200-$6,800**

Portrait Face: Painted eyes, molded eyelids, 17in (43cm) at auction **$22,000**

*Allow extra for fancy original clothing and/or bisque lower arms.

17½in (44cm) *Poupée Peau*, Barrios-type shoulder head. *H & J Foulke, Inc.*

7½in (19cm) tiny *Poupée Peau. H & J Foulke, Inc.*

E.B. Poupée: E. Barrois, 1862-1877.
Mark:

14-16in (36-41cm)	**$2,800-$3,200***
19-20in (48-51cm)	**$3,600-$3,900***
23in (58cm)	**$4,500-$4,750**
Wood body: 18in (46cm)	**$6,500**

B.V. Poupée: Brasseur-Videlier, wood
body, 15in (38cm) at auction   **$7,500**
A. Dehors: 1860. 17in (43cm) swivel
neck, bisque lower arms
$18,000-$19,000
Nicholas Joliet: Portrait lady with
special neck joint.
28in (71cm) at auction   **$27,500**
Marked Huret Poupée: Ca. 1850.
China or bisque shoulder head.

16-17in (41-43cm)	**$15,000-$20,000**
Wood body	**$25,000-$30,000**
Gutta-percha body	**$20,000-$25,000**

L.D. Poupée: Louis Doleac.
Kid body, 20in (51cm)   **$5,250***
Wood body,
18in (46cm) at auction   **$9,000**
Lavallée-Peronne: Kid body,
17in (43cm) with trousseau   **$9,500**
Radiquet and Cordonnier: Molded
breasts, bisque arms, one bent at elbow,
bisque lower legs, original signed
stand: 17in (43cm)   **$12,500-$13,500**
Rohmer Poupée: Ca. 1857-1880.
China or bisque swivel or shoulder
head.
16-18in (41-46cm)   **$4,000-$4,500**
Mark:

Leverd & Cie Poupée: Rare body style
with slant jointed hips,
18in (46cm) at auction   **$18,700**
B.S. Poupée: Blampoix.
16in (41cm) $3,000
Simonne Poupée:
Kid body:
16-17in (41-43cm) **$3,300-$3,800**
Wood body:
18in (46cm)   **$6,000-$6,500**
Period Clothes, Fashion Lady
clothing:

Dress	**$500-$1,000 up**
Boots	**$300-$350**
Elaborate wig	**$300-$400**
Nice wig	**$150-$250**

*Allow extra for fancy original clothing
and/or bisque lower arms.

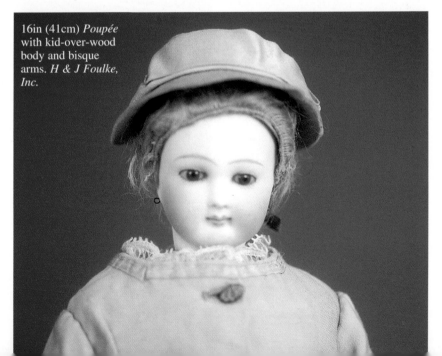

16in (41cm) *Poupée*
with kid-over-wood
body and bisque
arms. *H & J Foulke,
Inc.*

Frozen Charlotte
(Bathing Doll)

Frozen Charlotte: All-china doll, black or blonde molded hair, painted features; arms extended, legs separated but not jointed; no clothes; perfect condition. Good quality.

2-3in (5-8cm)	**$50-$65***
4-5in (10-13cm)	**$140-$165***
6-7in (15-18cm)	**$200-$225***
9-10in (23-25cm)	**$275-$325***
14-15in (36-38cm)	**$550-$600**
17in (43cm)	**$700-$750**

Pink tint, early hairdo:

2½-3½in (6-9cm)	**$300-$325**
3½in (9cm) *café-au-lait* hair	**$425**
5in (13cm)	**$425-$450**
8-10in (20-25cm)	**$800-$1,000**

Pink tint with bonnet:

3½in (9cm)	**$400-$450**
5in (13cm)	**$525-$575**
Black china: 5in (13cm)	**$165-$195**

Black boy, molded turban and pants:

3in (8cm)	**$275-$300**

*Allow extra for pink tint, fine decoration and modeling, unusual hairdo.

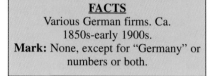

FACTS
Various German firms. Ca. 1850s-early 1900s.
Mark: None, except for "Germany" or numbers or both.

Black boy, molded shift:	
5in (13cm)	**$300-$350**
Blonde hair, molded bow:	
5½in (14cm)	**$200-$225**
Wig, lovely painted boots:	
5in (13cm)	**$200-$225**
All-Bisque:	
Child: 5in (13cm)	**$150-$175**
Parian-type (1860s style):	
5in (13cm)	**$225-$250**
Alice style with pink boots:	
5in (13cm)	**$325-$375**
Fancy hairdo and boots:	
4½in (11cm)	**$275-$300**
Molded clothes: 3¼in (9cm)	**$225**
Early boy, blonde hair:	
9in (23cm)	**$450-$500**

2-5/8in (6cm) early *Frozen Charlotte. H & J Foulke, Inc.*

Left: Very rare tiny *Frozen Charlotte* with molded hat and painted facial hair. *Private Collection.*

Fulper

Fulper Child Doll: Perfect bisque head, good wig, set or sleep eyes, open mouth; kid jointed or composition ball-jointed body; suitably dressed; all in good condition. Good quality bisque.

Kid body:
    18-21in (46-53cm)   **$275-$325***
Composition body:
    16-18in (41-46cm)   **$300-$350***
    22-24in (56-61cm)   **$400-$450***
Character Baby:
    16-18in (41-46cm)   **$400***
    22-24in (56-61cm)   **$500***
Toddler: 15-17in (38-43cm)**$650-$750**
Molded hair: 16in (41cm)
                $3,500-$4,000**

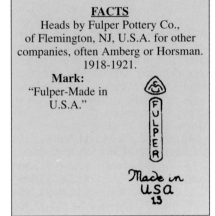

FACTS
Heads by Fulper Pottery Co., of Flemington, NJ, U.S.A. for other companies, often Amberg or Horsman. 1918-1921.
Mark:
"Fulper-Made in U.S.A."

*Allow more for an especially pretty or cute doll.
**Not enough samples to compute a reliable range.

20in (51cm) Fulper character baby. *H & J Foulke, Inc.*

Gaultier

Marked F.G. Fashion Lady (Poupée Peau): Ca. 1860-1930. Perfect bisque swivel head on bisque shoulder plate, original or good French wig, lovely glass stationary eyes, closed mouth, ears pierced; original kid body, kid arms with wired fingers or bisque lower arms and hands; appropriately dressed; all in good condition.

Mark: "F.G." on side of shoulder.

10-11in (26-28cm)	**$1,500-$1,650***
12-13in (30-33cm)	**$1,850-$2,000***
16-17in (41-43cm)	**$2,200-$2,500***
20in (51cm)	**$2,800-$3,000***
23-24in (58-61cm)	**$3,200-$3,500***
29-30in (71-76cm)	**$4,500-$5,000**
35in (89cm)	**$6,500**
37in (94cm)	**$7,200**

*Allow extra for original clothes.

FACTS
François Gauthier
(name changed to Gaultier in 1875);
St. Maurice,
Charenton, Seine, Paris, France.
(This company made
only porcelain parts, not bodies.)
1860 to 1899. (Then joined S.F.B.J.)

Wood body, *(Poupée Bois):*

16-18in (41-46cm)	**$4,800-$5,200**

Late doll in ethnic costume:

8-9in (20-23cm)	**$750-$850**

Painted eyes:

16-17in (41-43cm)	**$1,800-$2,000**

Painted eyes, molded hair:

14in (36cm)	**$3,800**

11in (28cm) early Gaultier *Poupée Peau,* all original. *H & J Foulke, Inc.*

Gaultier child with scroll mark, but face mold of block mark, exceptional model. *Mary Ann Spinelli.*

20in (51cm) early Gaultier child with block mark, kid body with bisque arms, exceptional model. *Mary Ann Spinelli.*

Early model:
13in (33cm) rare neck mechanism,
at auction **$7,700**
"Baggy pants," kid-over-wood arms:
15in (38cm) **$3,300**

Approximate size chart:
Size 3/0 = 10½in (27cm)
2/0 = 11½in (29cm)
1 = 13½in (34cm)
2 = 15in (38cm)
3 = 17in (43cm)
5 = 20in (51cm)
6 = 22in (56cm)

Marked F.G. Bébé: Ca. 1879-1887. Perfect bisque swivel head, large bulgy paperweight eyes, closed mouth, pierced ears; dressed; all in good condition. So-called "Block letter" mark.

Mark: F . 7.G

Composition body:
10in (25cm)	**$4,400-$4,700**
13-15in (33-38cm)	**$4,300-$4,600**
18-20in (46-51cm)	**$5,200-$5,700**
22-23in (56-58cm)	**$5,800-$6,100**
27-28in (69-71cm)	**$6,800-$7,200**
33-35in (84-89cm)	**$7,500-$8,000**

Kid body:
10in (25cm)	**$4,700-$4,900**
13-14in (33-36cm)	**$4,700-$5,200**
17-19in (43-48cm)	**$6,000**
22in (56cm)	**$7,000-$7,500**

Marked F.G. Bébé: Ca. 1887-1900. Bisque head, beautiful large set eyes; well dressed; all in good condition. So-called "Scroll" mark.

Mark:

Closed mouth, very good quality bisque:
5-6in (13-15cm)	**$750-$800**
15-17in (38-43cm)	**$2,800-$3,100***
22-24in (56-61cm)	**$3,600-$3,900***
27-28in(69-71cm)	**$4,300-$4,600***
32in (81cm)	**$5,000**

Open mouth:
14-17in (38-43cm)	**$1,750-$1,950**
20-22in(51-56cm)	**$2,100-$2,400**
31in (79cm)	**$3,300-$3,600**

*For grainy or high color bisque, deduct $500 to $1,000.

Gesland

Fashion Lady (Poupée): Perfect bisque swivel head, good wig, paperweight eyes, closed mouth, pierced ears; stockinette body on metal frame with bisque hands and legs; dressed; all in good condition.

Early face:
16-20in (41-51cm) **$5,500–$6,200***
F.G. face:
14in (36cm) **$3,600–$3,800***
16-20in (41-51cm) **$4,000–$4,500***
24in (61cm) **$5,500-$5,700***
28in (71cm) **$6,000–$6,500***
Body only, for 14in (36cm) **$1,100**

Bébé: Perfect bisque swivel head, composition shoulder plate, good wig, paperweight eyes, closed mouth, pierced ears; stockinette body on metal frame with composition lower arms and legs; dressed; all in good condition.

FACTS
Heads: François Gaultier, Paris, France.
Bodies: E. Gesland, Paris, France.
1860-1928.
Mark: Head:

F G

Body: Sometimes stamped "E. Gesland."

Beautiful early face:
14-16in (36-41cm) **$4,900–$5,100**
22-24in (56-61cm) **$5,900–$6,400**
29-30in (71-76cm) **$7,300-$7,500**
"Scroll" mark face:
14-16in (36-41cm) **$2,800–$3,100**
22-24in (56-61cm) **$4,000–$4,500**

*Allow extra for original clothes.

Gesland *poupée,*
all original. *Private Collection.*

Goebel

Goebel Child Doll: 1895 on. Perfect bisque socket head, good wig, sleep eyes, open mouth; composition jointed body; dressed; all in good condition. Some mold #120 or **B**.

16-18in (41-46cm)	**$350-$400**
23-25in (58-64cm)	**$425-$475**

Goebel Character Baby: Ca. 1910. Perfect bisque socket head, good wig, sleep eyes, open mouth; composition jointed baby body; dressed; all in good condition.

13-15in (33-38cm)	**$275-$325**
19-21in (48-53cm)	**$400-$450**

Goebel Character Doll: Ca. 1910. Perfect bisque head with molded hair in various styles, some with ornamentation, some with hats; character face with painted features; papier-mâché five-piece body; all in good condition.

6½in (7cm)	**$275-$300**

FACTS
F & W Goebel porcelain factory, near Coburg, Thuringia, Germany. 1879 on.
Marks:

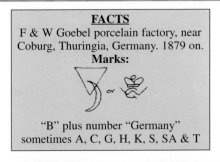

"B" plus number "Germany" sometimes A, C, G, H, K, S, SA & T

7in (18cm) Goebel character child. *Kay Jensen Antique Dolls.*

Left: 24in (61cm) Goebel child. *H & J Foulke, Inc.*

Googly-Eyed Dolls

All-Bisque Googly: Jointed at shoulders and hips, molded shoes and socks; mohair wig, glass eyes, impish mouth; undressed; in perfect condition.

Glass Eyes:

#217, 501, 330 and others:

4½-5in (11-13cm)	**$750-$800**
5½-6in (14-15cm)	**$900-$1,000**

#189, 192 swivel necks:

4½-5in (11-13cm)	**$900-$1,100**
5½-6in (14-15cm)	**$1,150-$1,250**
7in (18cm)	**$1,350-$1,450**

#112 Kestner, jointed elbows and knees, swivel neck:

5in (13cm)	**$3,250**
7in (18cm)	**$4,500****

FACTS

J.D. Kestner; Armand Marseille; Hertel, Schwab & Co.; Heubach; H. Steiner; Goebel and other German and French firms. Ca. 1911-on.

#111 Kestner, jointed elbows and knees, stiff neck: 5½in (13cm) **$3,250**
Baby: 4½in (12cm) **$550-$600**
S.W.C. **#405:** 6½in (17cm) **$1,350****
K★R 131:

7in (18cm)	**$3,500-$3,800****

Painted eyes, molded hair or wigged:

#217, 179 and others:

4½in (12cm)	**$400**
6in (15cm)	**$500-$550**
7in (18cm)	**$600-$650**

S.W.C. **#408:** 5in (13cm) **$350-$400***
#218, baby with wig: 6in (15cm) **$525**

Painted eyes, composition body: Perfect bisque swivel head; five-piece composition toddler or baby body; cute clothes; all in good condition.

A.M., E. Heubach, Goebel, R.A.:

6½-7½in (16-19cm)	**$400-$450***
9-10in (23-25cm)	**$750***
12in (31cm)	**$1,000***

#252 A.M., Kewpie-type baby:

9in (23cm)	**$1,200-$1,400****

Gebrüder Heubach:

6-7in (15-18cm)	**$575-$625***
7in (18cm) Winker	**$850-$900**
9in (23cm) top knot	**$1,500-$1,600**

#246 G.K. Winker with molded hat:

20in (51cm) at auction	**$2,100**

#10790: 4in (10cm) head only,

at auction	**$3,920**

*Allow extra for unusual models.
**Not enough price samples to compute a reliable range.

5in (12cm) 112 Kestner googly with jointed elbows and knees. *H & J Foulke, Inc.*

Glass eyes, composition body: Perfect bisque head; original composition body; cute clothes; all in nice condition. A.M. #323 and other similar models by H. Steiner, E. Heubach, Goebel and Recknagel:

7-8in (18-20cm)	**$900-$1,100**
10in (25cm)	**$1,400-$1,600**
13in (33cm)	**$2,500**
Baby body:	
10-11in (25-28cm)	**$1,200-$1,400**

Armand Marseille:
#253 (watermelon mouth):

7-8in (18-20cm)	**$1,200-$1,500**
11in (28cm)	**$2,300-$2,600**
#200:	
8in (20cm)	**$1,200-$1,500**
11-12in (28-31cm)	**$2,100-$2,300**
#240:	
10in (25cm) toddler	**$3,000-$3,200**
#241: 10in (25cm)	**$3,500****

Bähr & Pröschild 686:

10½in (26cm) at auction	**$3,900****

Demalcol (Dennis, Malley & Co., London, England):

9-10in (23-25cm)	**$750-$850**

Max Handwerck (Elite):
Molded hat:

10-13in (25-33cm)	**$1,700-$1,800**
Uncle Sam	**$2,500**
Double-faced	**$2,200**

Hertel, Schwab & Co.:
#163, red molded hair:

15in (38cm) baby	**$6,000-$6,500**
Toddler:	
12in (31cm)	**$4,000-$4,500**
16in (41cm)	**$7,000-$7,500**
20in (51cm) at auction	**$27,000**
#165, baby:	
11-12in (28-31cm)	**$3,500-$3,800**
16in (41cm)	**$5,500**
Toddler:	
11-12in (28-31cm)	**$4,500**
16in (41cm)	**$6,500**
21in (53cm) at auction	**$25,000**
#172, baby:	
15in (38cm)	**$6,800-$7,200****
Toddler: 18in (46cm)	**$12,000****
#173, baby:	
10-11in (26-28cm)	**$3,500-$3,800****
16in (41cm)	**$6,000-$6,500****
Toddler:	
10-12in (26-31cm)	**$4,000-$5,000****
16in (41cm)	**$7,000-$7,500****

**Not enough price samples to compute a reliable range.

13½in (34m) J.D.K. 221 googly. *Connie & Jay Lowe.*

19in (48cm) Einco googly. *Connie & Jay Lowe.*

9in (23cm) Gebrüder Heubach 9573 googly. *H & J Foulke, Inc.*

8in (20cm) S.F.B.J. 245 googly, five-piece composition body. *Kay Jensen Antique Dolls.*

Ernst Heubach:
  #291, 7in (18cm) matching pair with
  dimples, at auction   **$2,800**
  #310, 13-14in (33-36cm) at auction
                         $4,000-$4,500
  #322
    8½-9in (21-23cm) **$2,100-$2,400**
Gebrüder Heubach:
  Einco: 11in (28cm) five-piece body
                         $3,500-$3,800
    18in (46cm) at auction   **$13,500**
  Elizabeth: 7-9in (18-23cm) **$1,850**
  #8678, 9573:
    6-7in (15-18cm)   **$900-$1,100**
    9in (23cm)   **$1,500-$1,700**
  #10542: 8in (20cm)   **$850**
Oscar Hitt:
  13in (33cm) at auction   **$26,000**
K ★ R 131: 15-16in (38-41cm) **$13,000**
J.D.K. 221:
  12-13in (31-33cm)   **$5,800-$6,800**
  16½in (43cm) largest size
                       $13,000-$14,500
Kley & Hahn 180: 16½in (43cm)
                             $3,500**
Limbach SK: 8in (20cm)   **$1,600**
P.M. 950:
  11in (28cm)   **$3,100-$3,300****
S.F.B.J. #245:
  8in (20cm), five-piece body
                       $2,700-$3,200
  15in (38cm)   **$4,500-$4,600****
Schieler: 15in (38cm)   **$3,200****

Disc Eyes:
DRGM 954642 black or white:
  11-12in (28-31cm) **$1,250-$1,500****

Composition face: 1911-1914.
Hug Me Kids, Little Bright Eyes and
other trade names. Round all-composition or composition mask face, wig,
round glass eyes looking to the side,
watermelon mouth; felt body; original
clothes; all in very good condition.
  10in (25cm)   **$700-$800**
  12in (31cm)   **$950**
  16in (41cm)   **$1,250**

**Not enough price samples to compute a
reliable range.

Greiner

Marked Greiner: Papier-mâché shoulder head with blonde or black molded hair, painted features; homemade cloth body, leather arms; nice old clothes; entire doll in good condition, some wear acceptable.

'58 label:

15-17in (38-43cm)	**$900-$1,000**
20-23in (51-58cm)	**$1,250-$1,500**
28-30in (71-76cm)	**$1,750-$2,000**
38in (97cm)	**$2,800**
Much worn:	
20-23in (51-58cm)	**$650-$750**
28-30in (71-76cm)	**$850-$950**
Glass eyes: 20-23in (51-58cm)	
	$2,200-$2,500**

**Not enough price samples to compute reliable range.

'72 label:

19-22in (48-56cm)	**$500-$550**
29-31in (71-79cm)	**$800-$900**
35in (89cm)	**$1,100-$1,200**

FACTS

Ludwig Greiner of Philadelphia, PA, U.S.A. 1858-1883, but probably as early as 1840s.

Mark: Paper label on back shoulder:

GREINER'S
IMPROVED
PATENTHEADS
Pat. March 30th'58
or

GREINER'S
PATENT DOLL HEADS
No7
Pat. Mar. 30'58. Ext.'72

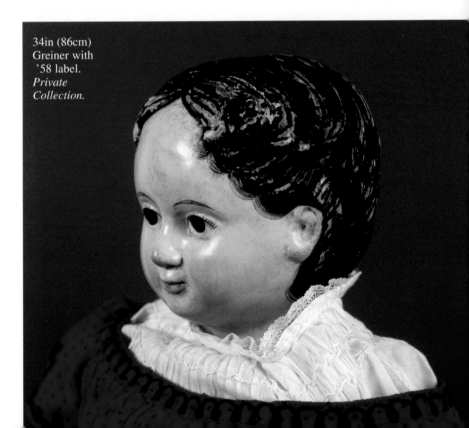

34in (86cm) Greiner with '58 label. *Private Collection.*

Heinrich Handwerck

Marked Handwerck Child Doll: Ca. 1885-on. Perfect bisque socket head, original or good wig, sleep or set eyes, open mouth, pierced ears; composition ball-jointed body with Handwerck stamp; dressed; entire doll in good condition.

#69, 79, 89, 99, 109, 119 or no mold #:
10-12in (25-31cm), all original
$550–$650
14-16in (36-41cm) $650-$700
19-21in (43-53cm) $550-$600
23-25in (58-64cm) $700-$750
28-30in (71-76cm) $800-$1,000
32in (79cm) $1,200-$1,350
36in (91cm) $1,800-$2,200
40in (102cm) $3,500-$3,750
42in (107cm) $4,200

Bébé Cosmopolite: 19in (48cm) all original, boxed $1,000
Ladies' Home Journal "Daisy," blonde mohair wig, blue eyes:
18in (46cm) only $1,500
#139 and other shoulder heads, kid body:
16-18in (41-46cm) $325-$350
22-24in (56-61cm) $425-$450
#79, 89, closed mouth:
18-20in (46-51cm) $2,300-$2,500**
24in (61cm) $2,800-$3,200**
#189, open mouth:
6½in (16cm), fully-jointed body
$700
18-20in (46-51cm) $900-$950

**Not enough price samples to compute a reliable range.

FACTS
Heinrich Handwerck, doll factory, Waltershausen, Thuringia, Germany. Heads by Simon & Halbig. 1855-on.
Trademarks: Bébé Cosmopolite, Bébé de Réclame, Bébé Superior.
Mark:

Germany

tcwacx handwfrcx
.ngcw S H & B-G

HANDWERCK
109-N
Germany

21in (53cm) 109 child. *H & J Foulke, Inc.*

Max Handwerck

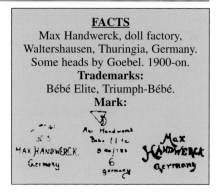

Marked Max Handwerck Child Doll: Perfect bisque socket head, original or good wig, set or sleep eyes, open mouth, pierced ears; original ball-jointed body; well dressed; all in good condition.

#283, 287, 297:

16-18in (41-46cm)	$300-$325
22-24in (56-61cm)	$400-$450
31-32in (79-81cm)	$700-$800
#421: 21in (53cm)	$650-$700

Bébé Elite Character Baby:

19-21in (48-53cm)	$400-$450

Hertel, Schwab & Co.

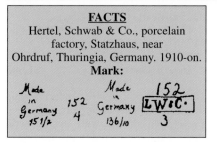

Marked Character Baby: Ca. 1910. Perfect bisque head; bent-limb baby body; dressed; all in good condition.

#130, 142, 150, 151, 152:

10-12in (25-31cm)	$250-$275*
15-17in (38-43cm)	$350-$400*
19-21in (48-53cm)	$450-$550*
24-25in (61-64cm)	$700-$800*

*Allow 25 percent extra for a jointed toddler body.

22in (56cm) Max Handwerck 287 child. *H & J Foulke, Inc.*

Left: 15in (38cm) Hertel, Schwab & Co. 151 character baby. *H & J Foulke, Inc.*

#150, all-bisque: 6in (15cm) **$400-$450**
#142, all-bisque, painted eyes:
  11in (28cm)   **$850-$900**
#159, two faces:
  10in (25cm) at auction   **$850**
#125 (so-called **Patsy Baby**):
  12-13in (30-33cm)   **$950-$1,000**
#126 (so-called **Skippy**):
  9in (23cm) baby   **$850**
  16in (41cm) toddler   **$1,500**

Child Doll: Ca. 1910. Perfect bisque head, mohair or human hair wig, sleep eyes, open mouth with upper teeth; good quality jointed composition body (some marked "K & W"); dressed; all in good condition.
Mold **#136:**
  7in (18cm) five-piece body
                    $250-$300
  18-20in (46-51cm)   **$400-$450**
  24-25in (61-64cm)   **$525-$575**

All-Bisque #208 Prize Baby: glass eyes, wig.
  4in (10cm)   **$225**
  7in (18cm)   **$400**

Marked Character Child: Perfect bisque head, painted or sleep eyes, closed mouth; jointed composition body; dressed; all in good condition.
#127 (so-called **Patsy**):
  17in (43cm)   **$2,100-$2,500**
#134, 141:
  13-14in (33-36cm)   **$3,500-$4,000**
#140:
  15in (38cm)   **$4,200**
#148, glass eyes, frowning face:
  18in (46cm) at auction   **$13,500**
#149:
  16-18in (41-46cm)   **$8,000-$9,000**
#154: See Kley & Hahn, page 130.
#166: See Kley & Hahn, page 130.
#169: See Kley & Hahn, page 130.

15in (38cm) 140 character boy. *McMasters Harris Premier Doll Auctions.*

Hertwig & Co.

Half-Bisque Dolls: 1911-on. Head and body to waist of one-piece bisque, molded hair, painted features; bisque hands, lower legs with white stockings and painted shoes, some with heels and bows; other parts of body are cloth; appropriate clothes; all in good condition.

4½in (11cm) children	**$225-$275**
6½in (17cm) adults	**$325-$375**
Family of seven dolls, boxed, at auction	**$3,300**

All-Bisque Children, painted eyes:
  Boy with molded hair, pouty face:
  4in (10cm) **$90-$110**
  Girl with molded hair and blue hair bows, 5in (12cm) **$90-$110**

See the "All-Bisque" section for Hertwig children with molded clothes, pink bisque characters and nodders.

See the "Bisque, German" section for shoulder heads with molded bonnets.

See the "China" section for china heads with gold-painted names.

See the "Amberg" section for all-bisque characters.

FACTS
Hertwig & Co., porcelain factory, Katzhutte, Thuringia, Germany. 1864-on.
Mark: "Germany"

6¾in (17cm) half-bisque gentleman. *H & J Foulke, Inc.*

7in (18cm) all-bisque child. *H & J Foulke, Inc.*

Ernst Heubach

Heubach Child Doll: Ca. 1888-on. Perfect bisque head; dressed; all in good condition.

#275 or horseshoe, kid or cloth body:
14in (36cm)	**$175-$200**
19-21in (48-53cm)	**$250-$300**
24in (61cm)	**$400**

#250, 251, composition body:
8-9in (20-23cm) five-piece body	**$210-$235**
16-18in (41-46cm)	**$300-$350**
23-24in (58-61cm)	**$400-$450**

#250, 407: Painted bisque:
7-8in (18-20cm)	**$110-$135**

#312 SUR (for Seyfarth & Reinhard):
14in (36cm)	**$300-$325**
28in (71cm)	**$600-$650**
45-46in (113-115cm)	**$3,500****

**Not enough price samples to compute a reliable range.

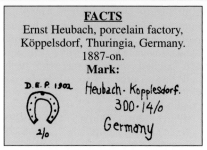

FACTS
Ernst Heubach, porcelain factory, Köppelsdorf, Thuringia, Germany. 1887-on.
Mark:

Character Children: 1910-on. Painted eyes, open/closed mouth.

#261, 262, 271 and others: Bisque shoulder head with molded hair, cloth body with composition lower arms.
12in (31cm)	**$300-$400**

#276, bug on nose:
7½in (19cm) at auction	**$625**

#417, Just Me-type:
12in (31cm) at auction	**$975**

15in (38cm) 275 child, all original. *H & J Foulke, Inc.*

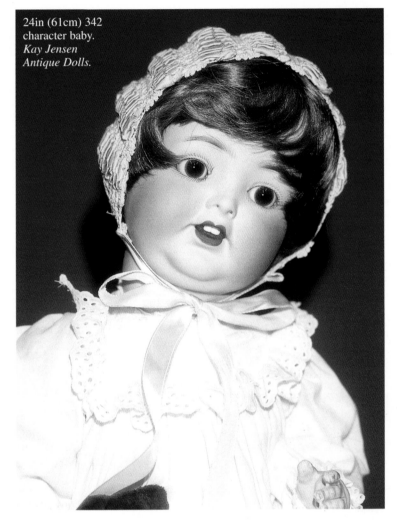

24in (61cm) 342
character baby.
*Kay Jensen
Antique Dolls.*

Character Baby: 1910-on. Perfect bisque head, good wig, sleep eyes, open mouth (sometimes also wobbly tongue and pierced nostrils); composition bent-limb baby; dressed; all in good condition.

#300, 320, 342 and others:

5½-6in (14-15cm)	**$250-$275**
8-10in (20-25cm)	**$250-$275**
14-17in (36-43cm)	**$325-$375**
19-21in (48-53cm)	**$400-$450**
24-25in (61-64cm)	**$550-$650**

Toddler: 9-10in (23-25cm) five-piece body **$375-$425**

Fully-jointed body:

15-17in (38-43cm)	**$475-$525**
23-25in (58-64cm)	**$800-$900**

Painted Bisque Toddler: 11in (28cm) factory original **$350-$400**

Infant: Ca. 1925. Perfect bisque head; cloth body.

#349, 339, 350:

10½in (26cm)	**$350-$400**
13-16in (33-41cm)	**$500-$550**

#338, 340:

14-16in (36-41cm)	**$725-$825****

**Not enough price samples to compute a reliable range.

Gebrüder Heubach

Heubach Character Child: Ca. 1910. Perfect bisque head; jointed composition or kid body; dressed; all in good condition. (For more photographs of Heubach dolls see *Focusing on Dolls*, pages 30-68 and previous *Blue Books*.)
#5636, 7663, laughing child, glass eyes:

12-13in (31-33cm)	**$1,600-$1,700**
15-18in (38-46cm)	**$2,200-$2,500**

#5689, smiling child:

26in (66cm)	**$4,000-$4,500***

#5730 Santa:

22-24in (56-61cm)	**$2,000-$2,400**

#5777 Dolly Dimple:

12in (31cm)	**$2,200**
19-22in (48-56cm)	**$3,000-$3,200**
Shoulder head, 17-19in (43-48cm)	**$900-$1,100**

#6969, 6970, 7246, 7347, 7407, 8017, pouty child (must have glass eyes):

7-9in (18-23cm)	**$850-$950**
12-13in (31-33cm)	**$2,250-$2,500**
18-20in (46-51cm)	**$3,800-$4,200**

FACTS
Gebrüder Heubach, porcelain factory, Licht and Sonneberg, Thuringia, Germany. 1820-on; doll heads, 1910-on.
Mark:

24in (61cm)	**$5,000-$5,500**
28in (71cm)	**$8,500***

#6969, painted eyes:

16in (41cm)	**$1,800**

#6692 and other shoulder head pouties:

14-16in (36-41cm)	**$550-$650**
20in (51cm)	**$900**

#7054 and other smiling shoulder heads:

12-14in (30-36cm)	**$450-$550**
19in (48cm)	**$800-$900**

#7407, painted eye, wigged:

16in (41cm)	**$2,000**

#7604, 7820 and other smiling socket heads:

14-16in (36-41cm)	**$700-$800**
20in (51cm)	**$1,250**

#7602, 6894, 7622 and other socket head pouties:

16-18in (41-46cm)	**$800-$900**

#7658, smiling face, molded short curly hair, bangs:

15in (38cm) at auction	**$6,400**

#7661, squinting eyes, crooked mouth:

19in (48cm)	**$6,750***

#7665, Smiling: 16in (41cm) **$1,800**
#7679, 8774 Whistler:

10in (25cm)	**$700-$800**
14in (36cm)	**$1,100**

#7684 Screamer: 10in (25cm) **$1,500**
16-19in (41-48cm) **$2,500-$3,000***
#7711:

9in (23cm)	**$800-$900**
12-14in (31-36cm)	**$1,400**

12in (31cm) 7246 pouty girl with glass eyes. *H & J Foulke, Inc.*

**Not enough price samples to compute a reliable range.

13in (33cm) 7711 character girl with open mouth. *H & J Foulke, Inc.*

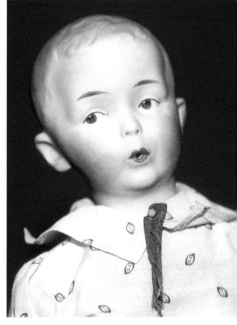

14in (36cm) 8774 whistling boy. *Kay Jensen Antique Dolls.*

#7743, big ears:
   17in (43cm)   **$5,500-$6,000****
#7764, singing girl:
   16in (41cm)   **$10,000****
#7788, 7850 Coquette:
   11in (28cm)   **$850-$900**
   14in (36cm)   **$1,000-$1,100**
   20in (51cm)   **$1,300-$1,400**
   Shoulder head,
   12in (31cm)   **$600-$700**
#7852, shoulder head, molded coiled braids: 16in (41cm)   **$2,200****
#7853, shoulder head, downcast eyes:
   14in (36cm)   **$1,650-$1,850**
#7911, 8191, grinning:
   11in (28cm)   **$650-$700**
   15in (38cm)   **$900-$1,000**
#7920: 18in (46cm)   **$2,700****
#7925, 7926, lady:
   11in (28cm)   **$1,200-$1,300**
   18-19in (46-48cm)   **$2,800-$3,100**
#8035, pouty boy, big ears:
   17in (43cm) at auction   **$11,000**

**Not enough price samples to compute a reliable range.

11in (28cm) character girl. *H & J Foulke, Inc.*

#8050, smiling girl with hair bow:
  18in (46cm)   **$10,000-$12,500****
#8192:
  9-11in (23-28cm)   **$350-$375**
  14-16in (36-41cm)   **$500-$550**
  18-22in (46-56cm)   **$750-$800**
#8381 Princess Julianna:
  16in (41cm)   **$12,000****
#8420, pouty with glass eyes:
  13in (33cm)   **$1,750-$1,950**
  16in (41cm)   **$2,200-$2,500**
#8548 Grumpy:
  25in (64cm)   **$13,500****
#8550, molded tongue sticking out:
  13in (33cm) intaglio eyes **$850-$950**
  13in (33cm) glass eyes
       $1,100-$1,200
#8556, googly-type face   **$11,500****
#9102 Cat:
  6in (15cm)   **$1,000-$1,150****
#9141 Winker:
  9in (23cm) glass eye   **$1,500**
  7in (18cm) painted eye   **$850-$950**
#9145: 23in (58cm) at auction **$20,500**
#10532:
  8½in (21cm) chubby five-piece
  toddler, all original   **$800-$900**

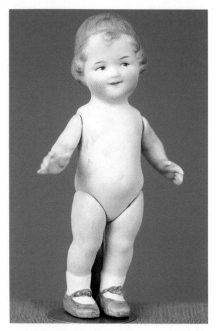

6in (15cm) all-bisque *Coquette* with hair band. *H & J Foulke, Inc.*

  20-22in (51-53cm)   **$1,000-$1,100**
  28in (71cm)   **$1,800**
#10586, 10633:
  12in (30cm)   **$375-$425**
  18-20in (46-51cm)   **$600-$650**
#11173 Tiss Me:
  8in (20cm)   **$1,850-$2,000****
Baby Bo Kaye, Bonnie Babe:
  7-8in (18-20cm)   **$900-$950**
#1907 Jumeau:
  16in (41cm)   **$1,800-$2,000**
  20-22in (51-56cm)   **$2,400-$2,500**

All-Bisque:
Position Babies and Action Figures:
  5in (13cm)   **$400-$450**
Girl with bobbed hair:
  9in (23cm)   **$800-$900**
Girl with headband (Coquette):
  6in (15cm) swivel neck   **$795-$895**
  9in (23cm)   **$900-$1,000**
Girl with three bows:
  6in (15cm)   **$1,350**
  9in (23cm)   **$1,650**
  9in (23cm) swivel neck   **$2,400**
Boy: 8in (20cm)   **$1,200**
Boy or girl: 4½in (11cm)   **$300-$350**
Chin Chin: 4½in (11cm)   **$300-$325**

Heubach Babies: Ca. 1910. Perfect bisque head; composition bent-limb body; dressed; all in nice condition.
#6894, 7602, 6898, 7759 and other pouty babies; **#7604** laughing:
  4½in (12cm)   **$225**
  6in (15cm)   **$250**
  10-12in (25-31cm)   **$350-$450**
  14in (36cm)   **$550-$650**
  20in (51cm)   **$1,000**
#7877, 7977 Baby Stuart:
Painted eyes:
  9in (23cm)   **$800-$850**
  13-15in (33-38cm)   **$1,300-$1,500**
Glass eyes: 13in (33cm)   **$2,250****
#8649, blue quilted bonnet:
  12in (31cm)   **$1,400**
#8420, glass eyes:
  14in (36cm)   **$1,100-$1,200**
#7959, molded pink cap:
  14in (36cm) at auction   **$4,200**

**Not enough price samples to compute a reliable range.

Indian Dolls
Bisque Heads

FACTS
Various German factories. Ca 1895-on.

American Indian Doll: Perfect bisque head, tinted complexion, wrinkles between eyebrows, wavy eyebrows, set brown glass eyes, black mohair wig; original clothes, head feathers, moccasins or molded shoes; all in good condition.
Marked "A.M." (Armand Marseille) or unmarked.

7-8in (18-20cm)	**$175-$225**
12in (30cm)	**$375-$425**
15in (38cm)	**$500-$550**
18in (46cm)	**$750-$850**

Bähr & Pröschild 244, closed mouth:
14-15in (36-38cm) **$1,800**
Gebrüder Heubach 8457, 9467, shoulder head on cloth body:
14in (36cm) **$2,500**
Simon & Halbig 1303:
15in (38cm) at auction **$6,750**

Jullien

FACTS
Jullien, Jeune of Paris, France.
1875-1904 when joined with S.F.B.J.
Mark: "JULLIEN" with size number

$$JuLLiEN$$
$$1$$

Marked Jullien Bébé: Perfect bisque head, lovely wig, paperweight eyes, closed mouth, pierced ears; jointed wood and composition body; pretty old clothes; all in good condition.

17-19in (43-48cm)	**$2,800-$3,000**
24-26in (61-66cm)	**$3,500-$4,000**

14in (36cm) factory dress and box, at auction **$3,600**
Open mouth:

19-21in (48-53cm)	**$1,500-$1,600**
29-30in (74-76cm)	**$2,200-$2,400**

19in (48cm) Jullien *bébé. Private Collection.*

Left: 14in (36cm) Bähr & Pröschild 224 Indian Brave. *H & J Foulke, Inc.*

Jumeau

Poupée Peau **Fashion Lady:** Late 1860s-on. Perfect bisque swivel head on shoulder plate, old wig, paperweight eyes, closed mouth, pierced ears; all-kid body; appropriate old clothes; all in good condition.

Mark on body: JUMEAU
MEDAILLE D'OR
PARIS

FACTS
Maison Jumeau, Paris, France.
1842-on.
Trademark:
Bébé Jumeau (1886)
Bébé Prodige (1886)
Bébé Français (1896)

Standard face:
 11½-13in (29-33cm) **$2,600-$3,000***
 17-18in (43-46cm) **$3,600-$3,800***
 20in (51cm) **$4,200-$4,600***
Head and shoulder plate only, size 2 **$950**

Poupée Bois, wood body with bisque limbs: 18in (46cm) **$6,500**
Later face with large eyes:
 10½-11in (27-28cm) **$2,000-$2,500***
 14-15in (36-38cm) **$2,800-$3,000***

So-called "Portrait Face:"
 19-21in (48-53cm) **$7,000-$7,250***
 28in (71cm) **$10,500**
 Wood body (*poupée bois*):
  19-21in (48-53cm)
 $10,000-$11,100*
Portrait Face with adult look:
 29in (74cm) **$34,300**

*Allow extra for original clothes.

18in (46cm) early *Poupée Peau* with portrait-type face. *H & J Foulke, Inc.*

12in (31cm) *Poupée Peau.*
H & J Foulke, Inc.

Period Clothes for Bébés:
Jumeau shift	**$400-$600**
Jumeau shoes	**$350-$450**
Jumeau dress and hat	**$1,000 up**

Portrait Jumeau: 1877-1883. Usually marked with size number only on head, blue stamp on body; skin or other good wig, spiral threaded enamel paperweight eyes, closed mouth, pierced ears; jointed composition body with straight wrists and separate ball joints; nicely dressed; all in good condition.

Almond-Eyed or First Series:

Sizes:
4/0 =	12in (30cm)
3/0 =	13½in (34cm)
2/0 =	14½in (37cm)
0 =	16in (41cm)
1 =	17in (43cm)
2 =	18½in (47cm)
3 =	20in (51cm)
4 =	23in (58cm)
5 =	25in (64cm)

12-14½in (30-37cm)	**$13,000-$15,000***
16-18½in (41-47cm)	**$18,000-$22,000***
20in (51cm)	**$25,000-$30,000***
23in (58cm)	**$33,000-$38,000***
25in (64cm)	**$55,000-$65,000***

*Allow extra for unusually large eyes.

10½in (26cm) *Poupée Peau* all original in regional French outfit. *H & J Foulke, Inc.*

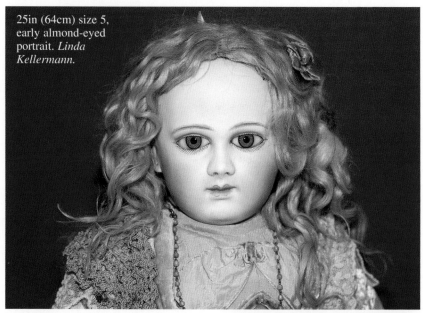

25in (64cm) size 5, early almond-eyed portrait. *Linda Kellermann.*

Second Series, excellent quality, larger dolls have applied ears:

Sizes:
    4 = 11-12in (28-31cm)
    5 = 13-14in (33-36cm)
    6 = 15in (38cm)
    7 = 16in (41cm)
    8 = 18in (46cm)
    9 = 20in (51cm)
    10 = 22in (56cm)
    12 = 25in (64cm)

11-12in (28-31cm)	**$5,000-$5,500**
13-15in (33-38cm)	**$5,500-$6,000**
18-20in (46-51cm)	**$7,000-$8,000**
22in (56cm)	**$9,000-$10,000**
25in (64cm)	**$12,000-$13,000**

Premiere, Early Unmarked Bébé:
Ca. 1880.
    9in (23cm) size 0   **$6,500-$7,000**
    10-11in (25-28cm) size 1   **$7,000**
    12in (31cm) size 2   **$7,000**

Incised Jumeau in Cartouche Bébé:
    12-13in (31-33cm)   **$5,500-$6,500**

15in (38cm) size 6, Second Series portrait. *H & J Foulke, Inc.*

17in (43cm) E.J. size 7, original French regional costume. Laraine & Gangolf Freisberg.

Long-Face Triste Bébé: 1879-1886. Designed by Carrier-Belleuse. Marked with size (9 to 16) number only on head, blue stamp on body. Perfect bisque socket head with beautiful wig, paperweight eyes, closed mouth, applied pierced ears; jointed composition body with straight wrists (separate ball joints on early models); lovely clothes; all in good condition.

21-23in (53-58cm)	**$20,000-$22,500**
26-27in (66-69cm)	**$25,000**
31-33in (79-84cm)	**$27,000**

Size
9 = 21in (53cm)
11 = 24in (61cm)
13, 14 = 29-30in (74-76cm)

E.J. Bébé: 1881-1886. Perfect bisque socket head with good wig, paperweight eyes, closed mouth, pierced ears; jointed composition body with straight wrists, early models with separate ball joints; lovely clothes; all in good condition.

Early Mark: 8
E.J.

17-18in (43-46cm) size 6	
	$8,500-$9,000
19-21in (48-53cm) size 8	**$11,000**
23-24in (58-61cm) size 9	**$14,000**
E.J.A.: 25in (64cm)	**$24,000-$26,000**

Mid to Late Period Mark:

"DÉPOSÉ"
E. 8 J.

9in (23cm)	**$6,500**
11in (28cm)	**$5,750-$6,000**
14-16in (36-41cm)	**$6,500-$6,800**
19-21in (48-53cm)	**$7,850-$8,250**
25-26in (64-66cm)	**$9,500-$10,500**
30in (76cm)	**$11,500-$13,000**

Déposé 9 or 9x:

20-21in (51-53cm)	**$6,500-$7,500**
10x: 22in (56cm)	**$8,000**
All-original couturier outfit, at auction	
	$15,000

Incised "Jumeau Déposé" Bébé: 1886-1889. Head incised as below, blue stamp on body. Perfect bisque socket head with good wig, paperweight eyes, closed mouth, pierced ears; jointed composition body with straight wrists; lovely clothes; all in good condition.

Mark: Incised on head:

DÉPOSÉ
JUMEAU
8

14-15in (36-38cm)	$4,000-$4,500
18-20in (46-51cm)	$5,000-$5,250
23-25in (58-64cm)	$5,500-$6,000

27in (69cm) boxed with original outfit, wig, shoes, at auction **$10,500**

Approximate sizes of E.J.s and Têtes:
1 = 10in (25cm)
2 = 11in (28cm)
3 = 12in (31cm)
4 = 13in (33cm)
5 = 14-15in (36-38cm)
6 = 16in (41cm)
7 = 17in (43cm)
8 = 19in (48cm)
9 = 20in (51cm)
10 = 21-22in (53-56cm)
11 = 24-25in (61-64cm)
12 = 26-27in (66-69cm)
13 = 29-30in (74-76cm)

Tête Jumeau Bébé: 1885-1899, then through S.F.B.J. Red stamp on head as indicated below, blue stamp or "Bébé Jumeau" oval sticker on body. Perfect bisque head, original or good French wig, beautiful stationary eyes, closed mouth, pierced ears; jointed composition body with jointed or straight wrists; original or lovely clothes; all in good condition.

Mark: TETE JUMEAU
DÉPOSÉ
B^{TE} SGDG
6

9-10in (23-25cm) #1	$6,000
12-13in (31-33cm)	$3,200-$3,800*
15-16in (38-41cm)	$3,500-$4,000*
18-20in (46-51cm)	$4,000-$4,200*
21-23in (53-58cm)	$4,300-$4,500*
25-27in (64-69cm)	$5,200-$5,500*
30in (76cm)	$5,800-$6,200*
34-36in (86-91cm)	$7,000-$7,500*
41in (104cm)	$10,000-$11,000*
Lady body, 20in (51cm)	$6,000*

Open mouth:
14-16in (36-41cm)	$2,350-$2,450*
20-22in (51-56cm)	$2,800-$3,000*
24-25in (61-64cm)	$3,200-$3,300*
27-29in (69-74cm)	$3,500*
32-34in (81-86cm)	$3,800*

*Allow extra for original clothes.

Large *Tête Jumeau.*
Dr. Carole Stoessel
Zvonar Collection.

Bébé Phonographe: 1894-1899.
  24-25in (61-64cm) **$6,500-$7,500**

Marked E.D. Bébé: Mark used during the Douillet management, 1892-1899. Perfect bisque head, closed mouth.
  17-19in (43-48cm) **$4,000-$4,200**
Mark:

Marked B.L. Bébé: 1892 on. For the Louvre department store. Perfect bisque socket head, closed mouth.
Mark: B. 9 L.
  13in (33cm) **$3,200-$3,800**
  18-21in (46-53cm) **$4,000-$4,500**

Marked R.R. Bébé: 1892 on. Perfect bisque head, closed mouth.
Mark: R 10 R
  21-23in (53-58cm) **$4,200-$4,500**
  26in (66cm) open mouth **$3,200**

#230 Character Child: Ca. 1910. Perfect bisque socket head, good wig, open mouth, set or sleep eyes; jointed composition body; dressed; all in good condition.
  12in (31cm) **$850-$950**
  21-23in (55-58cm) **$1,500-$1,600**

#1907 Jumeau Child: Ca. 1907-on. Sometimes red-stamped "Tête Jumeau." Perfect bisque head, open mouth.
  16in (40cm) **$2,000-$2,200**
  19-22in (48-56cm) **$2,500-$2,700**
  25-27in (64-69cm) **$3,000-$3,200**
  32-33in (81-84cm) **$3,800-$3,900**
Papier-mâché face:
  22-24in (56-61cm) **$800-$1,000****

DEP Tête Jumeau: See page 77 for details.
SFBJ Tête Jumeau: See page 169 for details.
Jumeau Characters: 1892-1899. Perfect bisque head with glass eyes, character expression:
  #203, 208 and others **$50,000 up**

#221 Great Ladies: 10-11in (25-28cm)
all original **$600-$700**
Double-faced Crying and Smiling:
  17in (43cm) at auction **$10,500**

Princess Elizabeth Jumeau: 1938 through S.F.B.J. Perfect bisque socket head highly colored, glass flirty eyes.
Mark:

UNIS
FRANCE 149
306

Body Incised: JUMEAU
PARIS
Princess

  18-19in (46-48cm) **$1,600-$1,800**
  32-33in (81-84cm) **$2,700-$3,200****

Bleuette: First model, incised "1."
  11in (27cm) only **$4,000-$4,200**

**Not enough price samples to compute a reliable range.

24in (61cm) *Tête Jumeau,* all original. *H & J Foulke, Inc.*

Marked Kamkins: Molded mask face with painted features, wig; cloth body and limbs; original clothing; all in excellent condition.

18-20in (46-51cm)	**$2,500**
Good	**$1,200-$1,500**
Fair to good condition	**$850-$950**
Dirty, face wear, naked	**$500-$600**
With swivel joints or molded derriére	**$2,500-$3,500**

19in (48cm) *Kamkins. H & J Foulke, Inc.*

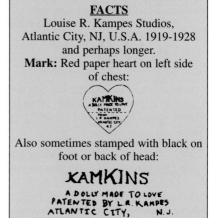

FACTS
Louise R. Kampes Studios, Atlantic City, NJ, U.S.A. 1919-1928 and perhaps longer.
Mark: Red paper heart on left side of chest:

Also sometimes stamped with black on foot or back of head:

KAMKINS
A DOLLY MADE TO LOVE
PATENTED BY L.R. KAMPES
ATLANTIC CITY,   N.J.

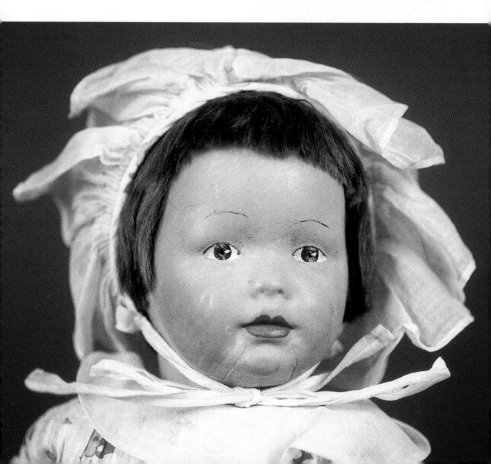

Kämmer & Reinhardt

Child Doll: 1886-1895. Perfect bisque head; ball-jointed composition body; appropriate clothes; all in good condition.

#192:

Closed mouth:

5in (13cm) five-piece body	**$550**
6-7in (15-18cm)	**$600-$700***
11in (28cm)	**$1,200-$1,300**
16-18in (41-46cm)	**$2,200-$2,500**
22-24in (56-61cm)	**$2,700-$2,900**

Open mouth:

7-8in (18-20cm)	**$550-$600***
12in (31cm)	**$700**
14-16in (36-41cm)	**$750-$850**
20-22in (51-56cm)	**$1,000-$1,100**
26-28in (66-71cm)	**$1,400-$1,600**
9in (23cm) doll in original dressmaker set	**$2,100**

Child Doll: 1895-1930s. Perfect bisque head, open mouth; Kämmer & Reinhardt ball-jointed composition body; appropriate clothes; all in good condition.

#191, 290, 402, 403 or size number only+:

Five-piece body:

4½-5in (12-13cm)	**$450-$495**
7-8in (18-20cm)	**$450-$500**
10in (25cm)	**$650-$700**

+Numbers 15 to 100 low on neck are centimeter sizes, not mold numbers.
*Allow $100 to $200 additional for flirty eyes; allow $200 extra for flapper body; allow $100 for walking body.

18½in (47cm) 192 child with open mouth. *H & J Foulke, Inc.*

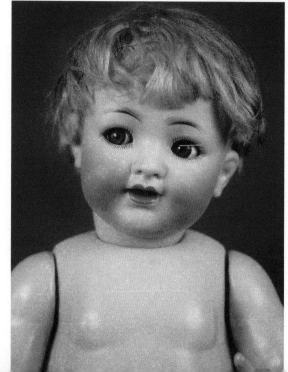

Above left: 13in (33cm) 118A character baby. *H & J Foulke, Inc.*

Above: 8¾in (22cm) 126 toddler with "starfish" hands. *H & J Foulke, Inc.*

Left: 18in (46cm) 22 toddler. *H & J Foulke, Inc.*

Fully-jointed body:

8-10in (20-25cm)	**$700-$800**
12-14in (31-36cm)	**$550-$600**
16-17in (41-43cm)	**$625-$650***
19-21in (48-43cm)	**$700-$750***
23-25in (58-64cm)	**$800-$900***
28in (71cm)	**$1,100-$1,200***
30-31in (76-79cm)	**$1,300-$1,500***
33-34in (84-86cm)	**$1,800-$2,000**
36in (91cm)	**$2,500-$2,800**
39-42in (99-107cm)	**$4,100-$4,600**

Closed mouth: 6in (15cm) five-piece body **$550-$600**

Child Doll: Shoulder head, kid body; all in good condition.

19-22in (48-56cm) **$350-$400**

Character Babies or Toddlers: 1909-on. Perfect bisque head; Kämmer & Reinhardt composition body; nicely dressed; all in good condition. (See *Simon & Halbig Dolls, The Artful Aspect* for photographs of mold numbers not shown here.)

#100 Baby, painted eyes:

11-12in (28-31cm)	**$400-$425**
14-15in (36-38cm)	**$500-$600**
18-20in (46-51cm)	**$800-$900**

Glass eyes:

16in (41cm)	**$1,800-$2,000*****

#118A, baby body: 11in (28cm) **$1,200**

#119, baby body:

24in (61cm), at auction **$16,000**

#121, 122, baby body:

10-11in (25-28cm)	**$500-$525**
15-16in (38-41cm)	**$700-$800**
23-24in (58-61cm)	**$1,100-$1,200**

#121, 122, toddler body:

10in (25cm) five-piece body	**$900-$1,000+**
13-14in (33-36cm)	**$1,200-$1,300**
20-23in (51-58cm)	**$1,700-$1,900**
28in (71cm)	**$2,200**

#126, 22, baby body:

10-12in (25-31cm)	**$400-$425****
14-16in (36-41cm)	**$450-$500****
18-20in (46-51cm)	**$550-$650****
22-24in (56-61cm)	**$700-$800****
28in (71cm)	**$1,200**

#126, all-bisque baby:

6-7½in (15-19cm)	**$750-$950**
10in (25cm) at auction	**$1,650**

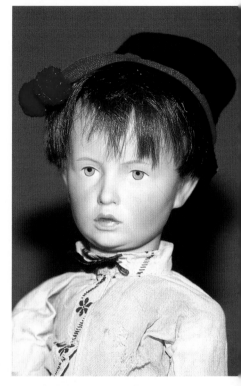

107 character child. *Floyd Jones.*

#126, all-bisque toddler:

7in (18cm)	**$1,400-$1,500*****

#126, 22, five-piece toddler body:

6-7in (15-18cm)	**$750-$850+**
9-10in (23-25cm)	**$950-$1,000+**
15-17in (38-43cm)	**$575-$675**
23in (58cm)	**$850-$950**

#126, toddler, fully-jointed:

12-13in (31-33cm)	**$550-$650****
15-17in (38-41cm)	**$850-$950****
23-25in (58-64cm)	**$1,200-$1,500****
28-30in (71-76cm)	**$1,650-$1,850****

+With "starfish" hands.
*Allow $100 to $200 additional for flirty eyes; allow $200 extra for flapper body; allow $100 extra for walking body.
**Allow $50 to $100 additional for flirty eyes.
***Not enough price samples to compute a reliable range.

#128, baby body:

10in (25cm)	**$550***
15-16in (38-41cm)	**$750-$850***
20in (51cm)	**$1,200-$1,300***
24in (61cm)	**$1,700-$1,800***

#128, toddler body:

16-18in (41-46cm)	**$1,650****

Composition Heads:

#926, five-piece toddler body:

18in (46cm)	**$400-$500***

"Puz" baby, cloth body:

16-17in (41-43cm)	**$350-$400***
25in (64cm)	**$550-$600***

Character Children: 1909-on. Perfect bisque socket head; Kämmer & Reinhardt composition ball-jointed body; nicely dressed; all in good condition. (See *Simon & Halbig, The Artful Aspect* for photographs of mold numbers not shown here.)

Boxed Set: One doll with four heads, at auction **$16,000**

#101 (Peter or Marie):

8-10in (20-25cm)	**$2,000-$2,300**
12in (31cm)	**$2,700-$3,000**
14-15in (36-38cm)	**$3,500-$3,600**
17in (43cm)	**$4,350-$4,650**
19-20in (48-51cm)	**$5,500-$6,000**

Glass eyes:

15in (38cm)	**$9,000-$10,000**
20in (51cm)	**$12,500**

#101X, flocked hair:

15in (38cm) at auction	**$6,000**

#102:

12in (31cm)	**$20,000 up****
22in (55cm)	**$75,000 up****

#103, 104: 22in (56cm)	**$100,000 up****
#105: 22in (56cm)	**$170,000****
#106: 22in (56cm)	**$145,000****

#107 (Carl):

12in (30cm)	**$12,000-$14,000**
22in (56cm)	**$50,000-$55,000**

*Allow $50 to $100 additional for flirty eyes.

**Not enough price samples to compute a reliable range.

22in (56cm) 117n character girl. *H & J Foulke, Inc.*

#109 (Elise):
7in (18cm)	**$2,500-$2,800**
9-10in (23-25cm)	**$3,000-$3,500**
14in (36cm)	**$7,500-$8,500**
21in (53cm)	**$20,000**

Glass eyes:
20in (51cm)	**$25,000-$26,000**

#112, 112x:
14in (36cm)	**$8,500-$9,500**
17-18in (43-46cm)	**$12,000-$15,000**

Glass eyes:
10-11in (25-28cm)	**$8,000** **
23in (58cm) at auction	**$22,000**

#114 (Hans or Gretchen):
8-9in (20-23cm) jointed body	**$1,800-$2,200**
12in (31cm)	**$2,700-$3,200**
15-16in (38-41cm)	**$4,000-$4,500**
19-20in (48-51cm)	**$5,500-$6,000**
21-22in (53-56cm)	**$6,200-$6,600**
25in (64cm) at auction	**$9,500**

Glass eyes:
15in (38cm)	**$9,250**
24in (61cm)	**$18,000**

#115: 15-16in (38-41cm) toddler
$5,000-$5,500

#115A:
Baby:
10-12in (25-31cm)	**$2,000-$2,200**
14-16in (36-41cm)	**$2,700-$3,000**

Toddler:
15-16in (38-41cm)	**$3,700-$4,200**
19-20cm (48-51cm)	**$4,800-$5,200**
23in (58cm)	**$6,000**

#116:
16in (41cm) toddler **$3,500-$4,000** **

#116A, open/closed mouth:
Baby:
10-11in (25-28cm)	**$1,600-$1,800**
14-16in (36-41cm)	**$2,200-$2,700**

Toddler:
12-13in (31-33cm)	**$2,800-$3,000**
16-18in (41-46cm)	**$3,000-$3,500**

#116A, open mouth:
Baby:
14-16in (36-41cm)	**$1,200-$1,500**
Toddler: 16in (41cm)	**$1,900**

**Not enough price samples to compute a reliable range.

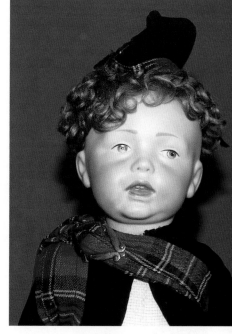

18in (46cm) 112 character child. *Laraine & Gangolf Friesberg.*

18½in (47cm) 114 character child. *Linda Kellermann.*

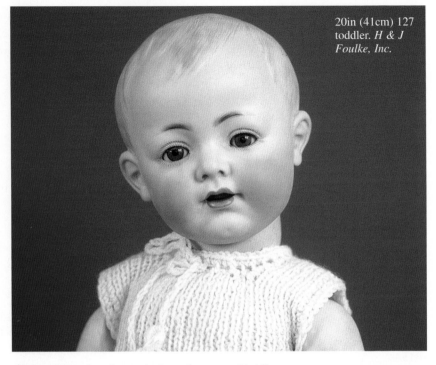

20in (41cm) 127 toddler. *H & J Foulke, Inc.*

#117, 117A, closed mouth (may have an H. Handwerck body):

8in (20cm)	**$2,400-$2,500**
12in (30cm)	**$3,500-$3,800**
14-16in (36-41cm)	**$4,300-$4,800**
18-20in (46-51cm)	**$5,000-$5,500**
22-24in (56-61cm)	**$5,750-$6,250**
30-32in (76-81cm)	**$7,000-$7,500**

#117n, flirty eyes:

14-16in (36-41cm)	**$1,100-$1,200**
20-22in (51-56cm)	**$1,600-$1,800**
28-30in (71-76cm)	**$2,000-$2,300**

#117n, sleep eyes:

14-16in (36-41cm)	**$850-$950**
22-24in (56-61cm)	**$1,200-$1,300**
30-32in (76-81cm)	**$1,500-$1,700**
39in (100cm)	**$3,900-$4,100**

#117, open mouth:

27in (69cm)	**$4,000-$4,500**

#123, 124 (Max & Moritz): Must have special body with molded shoes.

17in (43cm) each	**$20,000-$23,000****

#127:

Baby: 10in (25cm)	**$700-$750**
14-15in (36-38cm)	**$1,000-$1,100**
20-22in (51-56cm)	**$1,300-$1,600**

Toddler:

15-16in (38-41cm)	**$1,100-$1,300**
20-23in (51-58cm)	**$1,500-$1,700**

#135, child:

14-16in (36-41cm)	**$1,000-$1,200**

#201: 13in (33cm) **$1,500****

#214: 15in (38cm) **$2,100-$2,500****

Infant: 1924-on. Perfect bisque head; cloth body, composition hands; nicely dressed; all in good condition.

#171, 172:

14-15in (36-38cm)	**$3,000-$3,500****

#173, toddler (composition body):

14in (36cm)	**$1,650****

#175: 11in (28cm) head circumference **$1,100-$1,200****

Cloth Characters: 1927. Stockinette faces with needle-sculpted and hand-painted features; straw-filled torso; wire-armature arms and legs, wood feet; all original; excellent condition.

12in (31cm)	**$350-$400**

**Not enough price samples to compute a reliable range.

Kestner

Child doll, early socket head: Ca. 1880. Perfect bisque head, plaster dome; Kestner composition ball-jointed body, some with straight wrists and elbows; well dressed; all in good condition. Many marked with size numbers only.

#169, 128, long face and round face with closed mouth; no mold number:

7in (18cm)	**$1,200-$1,500**
10in (25cm)	**$1,500-$1,800**
12in (31cm)	**$1,800-$2,000**
14-16in (36-41cm)	**$2,000-$2,200**
19-21in (48-53cm)	**$2,300-$2,500**
24-25in (61-64cm)	**$2,750-$3,000**
29in (74cm)	**$3,500**
33in (84cm)	**$4,000**

Face with square cheeks or white space between lips, closed mouth; no mold number:

14-16in (36-41cm)	**$1,800-$2,200**
19-21in (48-53cm)	**$2,400-$2,500**
24-25in (61-64cm)	**$2,600-$2,800**

FACTS
J.D. Kestner, Jr., doll factory, Waltershausen, Thuringia, Germany. Kestner & Co., porcelain factory, Ohrdruf. 1816-on.

Very pouty face, closed mouth:

7in (18cm)	**$1,700-$1,900**
9in (23cm)	**$2,000-$2,300**
10-12in (25-31cm)	**$2,800-$3,000**
14-16in (36-41cm)	**$3,000-$3,200**
19-21in (48-53cm)	**$3,400-$3,800**
24in (61cm)	**$4,200-$4,500**
#X: 15in (38cm) only	**$3,200-$3,800**
#XI: 16in (41cm) only	**$3,900-$4,500**
#XII: 17in (43cm)	**$4,500**

#103, closed mouth:

28-32in (71-78cm)	**$3,000-$3,500**

A.T.-type, closed mouth:

12in (31cm)	**$5,000-$6,000**
21in (31cm)	**$10,000-$12,500**

22in (56cm) very pouty closed mouth. *H & J Foulke, Inc.*

Bru-type, molded teeth, jointed ankles:
  17in (43cm)   **$4,250**
Open mouth, square cut teeth:
  12-14in (31-36cm)   **$1,000**
  16-18in (41-46cm)   **$1,200-$1,400**
  24-25in (61-64cm)   **$1,500-$1,700**
Wax-over papier-mâché head: 11in
(38cm) all original, at auction   **$1,000**

Child doll, early shoulder head: Ca.
1880s. Perfect bisque head, plaster
dome, good wig, set or sleep eyes;
sometimes head is slightly turned; kid
body with bisque lower arms; marked
with size letters or numbers. (No mold
numbers.)
Closed mouth:
  12in (31cm)   **$450-$475***
  14-16in (36-41cm)   **$550-$650***
  20-22in (51-56cm)   **$700-$750***
  26in (66cm)   **$900-$950***
A.T.-type, closed mouth:
  21in (53cm)   **$7,000**
Open/closed mouth:
  16-18in (41-46cm)   **$550-$650**
Open mouth (turned shoulder head):
  16-18in (41-46cm)   **$350-$400**
  22-24in (56-61cm)   **$500-$550**
Open mouth, square cut teeth:
  14-16in (36-41cm)   **$1,000-$1,200**

**Child doll, bisque shoulder head,
open mouth:** Ca. 1892. Plaster dome,
good wig, sleep eyes, open mouth; kid
body, some with rivet joints; dressed,
all in good condition. (See *Kestner,
King of Dollmakers* for photographs of
mold numbers not shown here.)
Head Mark: 154 8 dep
        D made in Germany

Body Mark:

#145, 154, 147, 148, 166, 195:
  12-13in (31-33cm)   **$225-$250****
  16-18in (41-46cm)   **$300-$350****
  20-22in (51-56cm)   **$400-$450****
  26-28in (66-71cm)   **$550-$650****

*Allow $100 to $200 extra for a very
pouty face or swivel neck.
**Allow $50 to $75 additional for a rivet
jointed body and/or jointed composition
arms. Allow 30 percent additional for
original clothes, wig and shoes.

19½in (49cm) early
open mouth child,
chunky early body.
H & J Foulke, Inc.

Child doll, socket head, open mouth: Kestner ball-jointed body; dressed; all in good condition. (See *Kestner, King of Dollmakers* for photographs of mold numbers not shown here.)

Head Mark: *made in Germany. 8. 162.*

Body Mark:

Germany	or	Excelsior
5-1/2		DRP № 70686 Germany

Mold numbers #142, 144, 146, 164, 167, 171, 214:

10-12in (25-31cm)	**$550-$650***
14-16in (36-41cm)	**$600-$650***
18-21in (46-43cm)	**$650-$750***

24-26in (61-66cm)	**$800-$850***
28in (71cm)	**$900-$950***
32-33in (81-84cm)	**$1,200-$1,400***
36in (91cm)	**$2,200-$2,500**
42in (107cm)	**$3,750-$4,250**

Harder to find molds #128, 129, 149, 152, 160, 161, 173, 174:

10-12in (25-31cm)	**$700-$800***
14-16in (36-41cm)	**$700-$800***
18-21in (46-53cm)	**$850-$950***
24-26in (61-66cm)	**$1,100-$1,200***

#133, five-piece body: 6in (15cm) **$350**

#155, fully-jointed body:

7-8in (18-20cm)	**$700-$800**
10in (25cm) five-piece body	**$650-$700**

*Allow 30 percent additional for all-original clothes, wig and shoes.

Left: 16½in (42cm) 167 child, all original. *H & J Foulke, Inc.*

16in (41cm) 152 child. *H & J Foulke, Inc.*

18in (46cm) 186 character child, painted eyes. *Floyd Jones.*

16in (41cm) 183 character child with glass eyes. *Kay Jensen Antique Dolls.*

#171 Daisy, blonde mohair wig, blue sleep eyes:

18in (46cm) only	**$1,500-$1,600**
All-original shift, shoes, socks, wig	**$2,000**

#168, 196, 215:

18-21in (46-53cm)	**$550-$650**
26-28in (66-71cm)	**$700-$750**
32in (81cm)	**$800-$900**

Character Child: 1909-on. Perfect bisque head character face, plaster pate, wig, painted or glass eyes, closed, open or open/closed mouth; Kestner jointed composition body; dressed; all in good condition. (See *Kestner, King of Dollmakers* for photographs of mold numbers not shown here.)

#143 (Pre-1897):

7-8in (18-20cm)	**$700-$750**
9-10in (23-25cm)	**$750-$800**
12-14in (31-36cm)	**$750-$850**
18-20in (46-51cm)	**$1,000-$1,400**
24-27in (58-69cm)	**$1,800-$2,100**

#178-190:

Painted eyes:

12in (31cm)	**$1,800-$2,200**
15in (38cm)	**$3,200-$3,600**
18in (46cm)	**$4,500-$5,000**

Glass eyes:

12in (31cm)	**$3,200-$3,500**
15in (38cm)	**$4,800-$5,200**
18in (46cm)	**$6,000-$6,500**

Boxed set, doll with three character heads:

Painted eyes:

12in (31cm)	**$9,000**
15in (38cm)	**$12,500**
Glass eyes: 15in (38cm)	**$20,000****

#206:

12in (31cm)	**$10,000****
19in (48cm)	**$25,000****

#208:

Painted eyes:

12in (31cm)	**$10,000****
23-24in (58-61cm)	**$25,000****

#212: 12in (31cm) at auction **$8,750****

#220, toddler:

16in (41cm)	**$5,000-$5,500**
20in (51cm)	**$6,000-$6,500**
27in (69cm) size Q20	**$8,500-$9,500**

**Not enough price samples to compute a reliable range.

#239 toddler:
 15-17in (38-43cm) **$3,500-$4,000****
#241:
 17-18in (43-46cm) **$5,000-$5,500**
 21-22in (53-56cm) **$6,000-$6,300**
 28-30in (71-76cm) **$7,500-$8,000**
#249:
 15in (38cm) **$900-$1,000**
 22-24in (56-61cm) **$1,300-$1,400**
#260:
 Toddler, five-piece body:
  8-10in (20-25cm) **$900-$1,100**
  18-20in (46-51cm) **$900-$1,000**
 Jointed body:
  12-14in (31-36cm) **$650-$700**
  18-20in (46-51cm) **$750-$850**
  29-30in (74-76cm) **$1,100-$1,400**
  37in (95cm) at auction **$3,750**
  42in (107cm) **$4,250**

Character Baby: 1910-on. Perfect bisque head, molded and/or painted hair or good wig, sleep eyes, open or open/closed mouth; Kestner bent-limb body; well dressed; nice condition. (See *Kestner, King of Dollmakers* for photographs of mold numbers not shown here.)
Mark:

made in
F. Germany. 10
211
J.D.K.

#211, 226, 257:
 11-13in (28-33cm) **$550-$600***
 16-18in (41-46cm) **$700-$800***
 20-22in (51-56cm) **$900-$1,100***
 25in (64cm) **$1,500-$1,650**
#211, Toddler:
 16-20in (41-51cm) **$1,500-$1,600**
 24in (61cm) **$2,000-$2,200**
#257 Toddler:
 8in (20cm) **$1,000-$1,100**

JDK, solid dome:
 12-14in (31-36cm) **$450-$550**
 17-19in (43-48cm) **$600-$700**
 23-25in (58-64cm) **$1,000-$1,200**
 Painted eyes: 14in (36cm) **$375-$425**
#262, 263: See page 63.
#210, 234, 235, 238, shoulder heads:
 13in (33cm) **$800-$900**
Hilda, #237, 245 and solid dome baby **1070:**
 11-13in (28-33cm) **$1,800-$2,200**
 16-17in (41-43cm) **$2,400-$2,600**
 20-22in (51-56cm) **$3,200-$3,500**
 24in (61cm) **$4,000-$4,500**

*Allow $50 to $100 extra for an original skin wig.
**Not enough price samples to compute a reliable range.

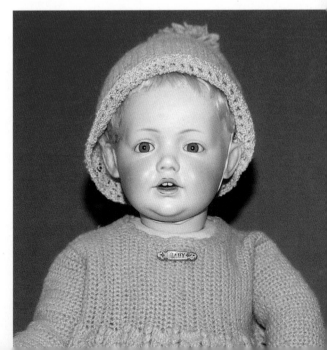

19in (48cm) 237 *Hilda* toddler. *H & J Foulke, Inc.*

Above: 17in (43cm) fat-cheeked baby. *H & J Foulke, Inc.*

Right: 6¾in (17cm) 184 all-bisque child. *H & J Foulke, Inc.*

20in (51cm) 247 toddler. *H & J Foulke, Inc.*

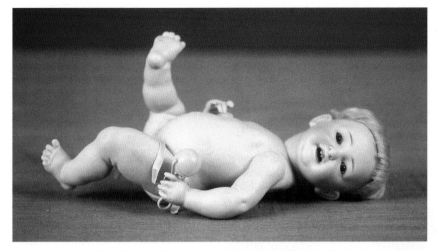

12in (31cm) 226 all-bisque baby. *H & J Foulke, Inc.*

Toddler:
14in (36cm)	**$3,200-$3,500**
17-19in (43-48cm)	**$4,200-$4,600**
21-23in (53-58cm)	**$4,800-$5,200**

#247:
14-16in (36-41cm)	**$1,500-$1,800**
Toddler:	
15in (38cm)	**$1,800-$1,900**
18-20in (46-51cm)	**$2,200-$2,300**

#267, molded hair:
22-24in (56-61cm)	**$3,000-$3,300**

JDK, solid dome, fat-cheeked (so-called Baby Jean):
12-13in (31-33cm)	**$850-$950**
17-18in (43-46cm)	**$1,100-$1,300**
22-24in (56-61cm)	**$1,500-$1,700**

All-Bisque Baby:
Painted eyes, stiff neck:
5-6in (13-15cm)	**$225-$275**

Swivel neck, painted eyes:
7½in (19cm)	**$450-$500**
9in (23cm)	**$650-$750**
12in (31cm)	**$850-$950**

Glass eyes, swivel neck:
5½in (23-25cm)	**$800-$1,000**

#177 Toddler:
8in (20cm)	**$1,000-$1,250**

#178 Toddler:
8in (20cm)	**$1,250-$1,400**

Immobile position baby, painted features, wig: 2½in (6cm) **$150-$165**

All-Bisque Child: Perfect all-bisque child, jointed at shoulders and hips; glass eyes; very good quality.

#130, 150, 160 and 208:
4-5in (10-13cm)	**$250-$350**
6in (15cm)	**$375-$425**
7in (18cm)	**$450-$500**
8in (20cm)	**$600-$650**
9in (23cm)	**$800-$850**
10in (25cm)	**$900-$1,100**
12in (31cm)	**$1,200-$1,400**

#184, 208, yellow boots:
4-5in (10-13cm)	**$400-$450**
7in (18cm)	**$650**

#208, swivel neck, yellow boots:
6in (15cm)	**$750-$850**
8in (20cm)	**$1,250-$1,500**

#310, yellow stockings:
5-6in (12-15cm)	**$550-$650**
8in (20cm)	**$1,265**

#620/130 or 208, swivel neck:
Glass eyes:
4in (10cm)	**$400-$425**
5-6in (13-15cm)	**$550-$650**
8in (20cm)	**$950**

Painted eyes:
4in (10cm)	**$175**
5-6in (13-15cm)	**$225-$275**

Early All-Bisque Dolls: See page 24.

Gibson Girl: Ca. 1910. Perfect bisque shoulder head with appropriate wig, closed mouth, up-lifted chin; kid body with bisque lower arms (cloth body with bisque lower limbs on small dolls); beautifully dressed; all in good condition; sometimes marked "Gibson Girl" on body.

#172:

10in (25cm)	**$950**
15in (38cm)	**$1,500-$1,600**
19-21in (48-53cm)	**$2,500-$3,000***
Head only to make a 20in (51cm) doll	**$825**

Lady Doll: Perfect bisque socket head, plaster dome, wig with lady hairdo; Kestner jointed composition body with molded breasts, nipped-in waist, slender arms and legs; appropriate lady clothes; all in good condition.

Mark: Siegfried
made in Germany
9

#162:

16-18in (41-46cm)	**$1,600-$1,800**
Naked: 16-18in (41-46cm)	**$1,000**

All-original clothes:

16-18in (41-46cm)	**$2,000-$2,200**

O.I.C. Baby: Perfect bisque solid dome head, wide open mouth with molded tongue; cloth body; dressed; all in good condition. Mold **#255.**

10in (25cm) head circumference	**$1,200-$1,300**

Siegfried: Perfect bisque head; cloth body with composition hands; dressed; all in good condition. Mold **#272.**

MARK: made in
D Germany. 8.
162.

10in (25cm)	**$1,500****
14in (36cm)	**$2,000****

Marked Century Doll Co. Infant: Ca. 1925. Perfect bisque head; cloth body. Some with smiling face are mold **#277.**

16-18in (41-46cm) long	**$650-$750**
Double-face	**$2,000-$2,500****

Mama doll, bisque shoulder head **#281:** 21in (53cm) **$650-$750****

*Allow extra for original clothes.
**Not enough price samples to compute a reliable range.

20in (51cm) 162 lady, all original. *H & J Foulke, Inc.*

Kewpie®

All-Bisque: 1913-on. Made by J.D. Kestner and other German firms. Often have manufacturing imperfections. Sometimes signed on foot "O'Neill." Standing, legs together, arms jointed, blue wings, painted features, eyes to side.

2-2½in (5-6cm)	**$110-$125**
4in (10cm)	**$135-$150***
5in (13cm)	**$165-$185***
6in (15cm)	**$235***
7in (18cm)	**$275-$325***
8in (20cm)	**$450-$500***
9in (23cm)	**$600-$700***
10in (25cm)	**$800***
12in (31cm)	**$1,300-$1,500***

Jointed hips:

4in (10cm)	**$500-$550**
6in (15cm)	**$850**
8in (20cm)	**$1,250**
Shoulder head: 3in (8cm)	**$350-$400**

Perfume bottle:

4½in (11cm)	**$550-$600**
Black Hottentot: 5in (13cm)	**$600-$700**
Buttonhole: 2in (5cm)	**$165-$175**
Pincushion: 2-3in (5-8cm)	**$250-$300**

Painted shoes and socks:

4-5in (10-13cm)	**$500-$600**
11in (28cm)	**$1,500-$1,800**

With glass eyes and wig:

6in (15cm)	**$1,250**
With wig: 6in (15cm)	**$425**

Action Kewpies (sometimes stamped "©"):

Thinker:

4in (10cm)	**$275-$325**
7in (18cm)	**$500-$550**

Kewpie with cat:

3½in (9cm)	**$600-$650**

Kewpie holding pen:

3in (8cm)	**$450-$475**

Kewpie with pen, sitting on "Kewpish Love" tray: 3in (8cm) **$750**

Kneeling, with outstretched arms:

3¾in (9cm)	**$1,100**

Reclining or sitting:

3-4in (8-10cm)	**$450-$500**

*Allow extra for original clothes.

FACTS
Designer: Rose O'Neill.
Mark: Red and gold paper heart or shield on chest and round label on back.

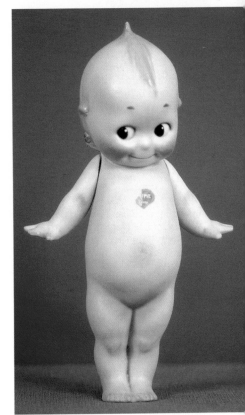

10½in (26cm) *Kewpie. H & J Foulke, Inc.*

10½in (26cm)
Kewpie with wig.
*Connie & Jay
Lowe.*

Crawling: 4in (10cm) **$800**
Tumbling: 3in (8cm) **$550-$600**
Farmer, Fireman (molded hats):
  4in (10cm) **$600-$750**
Kewpie: 2in (5cm) with rabbit, rose,
turkey, pumpkin, shamrock and others
$500-$550
Doodle Dog:
  1½in (4cm) **$1,000**
  3in (9cm) **$2,500**
  4½in (11cm) **$3,200**
Huggers: 3½in (9cm) **$200-$225**
Guitar player: 3½in (9cm) **$400-$500**
  With **Doodle Dog:** 4in (10cm)**$2,600**
Traveler: 3½in (9cm) **$325-$350**
Traveler with **Doodle Dog:**
  3½in (9cm) **$1,350-$1,650**
Baby Sister, molded blue hair bow: 3½in
(10cm), large chip on bow, at auction
$892
Kewpie with molded gray top hat and
red umbrella: 4½in (11cm) **$2,000**
Kewpie in egg shell: 2½in (6cm)**$3,000**
Kewpie Hero, soldier with nurse:
  5½in (14cm) **$8,400**
Kewpie with drum: 3½in (9cm) **$750**
Governor or **Mayor:**
  4in (10cm) **$450-$500**
Kewpie and **Doodle Dog** on bench:
  3½in (9cm) **$4,500**

Kewpie sitting on inkwell:
  3½in (9cm) **$750**
Soldiers:
  3½ (9cm) lying Confederate **$550**
  4in (10cm) **Hero** **$600**
  5-6in (13-15cm) standing
$900-$1,200
  3½in (9cm) sitting **$1,500**
Kewpie on sled: 2½in (6cm) **$1,000**
Two **Kewpies** reading book:
  3½in (9cm), standing **$850-$950**
  5½in (13cm) **$2,200**
Kewpie at tea table:
  4½in (11cm) **$3,200**
Kewpie with basket: 4in (10cm) **$750**
Kewpie Mountain: with 17 figures
$17,000 up
Kewpie, holding teddy bear:
  4in (10cm) **$850-$950**
Kewpie in bisque swing:
  2½in (6cm) **$4,000**
Glazed **Kewpie** shaker with animal:
  2in (5cm) each **$500**
Kewpie Bellhop in green:
  4in (10cm) **$850**
Place Card: 2in (5cm) **$425-$525**
Kewpie with broom and dustpan:
  5in (10cm) **$850**
Kewpie with bunting babies:
  3½in (9cm) **$4,000**

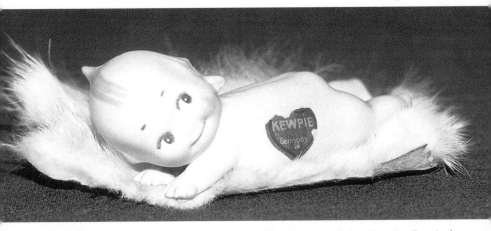

Bisque head on chubby jointed composition toddler body, glass eyes: Made by J.D. Kestner.

Mark:

"Ges. gesch.
O'Neill J.D.K."

10in (25cm) five-piece body **$5,000**
12-14in (31-36cm)   **$6,500**

Bisque head on cloth body: Mold #1377 made by Alt, Beck & Gottschalck.
12in (31cm) glass eyes
                $2,600-$2,800**
Painted eyes   **$1,600-$2,000****

Celluloid: Made by Karl Standfuss, Saxony, Germany.
2½in (6cm)   **$35-$40**
5in (13cm)   **$80-$90**
8in (20cm)   **$175-$200**
12in (31cm)   **$300**
22in (56cm)   **$550-$600****
Black: 2½in (6cm)   **$125**
5in (13cm)   **$200**
Kewpie/Billiken double face:
2½in (6cm)   **$150**
Made in Japan:
2½in (6cm) bride and groom, pair
                    $50
4in (10cm) boxed pair **$95**
16in (41cm)   **$235**
Soldier: 3½in (9cm) **$60**

**Not enough price samples to compute a reliable range.

4½in (11cm) reclining *Kewpie. Connie & Jay Lowe.*

12in (33cm) composition *Kewpie. H & J Foulke, Inc.*

All-Composition: Made by Cameo Doll Co., Rex Doll Co. and Mutual Doll Co. All-composition, jointed at shoulders, some at hips; good condition.

8in (20cm)	**$175-$200**
11-12in (28-31cm)	**$300-$350**
All original, boxed	**$550-$600**
Black: 12-13in (31-33cm)	**$400-$450**
Talcum container:	
7in (18cm)	**$225-$250**
Composition head, cloth body:	
12in (31cm)	**$250-$275**

All-Cloth: Made by Richard G. Krueger, Inc., or King Innovations, Inc., New York. Patent number 1785800. Mask face with fat-shaped cloth body.

10-12in (25-31cm)	**$275-$300**
18-22in (46-56cm)	**$600-$650**

Hard Plastic: Ca. 1950s.

Standing **Kewpie,** one-piece with jointed arms: 8in (20cm)   **$135-$150**

Boxed	**$225-$250**

Fully-jointed with sleep eyes; all-original clothes: 13in (33cm)   **$500**

Vinyl: Ca. 1960s. Cameo Dolls. All original and excellent condition.

12-13in (31-33cm), boxed	**$60-$75**
16in (41cm), boxed	**$95**
27in (68cm)	**$200**
Black:	
12in (31cm) boxed	**$100-$125**

Kewpie Baby with hinged body:

16in (41cm)	**$200-$250**

Kewpie Gal:

8in (20cm), boxed	**$65-$75**
14in (36cm), boxed	**$125**

Ragsy, molded clothes:

8in (20cm)	**$40-$45**

Jesco Dolls: 1980s. Boxed:

8in (20cm) black	**$40-$50**
12in (31cm)	**$50-$60**
18in (46cm)	**$75-$85**
24in (61cm)	**$150-$175**

Danbury Mint: 1990s. Porcelain, boxed: 12in (31cm)   **$60-$80**

15in (38cm) cloth Krueger *Kewpie. H & J Foulke, Inc.*

12in (31cm) hard plastic *Kewpie. H & J Foulke, Inc.*

Kley & Hahn

Character Baby: Perfect bisque head; bent-limb baby body; nicely dressed; all in good condition.

#138, 158, 160, 167, 176, 458, 525, 531, 680 and others:

11-13in (28-33cm)	**$350-$400**
18-20in (46-51cm)	**$475-$525**
24in (61cm)	**$750**
28in (71cm)	**$1,000-$1,200**
Toddler:	
14-16in (36-41cm)	**$1,000-$1,250**
18-20in (46-51cm)	**$1,500-$1,600**

#567, Two-face toddler: 18in (46cm)
$2,400

FACTS
Kley & Hahn, doll factory, Ohrdruf, Thuringia, Germany. Heads by Hertel, Schwab & Co. (100 series), Bähr & Pröschild (500 series) and J.D. Kestner (200 series, 680 and Walküre). 1902-on.
Trademarks: Walküre, Meine Einzige, Special, Dollar Princess.
Mark:

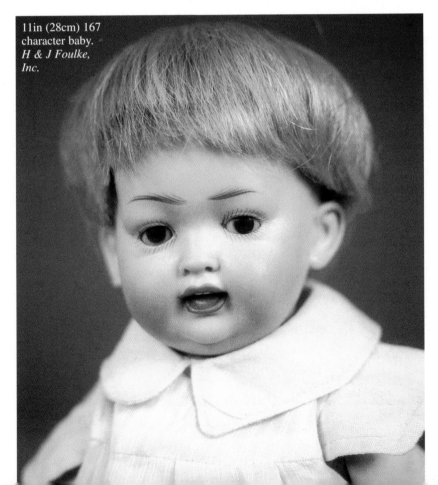

11in (28cm) 167 character baby. *H & J Foulke, Inc.*

Character Child: Perfect bisque head, closed mouth; jointed composition child or toddler body; fully dressed; all in good condition.

#520, 526:
15-16in (38-41cm)	**$3,500-$3,800**
19-21in (48-53cm)	**$4,500-$5,500**

#536, 546, 549:
15-16in (38-41cm)	**$4,200-$4,800**
19-21in (48-53cm)	**$5,200-$5,800**

#547: 18½in (47cm) at auction **$6,825**

#548, 568, Toddler:
21-23in (53-58cm)	**$1,600-$1,800**

#154, 166, closed mouth, toddler or jointed body:
14-16in (36-41cm)	**$1,800-$2,200**
19-20in (48-51cm)	**$2,500-$2,750**

#154, 166, open mouth, jointed body:
13in (33cm)	**$700-$800**
18-20in (46-51cm)	**$950-$1,100**
25in (64cm)	**$1,300-$1,500**

#169, closed mouth toddler:
13-14in (33-36cm)	**$1,800-$2,200**
19-21in (48-53cm)	**$2,750-$3,000**

#169, open mouth:
23in (58cm) baby	**$1,300-$1,500**

Child Doll: Perfect bisque head; jointed composition child body; fully dressed; all in good condition.

#250, 282 or **Walküre:**
7½in (19cm)	**$300-$350**
12-13in (31-33cm)	**$425-$450**
16-18in (41-46cm)	**$400-$500***
24-25in (61-64cm)	**$550-$600***
30-31in (76-79cm)	**$800-$900**
35-36in (89-91cm)	**$1,200-$1,400**

Special, Dollar Princess:
23-25in (58-64cm)	**$450-$495**

*Allow $100 to $150 additional for flapper body.

17in (43cm) 536 character girl. *Linda Kellermann.*

23in (58cm) 169 character toddler. *Mary Barnes Kelley.*

Kling

Bisque shoulder head: Ca. 1880. Molded hair, painted eyes, closed mouth; cloth body with bisque lower limbs; dressed; in all good condition. Mold numbers in **100** and **200** Series.

6in (15cm)	**$165-$185**
12-14in (31-36cm)	**$250-$300**
18-20in (46-51cm)	**$400-$450**
23-25in (58-64cm)	**$550-$600**

Glass eyes and molded hair:

15-16in (38-41cm)	**$500-$600***
22in (56cm)	**$900-$950***

Lady styles with decorated bodice, such as:

#135, 144, 170:

21-23in (53-58cm)	**$1,500 up**

#116, lady with molded blue bonnet:

16in (41cm) at auction	**$1,600**

China shoulder head: Ca. 1880. Black- or blonde-haired china head with bangs, sometimes with a pink tint; cloth body with china limbs; dressed; all in good condition.

#188, 189, 200, 203 and others:

13-15in (33-38cm)	**$275-$325**

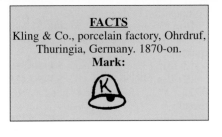

FACTS
Kling & Co., porcelain factory, Ohrdruf, Thuringia, Germany. 1870-on.
Mark:

18-20in (46-51cm)	**$350-$400**
24-25in (61-64cm)	**$475-$525**

Bisque head: Ca. 1890. Perfect bisque head, glass eyes; appropriate body; dressed; all in good condition.

#123, closed mouth shoulder head:

6½in (17cm)	**$250-$275**
8in (20cm) all-original pair	**$750**
12in (31cm):	
Original costume	**$500-$700**
Re-dressed	**$250-$300**

*Allow extra for unusual or elaborate hairdo.

10in (25cm) boy with glass eyes. *H & J Foulke, Inc.*

#152, 166 or 167, closed mouth shoulder head:
16-18in (41-46cm)   **$650-$750**
#182, 190, socket head, closed mouth, composition body:
14in (36cm)   **$1,400-$1,600**
#373, 377, 245, shoulder head, open mouth:
13-15in (33-38cm)   **$300-$350**
19-22in (48-56cm)   **$375-$425**
#370, 372, 182, socket head, open mouth:
14-16in (36-41cm)   **$375-$425**
22-24in (56-61cm)   **$450-$500**
27in (69cm)   **$600-$650**

All-Bisque: Glass eyes, wig.
#61, 71, pink or blue shirred hose:
5-6in (13-15cm)   **$400-$500***
#94, green shoes: 4in (10cm)   **$400**
#36, 69, black boots:
4-5in (10-13cm)   **$400-$500***
#36, 96, yellow boots:
4-5in (10-13cm)   **$400-$500***

*Allow extra for swivel neck.

4in (10cm) 94 Kling all-bisque child with green shoes and black stockings. *H & J Foulke, Inc.*

König & Wernicke

FACTS
König & Wernicke, doll factory, Waltershausen, Thuringia, Germany. Heads by Hertel Schwab & Co. and Bähr & Pröschild. 1912-on.
Trademarks: Mein Stolz, My Playmate
Mark:

K & W
1070

König & Wernicke Character: Perfect bisque head; composition baby or five-piece toddler body; appropriate clothes; all in good condition.
#98, 99, 100, 1070:
10-11in (25-28cm)   **$325-$350***
14-16in (36-41cm)   **$400-$450***
19-21in (48-53cm)   **$500-$600***
24-25in (61-64cm)   **$750-$850***
Toddler, fully-jointed body:
13-15in (33-38cm)   **$750-$850**
19-20in (48-51cm)   **$1,200-$1,400**

Child #4711, Mein Stolz (My Pride):
37in (94cm)   **$1,800-$2,000**

*Allow extra for flirty eyes.

König & Wernicke 1070 character baby. *Dr. Carole Stoessel Zvonar Collection.*

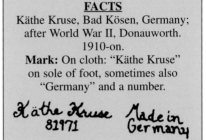

Käthe Kruse

Cloth Käthe Kruse: Molded muslin head, hand-painted; jointed at shoulders and hips:
Doll I: 1910-1929. 16in (41cm):
Early model, wide hips:

Mint, all original	**$4,600-$5,000**
Very good	**$3,200-$3,800**
Fair	**$1,600-$2,000**
Jointed knees, very good	**$6,500 up****
"Frog" hands, good	**$5,000**

Doll I: 1929-on. 17in (43cm):
Later model, slim hips:

Molded hair, mint	**$3,300-$3,500**
Very good	**$2,200-$2,600**

Doll 1H: 1930-on. (wigged):

Mint, all original	**$3,000-$3,500**
Very good	**$2,000-$2,300**
U.S. Zone, all original, excellent: 18in (46cm)	**$2,500-$2,800**

Doll II "Schlenkerchen" Smiling Baby: 1922-1936. 13in (33cm):

Excellent	**$10,000****
Very worn	**$4,000**

Doll V and VI Babies "Traumerchen": 1925-on. Five-pound weighted "Sand Baby" and **Du Mein,** unweighted:

Cloth head: 19½-23½in (50-60cm)	**$5,000-$6,000**
Magnesit head: 21in (53cm)	**$1,600**

Doll VII: 1926-1952. 14in (36cm), with **Doll I** head, 1930-on.

All original	**$2,000-$2,500**

With **Du Mein** head (1928-1930):
14in (36cm):

Good condition	**$1,800-$2,200**

Doll VIII "German Child": 1929-on. 20½in (52cm) wigged, turning head:

Mint, all original	**$1,700-$2,100**
Good condition, suitably dressed	**$1,200**

**Not enough price samples to compute a reliable range.

16in (41cm) early model *Doll I. H & J Foulke, Inc.*

FACTS
Käthe Kruse, Bad Kösen, Germany; after World War II, Donauworth. 1910-on.
Mark: On cloth: "Käthe Kruse" on sole of foot, sometimes also "Germany" and a number.

Käthe Kruse
81971
Made in
Germany

Hard plastic on back: Turtle mark and "Käthe Kruse."

Doll IX "Little German Child": 1929-on. Wigged, turning head, 14in (36cm):

Mint, all original	**$1,350-$1,650**
U.S. Zone: cloth head	**$1,100-$1,300**

Doll X (1930-1952), turning **Doll I** head:

14in (36cm) all original	**$2,000-$2,500**
U. S. Zone, cloth head	**$1,100-$1,300**

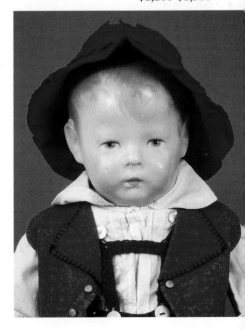

Dolls XII and XIII "Hampelchen": (1931-on). With dangling legs:

14in (36cm)	**$1,400-$1,600**
18in (45cm)	**$2,000-$2,500**

Hard Plastic (Synthetic) Head: Ca. 1948-on. Hard plastic head with human hair wig, painted eyes; pink muslin body; original clothes; all in excellent condition.

US. Zone:

14in (36cm)	**$600-$700**
21in (53cm)	**$950**

Ca. 1952-1975:

14in (36cm)	**$375-$425**
19-21in (48-53cm)	**$500-$575**

1975-on:

14in (36cm)	**$300-$350**
19-21in (48-53cm)	**$350-$400**
20in (51cm) Du Mein	**$600-$700**

Doll XIV Slim Grandchild:

18in (46cm), at auction	**$1,700**

Hanna Kruse Dolls:
  Däumlinchen 25H: 1957-on.

10in (25cm) with foam rubber stuffing	**$175-$200***

Rumpumpel Baby or **Toddler 32 H:** 1959-on. 13in (33cm)   **$250-$275**

Doggi: 1964-1967. Vinyl head:

10in (25cm)	**$225-$250**

Hard Plastic Baby:

14in (36cm)	**$100-$125**

All-Hard Plastic (Celluloid) Käthe Kruse: Wig or molded hair, sleep or painted eyes; jointed neck, shoulders and hips; original clothes; all in excellent condition. Turtle mark. 1955-1961.

16in (41cm)	**$400-$450**
Re-dressed	**$200-$225**
Vinyl head: 16in (41cm)	**$250-$300**

Mannikin: Ca. 1950.

46-52in (116-132cm)	**$2,200-$2,500**

14in (36cm) *Doll IX* with synthetic head, U.S. Zone model, all original. *H & J Foulke, Inc.*

18½in (47cm) model 47H with synthetic head based on *Hampelchen* face, all original. *H & J Foulke, Inc.*

Kruse-Type

Bing Art Dolls: Nurnberg, Germany. 1921-1932. Cloth head, molded face, hand-painted features; cloth body with jointed shoulders and hips (some with pinned joints), mitten hands; all-original clothing; very good condition. "Bing" stamped or impressed on sole of shoe.

Cloth head, painted hair:
    10-12in (25-30cm)   **$425-$475**
    14in (35cm)   **$850-$950**

Cloth head, wigged: 10in (25cm)
    $400-$450

Composition head, wigged:
    7in (18cm)   **$125-$135**

Heine & Schneider Art Doll: Bad-Kösen, Germany. 1920-1922. All-cloth or head of pressed cardboard covered with cloth, molded hair; cloth body with jointed shoulders and hips (some with cloth-covered composition arms and hands); appropriate or original clothes; all in good condition. Mark stamped on foot.

    17-19in (43-48cm)   **$1,600-$1,800**

Unmarked Child Dolls: Ca. 1920s.
    15-17in (38-43cm)   **$375 up***

*Depending upon quality.

10in (25cm) Bing child, all original.
H & J Foulke, Inc.

Gebrüder Kuhnlenz

Gebrüder Kuhnlenz doll with closed mouth: Ca. 1885-on. Perfect bisque socket head (some with closed Belton-type crown), inset glass eyes, closed mouth, round cheeks; jointed composition body; dressed; all in good condition.

#28, 31, 32, 39:

8-10in (20-25cm)	**$850-$1,100**
15-16in (38-41cm)	**$1,600-$1,700**
21-23in (53-58cm)	**$2,400-$2,600**

#34, Bru-type, French body:

15in (38cm)	**$3,500-$4,000****
18in (46cm)	**$5,200-$5,600****

#38 shoulder head, kid body:

12in (31cm)	**$500**
16-18in (41-46cm)	**$600-$650**
23-24in (58-61cm)	**$800-$900**

**Not enough price samples to compute a reliable range.

Left: 19in (48cm) 38 shoulder head child. *H & J Foulke, Inc.*

Below: 7½in (19cm) 56 all-bisque child with swivel neck, all original. *H & J Foulke, Inc.*

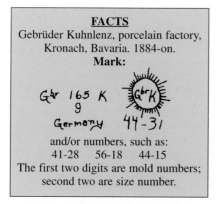

FACTS
Gebrüder Kuhnlenz, porcelain factory,
Kronach, Bavaria. 1884-on.
Mark:

Gᵇʳ 165 K   Gᵇʳ K

9   Germany   44-31

and/or numbers, such as:
41-28   56-18   44-15
The first two digits are mold numbers;
second two are size number.

Lanternier

FACTS
A Lanternier & Cie. Porcelain factory of
Limoges, France. 1915-1924.
Mark:

LIMOGES   FABRICATION FRANÇAISE

A L   AL ε Cⁱᵉ
LIMOGES
A   1

Gebrüder Kuhnlenz Child Doll: Ca. 1890-on. Perfect bisque socket head, sleep or paperweight-type eyes, open mouth, molded teeth; jointed composition body, sometimes French; dressed; all in good condition.

#41, 44, 56 (character-type face):

9-10in (23-25cm)	**$600**
16-19in (41-48cm)	**$700-$800**
24-26in (61-66cm)	**$1,000-$1,100**

#165:

18in (46cm)	**$300-$350**
22-24in (56-61cm)	**$400-$450**
30-32in (76-81cm)	**$750-$800**

#61, 47 shoulder head:

19-22in (48-56cm)	**$450-$500**

Gebrüder Kuhnlenz Tiny Dolls: Perfect bisque socket head, wig, stationary glass eyes, open mouth with molded teeth; five-piece composition body with molded shoes and socks; all in good condition. Usually mold **#44**.

7-8in (18-20cm):

Crude body	**$185-$210**
Better body	**$250-$300**

Black: See page 55.

All-Bisque: Swivel neck, usually mold **#31, #41, #44** or **56**:

Bootines:

7-8in (18-20cm)	**$1,500-$2,000**
9½in (24cm)	**$2,500-$2,750**

Mary Janes:

5in (13cm)	**$550-$650**
7in (18cm)	**$1,250**
8½in (22cm)	**$1,850**

Black: See page 55.

Marked Lanternier Child: Ca. 1915. Perfect bisque head, good or original wig, large stationary eyes, open mouth, pierced ears; papier-mâché jointed body; pretty clothes; all in good condition.

Cherie, Favorite or La Georgienne:

16-18in (41-46cm)	**$450-$550**
22-24in (56-61cm)	**$750-$800**
28in (71cm)	**$950**

Lorraine Lady: Ca. 1915.
Composition lady body:

16-18in (41-46cm)	**$650-$850***

Characters, "Toto" and others: Ca. 1915. Smiling character face:

17-19in (43-48cm)	**$750-$800**

*Depending upon costume and quality.

Lenci

Lenci: All-felt (sometimes cloth torso); pressed felt head, painted features, eyes usually side-glancing; jointed shoulders and hips; original clothes, often of felt or organdy; in excellent condition.

Miniatures and Mascottes:
8-9in (20-23cm) Regionals
$350-$400
Children or unusual costumes
$450-$600
Jackie Coogan with cigarette
$1,800
Purse **$250-$300**

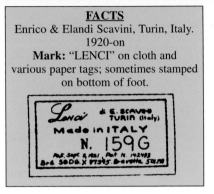

FACTS
Enrico & Elandi Scavini, Turin, Italy.
1920-on
Mark: "LENCI" on cloth and various paper tags; sometimes stamped on bottom of foot.

Left: 9½in (24cm) peasant girl with pig, all original. *H & J Foulke, Inc.*

Below: 13in (33cm) 149 model, all original. *H & J Foulke, Inc.*

Children #300, 109, 149, 159, 111:

13in (33cm)	**$850-$1,000**
17in (43cm)	**$1,500-$2,000**
19-22in (48-56cm)	**$1,600-$2,200**

Black Hottentot: 15in (38cm) **$2,500**

Clown, red felt hair:

18in (46cm)	**$2,700**

#252 Toddler:

20in (51cm) at auction	**$3,300**

#563 Bellhop with chubby face:

22in (56cm) at auction	**$2,500**

#1500, scowling face:

17-19in (43-48cm)	**$2,250-$2,750**

#500: 21in (53cm) **$1,650-$1,850**

Baby:

18-21in (46-53cm)	**$2,250-$2,750**

1930s Children:

"Lucia" face, 14in (36cm):

Child clothes	**$800-$1,200**
Regional outfits	**$600-$800**

"Laura" face: 16in (41cm) **$1,000 up**

"Mariuccia" face:

17in (43cm)	**$1,100 up**

"Benedetta" face:

9in (48cm)	**$1,300 up**

"Henriette" face:

25in (63cm)	**$1,700 up**

Above: 12in (31cm) *Little Orphant Annie,* all original and boxed. *H & J Foulke, Inc.*

Right: 20in (51cm) glass-eyed girl. *Kay Jensen Antique Dolls.*

1935 Round face:
11-12in (28-31cm)	**$750-$850**
20in (51cm)	**$1,250**

Becassine:
11in (28cm)	**$950**
20in (51cm) glass eyes	**$3,000**

Ladies and long-limbed novelty dolls:
24-28in (61-71cm)	**$1,500-$2,500**
40in (102cm), faded color	**$1,000-$1,250**
Pierrot (Dudovich):	
20in (51cm)	**$3,000-$3,500**
Opium Smoker:	
20in (51cm)	**$3,200**
Valentino:	
25in (63cm)	**$5,750**

Glass Eyes, 20in (51cm): Valentine, Widow Allegra and others
            $3,000-$4,000

"Surprised Eye" (round painted eyes), fancy clothes:
20in (51cm)	**$2,200-$2,600**
"Autumn," at auction	**$3,500**
Hand Puppet	**$400-$500**
Winkers:	
12in (31cm)	**$750-$950**
Black Bellhop, at auction	**$2,500**
Wood head: 6in (15cm)	**$60-$90**
Mask face, disc eyes:	
23in (58cm)	**$600-$700**
Flocked hard plastic:	
11in (28cm)	**$200-$250**
Celluloid-type, 6in (15cm)	**$65-$75**
Catalogs	**$900-$1,200**
1950 Characters	**$300 up**

> *Collector's Note:* Mint examples of rare dolls will bring higher prices. To bring the prices quoted, Lenci dolls must be clean and have good color. Faded and dirty dolls bring only about one-third to one-half of these prices.

Modern Series: 1979 on:
13in (28cm)	**$85-$110**
22-21in (51-53cm)	**$175-$225**
22in (56cm) surprised eyes	**$250-$275**
26in (66cm) lady	**$225-$250**
27-28in (69-71cm) long gown	**$250-$300**

Lenci-Type

Vintage Felt or Cloth Doll: Mohair wig, painted features; stuffed cloth body; original clothes or costume; excellent condition.

Child dolls: 16-18in (41-46cm) depending upon quality, up to   **$750**

Regional costume, very good quality:
7½-8½in (19-22cm)	**$40-$50**
12in (31cm)	**$90-$110**

Alma, Turin, Italy:
11in (28cm)	**$200-$250**
16in (41cm)	**$400-$500**

9in (23cm) *Serenella* by Alberani Vecchiotti, Milano, all original. *H & J Foulke, Inc.*

Dean's Rag Book Company, England:
14-16in (36-41cm) **$500-$600**
Composition face:
18in (46cm) **$600-$700**
Dancing Dolls:
12in (31cm) **$225-$250**

Ronnaug Pettersen, Norway: All-original Norwegian costume.
8in (20cm) **$125**
8in (20cm) girl in ski outfit
$250-$300
15in (38cm) **$1,000-$1,200**
17-18in (43-46cm) **$1,800-$2,200**

Vecchiotti, Milano, Italy:
9½in (24cm) all original **$195**

Baitz, Austria:
9in (23cm) all original **$30-$35**

Farnell's Alpha Toys, London, England:
Child: 14in (36cm) **$300-$350**
Black character:
14in (36cm) **$275-$300**
King George VI, 1937:
16in (41cm) **$400-$450**

Allwin Nightdress Case:
20in (51cm) **$400**

Eugenie Poir, Gre-Poir French doll makers, Paris and New York:
16-18in (41-46cm)
Cloth face **$300-$350**
Felt face **$450-$550**
Raynal, Venus, Marina, Clelia, Paris, France:
17-18in (43-46cm) mint **$500-$600**
Poupées Nicette: 14in (36cm)
Regional costumes **$250-$300**

9in (23cm) Baitz, Austria, all original. *H & J Foulke, Inc.*

8in (20cm) Ronnaug Petterssen, Norway, all original. *H & J Foulke, Inc.*

Liberty of London

FACTS
Liberty & Co. of London, England.
1906-on.
Mark: Cloth label or paper tag
"Liberty of London."

British Coronation Dolls: 1939. All-cloth with painted and needle-sculpted faces; original clothes; excellent condition. The **Royal Family** and **Coronation Participants:**

9-9½in (23-24cm)	**$175-$200**
Princess Margaret:	
7in (15cm)	**$400-$425**
Princess Elizabeth:	
7in (17cm)	**$400-$425**

English Historical and Ceremonial Characters:

9-10in (23-25cm)	**$150-$195**
Beefeater (Tower Guard)	**$85**

Armand Marseille (A.M.)

FACTS
Armand Marseille of Köppelsdorf,
Thuringia, Germany
(porcelain and doll factory).
1885-on.
Marks:

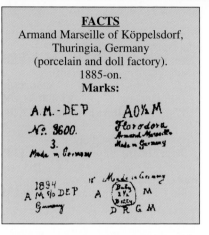

Child Doll: 1890-on. Perfect bisque head, nice wig, sleep eyes, open mouth; composition ball-jointed body; pretty clothes; all in good condition.
#390 (larger sizes marked only "A. [size] M."), **Florodora, 1894:**

9-10in (23-25cm)	**$225-$250**
12-14in (31-36cm)	**$175-$225**
16-18in (41-46cm)	**$225-$250**
20in (51cm)	**$275-$300**
23-24in (58-61cm)	**$325-$375**
28-29in (71-74cm)	**$450-$500**
30-32in (76-81cm)	**$550-$650**
35-36in (89-91cm)	**$1,000**
38in (96cm)	**$1,500**
40-42in (102-107cm)	**$2,000-$2,200**
15-18in (38-46cm) all-original factory clothes	**$500-$600**

Five-piece composition body, (excellent quality body):

6-7in (15-18cm)	**$200-$225**
9-10in (23-25cm)	**$260-$285**
Closed mouth:	
5-5½in (12-14cm)	**$250-$275**

Cardboard and stick leg body:

9-10in (23-25cm)	**$125**
12-14in (31-36cm)	**$135-$150**
16-18in (41-46cm)	**$175-$200**

Liberty of London *Shakespeare*, all original. *H & J Foulke, Inc.*

Above: 21in (83cm)
1894 child. *H & J
Foulke, Inc.*

27in (69cm) 390
child. *H & J Foulke,
Inc.*

#1894 (composition body; early pale bisque):

14-16in (36-41cm)	**$400-$450**
21-23in (53-58cm)	**$575-$675**
26in (66cm)	**$750-$775**

#370, 3200, 1894, Florodora, Anchor 2015, Rosebud Lily, Alma, Mabel, Darling, Beauty, Princess: shoulder heads on kid or cloth bodies

11-12in (28-31cm)	**$110-$125**
14-16in (36-41cm)	**$175-$200**
22-24in (56-61cm)	**$275-$300**
25-26in (64-66cm)	**$325-$350**

#2000: 14in (36cm)   **$900****

Queen Louise, Rosebud (composition body):

12in (31cm)	**$250-$275**
23-25in (58-64cm)	**$375-$425**
28-29in (71-74cm)	**$550**

Baby Betty:

14-16in (36-41cm) composition body   **$400-$450**

19-21in (48-53cm) kid body   **$325-$375**

12in (31cm) 700 character child. *Fritzi Bartlemay.*

#1894, 1892, 1896, 1897 shoulder heads (excellent quality):

19-22in (48-56cm)   **$375-$425**

Character Children: 1910-on. Perfect bisque head, molded hair or wig, glass or painted eyes, open or closed mouth; composition body; dressed; all in good condition. (For photographs of dolls not shown here, see previous *Blue Books*.)

#230 Fany (molded hair):

15-16in (38-41cm)	**$6,000-$7,000**
18in (46cm)	**$8,500-$9,500**

#231 Fany (wigged):

13-14in (33-36cm)	**$5,000-$5,500**
16in (41cm)	**$6,500**

#250: 11-13in (28-33cm)   **$500-$600**

#251/248 (open/closed mouth):

12in (31cm)	**$1,000-$1,200**
16-18in (41-46cm)	**$2,000-$2,200**

#340: 13in (33cm)   **$2,500****

#345, (wig, intaglio eyes):

12in (31cm) at auction   **$2,800**

#372 Kiddiejoy, shoulder head, "mama" body: 19in (48cm)   **$500****

#400 (child body):

13in (33cm)	**$1,600-$1,800****
17in (43cm)	**$2,600-$2,800****

#500, 600:

13-15in (33-38cm)   **$500-$600**

#550 (glass eyes):

12in (31cm)	**$1,500-$1,800**
18-20in (46-51cm)	**$2,800-$3,200**

#560: 11-13in (28-33cm)   **$750-$850**

#590, (open/closed mouth):

15-16in (38-41cm)   **$1,000-$1,100**

#620, shoulder head:

16in (41cm)   **$950****

#640, shoulder head (same face as **550** socket): 20in (51cm)   **$1,000-$1,200****

#700:

11in (28cm) painted eyes   **$2,100****

14in (36cm) glass eyes   **$3,500-$4,000****

A.M. (intaglio eyes):

16-17in (41-43cm)   **$6,000 up**

21in (53cm) solemn face, at auction   **$23,000**

24in (61cm) smiling face, at auction   **$27,000**

**Not enough price samples to compute a reliable range.

Character Babies and Toddlers:
1910-on. Perfect bisque head, good wig, sleep eyes, open mouth, some with teeth; composition bent-limb body; suitably dressed; all in nice condition.

Marks:

Armand Marseille
Germany
990
A ½ oM

Germany
326
A 11 M

Mold #990, 985, 971, 996, 1330, 326, (solid dome), 980, 991, 327, 329, 259 and others:

10-11in (25-28cm)	$200-$225
13-15in (33-38cm)	$250-$300
18-20in (46-51cm)	$350-$400
22in (56cm)	$500
24-25in (61-64cm)	$600

#233:
13-15in (33-38cm)	$500-$550
20in (51cm)	$700-$800

#251/248 (open/closed mouth):
11-12in (28-31cm)	$500-$600

#251/248 (open mouth):
12-14in (31-36cm)	$450-$500

#410 (two rows of teeth):
12in (31cm)	$600-$700

#518:
16-18in (41-46cm)	$400-$450
25in (64cm)	$800

#560A:
10-12in (25-31cm)	$375-$400
15-17in (38-43cm)	$475-$525

#580, 590 (open/closed mouth):
9in (23cm)	$450-$500
15-16in (38-41cm)	$1,000-$1,100

#590 (open mouth):
12in (31cm)	$450-$500
16-18in (41-46cm)	$650-$750

#920, shoulder head, "mama" body:
21in (53cm)	$650**

Melitta: 19in (48cm) toddler
$800-$900

**Not enough price samples to compute a reliable range.

11½in (29cm) 985 character baby. *H & J Foulke, Inc.*

9in (23cm) 590 character baby. *H & J Foulke, Inc.*

12½in (32cm) head circumference *Baby Phyllis. H & J Foulke, Inc.*

Infant: 1924-on. Solid-dome bisque head with molded and/or painted hair, sleep eyes; hard-stuffed jointed cloth body or soft-stuffed cloth body; dressed; all in good condition.

Mark:

A. M.
Germany.
351. 14K

#351, 341, Kiddiejoy and **Our Pet:**
Head circumference:

8-9in (20-23cm)	$200-$225
10in (25cm)	$250-$275
12-13in (31-33cm)	$325-$350
15in (38cm)	$450

Composition body (length):

5-6in (12-15cm)	$165-$185
8-10in (21-25cm)	$250-$275
13-15in (33-38cm)	$265-$285
23in (58cm)	$500-$550

Hand Puppet: 8½in (21cm) head circumference **$275-$300**
Boxed with label, at auction **$550**
#352:
17-20in (43-51cm) long **$450-$500**
#347, head circumference:
12-13in (31-33cm) **$400-$450**

Baby Phyllis, head circumference:

9in (23cm) black	$400-$425
12-13in (31-33cm)	$400-$450

Baby Gloria, RBL, New York:

12in (31cm)	$400-$450
15-16in (38-41cm)	$600-$650

Marked "Just Me" Character: Ca. 1925. Perfect bisque socket head, curly wig, glass eyes to side, closed mouth; composition body; dressed; all in good condition. Some of these dolls, particularly the painted bisque ones, were used by the Vogue Doll Company in the 1930s and will be found with original Vogue labeled clothes.

Mark:

Just ME
Registered
Germany
A 310/5/0 M

7½-8in (19-20cm)	$1,400-$1,500
9-10in (23-25cm)	$1,800-$2,100
11in (28cm)	$2,500-$2,600
13in (33cm)	$3,000
7½in (19cm) all original, in Easter egg	$2,500

Painted bisque:
7-8in (18-20cm) all original
$1,000-$1,250
10in (25cm) all original
$1,200-$1,400
9in (23cm) all original and boxed, at
auction **$3,000**

Lady: 1910-1930. Bisque head with
mature face, mohair wig, sleep eyes,
open or closed mouth; composition
lady body with molded bust, long slender arms and legs; appropriate clothes;
all in good condition.
#401 and **400** (slim body), 14in (36cm):
Open mouth **$1,250-$1,450**
Closed mouth **$2,250-$2,500**
Painted bisque **$900-$1,000**
All-original flapper outfit, at auction
$1,900

#300, (M.H.):
9in (23cm) **$1,400-$1,500****
All original **$1,650***
#400, flapper body: 16-19in (41-48cm)
$2,250-$2,750

**Not enough price samples to compute a
reliable range.

12½in (32cm) *Just Me. H & J Foulke,
Inc.*

Below: 15in (38cm) 400 flapper. *Sheila
Needle.*

Metal Dolls

Missionary Ragbabies

German Metal Head Child: Ca. 1888-on. Marked Minerva, Juno and Diana or unmarked. Metal shoulder head on cloth or kid body; dressed; very good condition, not repainted. Molded hair, painted eyes:

12-14in (31-36cm)	**$125-$150**
20-22in (51-56cm)	**$175-$195**

Molded hair or wig, glass eyes:

12-14in (31-36cm)	**$160-$185**
20-22in (51-56cm)	**$235-$265**

American All-Metal Child: Ca. 1917-on. Giebeler-Falk, Atlas Doll & Toy Co. and others. Wig, sleep eyes; fully-jointed body; dressed; all in good condition.

16-20in (41-51cm)	**$275-$325**

All-Metal Baby:

11-13in (28-33cm)	**$100-$125**

FACTS
Julia Beecher, Elmira, NY, U.S.A. 1893-1910. All-cloth. 16-23in (41-58cm) **Designer:** Julia Jones Beecher **Mark:** None

Beecher Baby: Handmade stuffed stockinette doll with looped wool hair, painted eyes and mouth, needle-sculpted face; appropriately dressed; all in good condition.

21-23in (53-59cm)	**$3,500-$4,000**
Excellent	**$5,000**
Fair	**$1,800-$2,000**

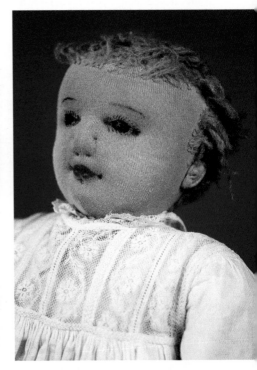

17in (43cm) Juno girl with metal shoulder head. *H & J Foulke, Inc.*

21in (53cm) *Missionary Ragbaby. H & J Foulke, Inc.*

Moravian

Moravian Cloth *Polly Heckewelder:*
All-cloth with flat face, hand-painted
hair and features, stitch-jointed limbs,
mitten hands with stitched fingers and
separate thumbs; original 1870s style
clothes – blue or pink checked cotton
dress with lace-trimmed white apron,
lace edging and crocheted outer bonnet
with bow in color to match dress, black
shoes and white stockings.

  16-18in (41-46cm)

Early model	**$2,500-$3,800**
1930s to 1940s model	
	$1,500-$2,000
Recent	**$150-$250**

FACTS
Ladies Sewing Society of Central
Moravian Church,
Bethlehem, PA, U.S.A..
1872 to present
Mark: None

Moravian Cloth *Benigna:* 1943. All-
cloth with painted features; depicting
Moravian females with different
colored caps designating their position.
Each doll carried a drawstring reticule
containing a paper identifying her.

  4-5in (10-12cm)   **$250****

**Not enough price samples to compute a
reliable range.

18in (41cm) early and later
Polly Heckewelder dolls, all
original except for the shoes
on the early one. *Connie
Blain Collection.*

Multi-Faced Dolls

Marked C.B. Doll: Carl Bergner, Sonneberg, Germany. Perfect bisque head with two or three different faces, usually sleeping, laughing and crying, papier-mâché hood hides the unwanted face(s); a ring through the top of the hood attached to a dowel turns the faces; cloth torso, composition limbs or jointed composition body; dressed; all in good condition.

Two or three faces:
12-13in (31-33cm) **$1,500-$1,800**
#202 dep, two-faced black and white:
13in (33cm) **$1,800-$2,200**
Simon & Halbig, two faces:
15in (38cm) at auction **$3,400**
Red Riding Hood, Grandmother and Wolf: 13in (33cm) **$6,000****

FACTS
Various German, French and American companies.
1888 and perhaps earlier.

German Character Babies: Ca. 1910. Perfect bisque head with two faces, usually crying, sleeping or smiling; swivel neck; composition or cloth body; dressed; all in good condition. Some have papier-mâché hoods to cover unwanted faces, while some use cloth bonnets.

HvB (von Berg) two-faced baby:
17in (43cm) **$1,200-$1,400**
Gebrüder Heubach three-faced baby:
13in (33cm) **$1,800-$2,000**
Kley & Hahn two-faced baby:
13in (33cm) **$1,600-$1,800**
Max Schelhorn two-faced baby:
9in (23cm) **$650-$750**
Herm Steiner topsy-turvy baby:
8in (20cm) **$500-$600**
American Composition Dolls:
    Trudy: 3-in-1 Doll Corp., New York; sleeping, crying, smiling, all original:
14in (36cm) **$225-$250**
    Johnny Tu-Face: Effanbee, New York; crying and smiling:
16in (41cm) **$400-$450**

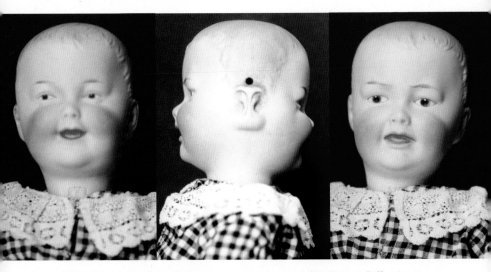

18in (46cm) Shelhorn character with two faces. *Helen Burton Collection.*

Munich Art Dolls

Nelke

FACTS
Marion Kaulitz. 1908-1912.
All-composition, fully-jointed bodies.
Designer: Paul Vogelsanger and others.
Mark:
Sometimes signed on doll's neck.

FACTS
The Nelke Corporation,
Philadelphia, PA, U.S.A.
1917-1930.
Mark: Woven label

Munich Art Dolls: Molded composition character heads with hand-painted features; fully-jointed composition bodies; appropriate regional or "country style" clothes; all in good condition.

13-14in (33-36cm) **$4,000-$5,000**
18-19in (46-48cm) **$7,500-$9,500**

Nelke or Nelke-type Dolls: One-piece stockinette dolls, some with attached limbs, hand-painted faces with large eyes and rosy cheeks, painted hair; clothing was an integral part of the body, but some had an added ribbon, collar, hat or other item; excellent condition.

8-10in (20-25cm) **$85-$95**
14-15in (36-41cm) **$150-$175**

16in (41cm) *Munich Art* character girl.
Dorothy Hunt, Sweetbriar.

Right: Nelke-type stockinette doll, all original. *H & J Foulke, Inc.*

Revalo Character Baby or **Toddler:**
Perfect bisque socket head, good wig,
sleep eyes, hair eyelashes, painted
lower eyelashes, open mouth; baby
bent-limb body; dressed; all in good
condition.

#22:

15-17in (38-41cm)	$350-$400
22in (56cm)	$600-$650
Toddler:	
22in (56cm)	$850-$950

Revalo Child Doll: Bisque socket
head, good wig, sleep eyes, hair eyelashes, painted lower eyelashes, open
mouth; ball-jointed composition body;
dressed; all in good condition. Mold
#150 or **#10727:**

14-15in (36-38cm)	$400-$425
18-20in (46-51cm)	$500-$550
24-25in (61-64cm)	$700-$750
28in (71cm)	$900-$950
Shoulder head:	
22-25in (56-64cm)	$500-$600

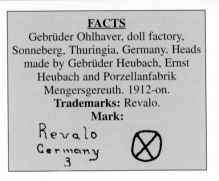

FACTS
Gebrüder Ohlhaver, doll factory,
Sonneberg, Thuringia, Germany. Heads
made by Gebrüder Heubach, Ernst
Heubach and Porzellanfabrik
Mengersgereuth. 1912-on.
Trademarks: Revalo.
Mark:

Revalo
Germany
3

Revalo Character Doll: Bisque head
with molded hair, painted eyes,
open/closed mouth; composition body;
dressed; all in good condition.

Coquette:	
12-13in (31-33cm)	$750-$850
Coquette with hair bows:	
13-14in (33-36cm)	$900-$1,000

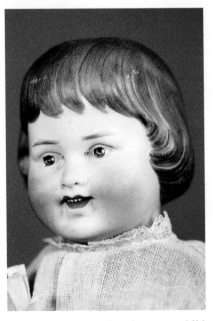

17½in (44cm) *Revalo* child. *H & J Foulke, Inc.*

13in (33cm) *Revalo* character child *Coquette. H & J Foulke, Inc.*

Oriental Dolls

Japanese Traditional Dolls:
Ichimatsu (play doll): 1868-on. Papier-mâché swivel head on shoulder plate, hips, lower legs and feet (early ones have jointed wrists and ankles); cloth midsection, cloth (floating) upper arms and legs; hair wig, dark glass eyes, pierced ears and nostrils; original clothes; all in very good condition.

Meiji Era (1868-1912):

3-5in (8-13cm)	**$300-$350**
12-14in (31-36cm)	**$550-$650***
18-20in (46-51cm)	**$800-$1,000***
24-26in (61-66cm)	**$1,800-$2,000***

Early three-bend body (**Mitsuore**):

14-16in (36-41cm)	**$2,000 up**

Ca. 1920s and 1930s:

13-15in (33-38cm)	**$350-$450****
17-18in (43-46cm)	**$550-$650****
24in (61cm)	**$850**

Ca. 1940s:

10-12in (25-31cm)	**$85-$95**
14-16in (36-41cm)	**$135-$165**
20in (51cm)	**$225**

Gosho Ningyo: Ca. 1900. Chubby immobile baby in various poses with accessory:

7in (18cm)	**$500**

Traditional Lady (**Kyoto** or **Fashion Doll**):

Ca. 1900: 12in (31cm)	**$500 up**

1920s:

10-12in (25-31cm)	**$150-$175**
16in (41cm)	**$235-$265**

1940s:

12-14in (31-36cm)	**$85-$95**
6½in (16cm) Geisha with six wigs, boxed	**$100-$110**

Traditional Warrior:

1880s: 16-18in (41-46cm)	**$800 up**
1920s: 11-12in (28-31cm)	**$250 up**

Royal Personages:

Ca. 1890: 10in (25cm)	**$800 up**

1920s-1930s:

4-6in (10-15cm)	**$100-$125**
12in (31cm)	**$350 up**

*Allow extra for a sexed boy.
**Allow extra for elaborate original outfits.

26in (66cm) early sexed *Ichimatsu*, all original. *H & J Foulke, Inc.*

Baby with bent limbs:
Ca. 1910: 11in (28cm)   **$250 up**
Ca. 1930s, souvenir dolls:
  8-10in (20-25cm)   **$65-$85**
  16in (41cm)   **$150-$175**
Carved Ivory: Ca. 1890.
  2-3in (5-8cm) fully-jointed, exquisite
  carving   **$350**
  Lesser quality   **$225**

Chinese Papier-mâché: Ca 1930-1940.
Opera Doll, all original:
  8in (20cm)   **$110-$135**
  26in (66cm)   **$500-$600**
Child Doll: Papier-mâché head, hands and feet, cloth body; all original:
  9-10in (23-25cm)   **$35-$45**

Oriental Bisque Dolls: Ca. 1900-on. Made by French and German firms. Bisque head tinted yellow; matching ball-jointed or baby body; original or appropriate clothes; all in excellent condition. (See previous *Blue Books* for photographs of dolls not shown here.)

7in (18cm) Gosho Ningyo, ca. 1900, all original. *Shogun.*

B.P. #220:
  11in (33cm)   **$2,300****
  16-17in (41-43cm) **$3,200-$3,500****
Belton-type: 12in (31cm) 127 **$1,700**
BSW #500:
  11in (28cm)   **$1,100-$1,300**
  14-15in (36-38cm) **$1,800-$2,200***

Bru Jne: 20in (51cm)   **$26,000****
Jumeau:
  Closed mouth: 19-20in (48-51cm)
    $48,000-$62,000**
  Open mouth: 18in (46cm) **$4,500****
French *Poupée*, wood body:
  15in (38cm)   **$7,250-$8,250**
JDK 243:
  13-14in (33-36cm)   **$4,300-$5,300**
  16-18in (41-46cm)   **$5,800-$6,500**
A.M. 353:
  9½ (24cm)   **$750-$800**
  12in (31cm)   **$900-$1,000**
  15-16in (38-41cm)   **$1,200-$1,400**
  10in (25cm) cloth body   **$700**
A.M. Girl: 8-9in (20-23cm)   **$650**

*Allow extra for elaborate original outfits.
**Not enough price samples to compute a reliable range.

S&H 1329:

14-15in (36-38cm)	**$1,600-$1,800***
18-19in (46-48cm)	**$2,200-$2,500***
24in (61cm)	**$3,200-$3,500***

S&H 1099, 1129, and **1199:**

9-10in (23-25cm)	**$1,200-$1,300***
12in (31cm)	**$1,900***
15-16in (38-41cm)	**$2,300-$2,600***
24in (61cm)	**$4,250**

S PB H:

9in (23cm)	**$650**
16in (41cm)	**$1,600**

#164:

16-17in (41-43cm)	**$1,850-$2,000***

Unmarked:

4½in (12cm) painted eyes	**$175-$195**
4¾in (12cm) glass eyes	**$400-$500**
11-12in (28-31cm) glass eyes	**$850**

All-Bisque Dolls:
JDK Baby: 7in (18cm) **$2,200****
Heubach Chin Chin:

4in (10cm)	**$300-$325**

S&H Child:

4½in (12cm)	**$625-$675**
5½in (14cm)	**$750-$775**
7in (18cm)	**$850-$950**

Man with molded hat and mustache:

3½in (6cm)	**$330**

Bisque Heads of Unknown Origin:
Lady with molded hair or hat, wood jointed body: 13in (33cm) **$750-$850****
Character man with molded mustache, jointed body: 11in (28cm) **$1,100****

German Papier-mâché: Ca. 1925.
August Möller: 14in (36cm) all original, boxed, at auction **$650**
#419, Papier-mâché man, molded hat and mustache, cloth body:

13in (33cm)	**$300-$350**

American Cloth: Oil painted stockinette in the Chase manner; original clothes: 16in (41cm) **$800-$1,000**

*Allow extra for elaborate original outfits.
**Not enough price samples to compute a reliable range.

7in (18cm) JDK all-bisque baby. *H & J Foulke, Inc.*

15in (38cm) Simon & Halbig 1329 pair, all original, in authentic costumes. *H & J Foulke, Inc*

Papier-Mâché
(So-Called French-Type)

French-type Papier-mâché: Shoulder head with painted black pate, brush marks around face, nailed-on human hair wig (often missing), set-in glass eyes, closed or open mouth with bamboo teeth, pierced nose; French pink kid body with stiff arms and legs; appropriate old clothes; all in good condition, showing some wear.

14-16in (36-41cm)	**$1,800-$2,200**
19-21in (48-51cm)	**$2,500-$2,600**
24-26in (61-66cm)	**$2,800-$3,000**
32in (81cm)	**$3,500-$3,800**
Painted eyes:	
6-8in (15-20cm)	**$550-$600**
14-16in (36-41cm)	**$1,200-$1,500**

FACTS
Heads by German firms such as Johann Müller of Sonneberg and Andreas Voit of Hildburghausen, were sold to French and other doll makers. 1835-1850. **Mark:** None.

Wood-jointed body:	
6in (15cm)	**$750-$800**
Shell decoration:	
8in (20cm) pair	**$1,300-$1,600**
18in (46cm) pair	**$2,500**
Poupard, molded bonnet and clothes:	
18in (46cm)	**$400-$500**

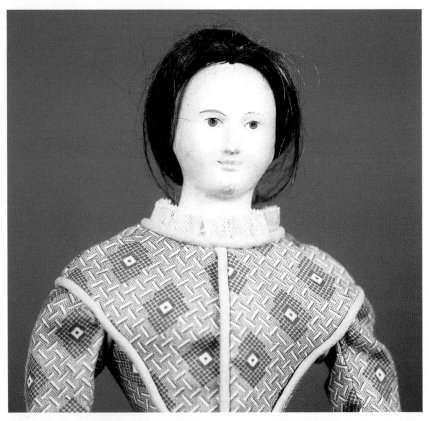

15in (38cm) French papier-mâché fashion, pink kid body. *H & J Foulke, Inc.*

Papier-Mâché
(German)

Papier-mâché Shoulder Head: Ca. 1840s-1860s. Johann Müller and others. Unretouched shoulder head, molded black hair, painted eyes; some wear and crazing; cloth or kid body; original or appropriate old clothing; entire doll in fair condition.

16-18in (41-46cm)	**$900-$1,000***
22-24in (56-61cm)	**$1,100-$1,300***
32in (81cm)	**$1,900-$2,200***
18½in (47cm) all original, exceptional model and condition	**$5,000**
Long curls: 19in (48cm)	**$2,300**

Brown hair with molded flowers and ornaments: 17in (43cm) **$3,190**

Glass eyes, short hair:

19in (48cm)	**$1,650-$1,850**
24in (61cm)	**$2,400**
21in (53cm) all-original provincial costume	**$2,600**

Glass eyes, long hair:

22in (56cm)	**$1,700-$2,000**

Glass eyes, bun and exposed ears:

20-22in (51-56cm)	**$4,000-$5,000**

Flirty eyes, long hair:

23in (58cm)	**$2,700-$3,000**

Unmarked So-called Pre-Greiner: Ca. 1850. Unknown makers, some may be American. Papier-mâché shoulder head; molded and painted black hair, pupil-less black glass eyes; stuffed cloth body, mostly homemade, wood, leather or cloth extremities; dressed in good old or original clothes; all in good condition, showing some wear.

18-22in (46-56cm)	**$1,200-$1,500**
28-32in (71-81cm)	**$2,200-$2,700**

Fair condition, much wear:

20-24in (51-61cm)	**$700-$800**

Flirty eye: 30in (76cm) **$3,000-$3,500**

Molded Hair Papier-mâché: So-called Milliners' Model: 1820s-1860s. Unretouched shoulder head, various molded black hairdos, blue, black or brown eyes, painted features; original kid body, wooden arms and legs; original or very old handmade clothing; entire doll in fair condition.

Long curls:

9in (23cm)	**$550****
13in (33cm)	**$675-$725****
23in (58cm)	**$1,400-$1,500****

Covered wagon hairdo:

7in (18cm)	**$275-$325****
11in (28cm)	**$500-$550**
15in (38cm)	**$675-$775****

*Allow extra for unusual model.
**Allow extra for excellent condition and original clothes.

31½in (80cm) early papier-mâché with glass eyes. *Laraine & Gangolf Freisberg.*

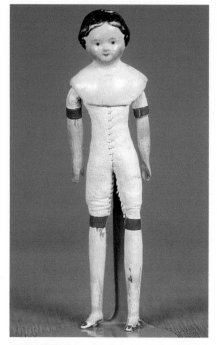

6½in (17cm) molded hair papier-mâché with covered wagon hairdo. *H & J Foulke, Inc.*

19½in (59cm) molded hair papier-mâché with braided coronet and painted side curls. *Greg Montcastle.*

Side curls with braided bun:
    9-10in (23-25cm)   **$900-$1,000***
    18in (46cm) at auction   **$3,850**
Center part with molded bun:
    7-8in (18-20cm)   **$575-$650**
    11in (28cm)   **$1,100-$1,200***
        Wood-jointed body   **$1,500**
Side curls with high beehive (Apollo knot):
    11-12in (28-31cm)   **$1,100-$1,300***
    18in (46cm)   **$2,000-$2,250***
Coiled braids at ears, braided bun:
    10-11in (25-28cm)   **$1,000-$1,100***
    20in (51cm)   **$2,000-$2,200***
Braided coronet:
    11in(28cm)   **$1,250-$1,450***
    17-18in (43-46cm)   **$3,200-$3,500**
Short wind-blown hair:
    11in (28cm)   **$1,100***
    18in (46cm)   **$1,750***
Molded bonnet:
    15in (38cm) at auction   **$3,525**

*Allow extra for excellent condition and original clothes.

Sonneberg Täufling So-called Motschmann Baby*: Ca. 1850-on. Heinrich Stier and other Sonneberg factories. Papier-mâché or wax-over-composition head with painted hair, dark pupil-less glass eyes; composition lower torso, composition and wood arms and legs, jointed at the ankles and wrists, cloth-covered midsection with voice box, cloth-covered upper arms and legs, called floating joints; dressed in shift and bonnet. (For body photograph, see *11th Blue Book*, page 336.)
Very good condition:
    6in (15cm)   **$650-$750**
    12-14in (31-36cm)   **$1,000-$1,200**
    18-20in (46-51cm)   **$1,800-$2,300**
    24-26in (61-66cm)   **$3,000-$3,250**
Fair condition, with wear:
    12-14in (31-36cm)   **$600-$750**
    18-20in (46-51cm)   **$1,200-$1,300**

*Some are found stamped "Ch. Motschmann," but he was the holder of the patent for the voice boxes, not the manufacturer of the dolls.

Patent Washable Dolls: 1880-1915. F.M. Schilling and other Sonneberg factories. Composition shoulder head with mohair or skin wig, glass eyes, closed or open mouth; cloth body with composition arms and lower legs, sometimes with molded boots; appropriately dressed; all in good condition.
Superior Quality:

12-14in (31-36cm)	**$500-$600**
16-18in (41-46cm)	**$700-$750**
22-24in (56-61cm)	**$850-$900**
30in (76cm)	**$1,200-$1,400**
17in (43cm) original costume, exceptional condition	**$1,300**

Standard Quality:

11-12in (28-31cm)	**$150-$175**
14-16in (36-41cm)	**$225-$250**
22-24in (56-61cm)	**$350-$375**
30-33in (76-84cm)	**$450-$500**
38in (97cm)	**$600-$700**
Lady: 13-16in (33-41cm)	**$750-$850**
Oriental: 12in (31cm)	**$250**

Sonneberg-type Papier-mâché: Ca. 1880-1910. Müller & Strasburger, A. Wislizenus, Cuno & Otto Dressel and other Sonneberg factories. Shoulder head with molded and painted black or blonde hair, painted eyes, closed mouth; cloth body, sometimes with leather arms; old or appropriate clothes; all in good condition, showing some wear.
Mark: Usually unmarked. Some marked:

```
M & S
Superior
2015
```

13-15in (33-38cm)	**$300-$350**
18-19in (46-48cm)	**$450-$500**
23-25in (58-64cm)	**$600-$700**
Glass eyes: 18in (46cm)	**$550-$600**
Topsy-Turvy: 7½in (19cm) all original	**$300**

Papier-mâché child: Ca. 1920-on. Papier-mâché head, good wig, painted features; hard stuffed body; original clothes, all in good condition.

10-12in (25-31cm)	**$75-$85**

12in (31cm) patent washable. *H & J Foulke, Inc.*

20in (51cm) Sonneberg-type papier-mâché lady. *Floyd Jones.*

Parian-Type
(Untinted Bisque)

Unmarked Parian: Pale or untinted shoulder head, sometimes with molded blouse, beautifully molded hairdo (may have ribbons, beads, comb or other decoration), painted eyes, closed mouth; cloth body; lovely clothes; entire doll in fine condition.

FACTS
Various German firms. Ca. 1860s through 1870s.
Mark:
Usually none, sometimes numbers.

Common, plain style:

8-10in (20-25cm)	**$135-$185**
16in (41cm)	**$300-$350**
24in (61cm)	**$475-$525**
Swivel neck: 17½in(45cm)	**$525-$575**

Molded white blouse, blue scarf:

22in (56cm)	**$550-$575**

Pretty hairdo, may have simple ribbon, comb or snood:

14-15in (36-38cm)	**$550-$650**
18-20in (46-51cm)	**$800-$900**

Decorated shoulder plate:

14in (36cm)	**$1,300-$1,500**
18-19in (46-48cm)	**$1,800-$2,300**
25in (64cm)	**$2,500-$2,600**

Lady, removable cluster of curls:

17-19in (43-48cm)	**$4,500-$5,000**

Alice hairdo:

11-14in (24-36cm)	**$450-$500**
21in (53cm)	**$650-$750**

"**Augusta Victoria**" (blonde hair, molded blouse):

14-16in (36-41cm)	**$1,200-$1,300**

"**Countess Dagmar**":

19in (48cm)	**$850-$950**

"**Dolly Madison**," glass eyes, swivel neck:

18in (46cm)	**$750-$800**
Decorated plate:	
17in (43cm)	**$1,250-$1,350**

11in (28cm) *Alice* parian. *H & J Foulke, Inc.*

"**Empress Eugenie,**" pink lustre hat and snood:
 13-15in (33-38cm)   **$1,100-$1,200**
"**Irish Queen,**" Limbach 8552:
 16in (41cm)   **$600-$700**
Child, short blonde hair:
 15-16in (38-41cm)   **$500-$550**
Child, glass eyes, molded blonde curls:
 14-16in (36-41cm)   **$1,150-$1,250**
Boy, molded hat and shoulder plate:
 19½in (49cm), at auction   **$2,750**
Man, molded collar and tie:
 16-17in (41-43cm)   **$650-$750**
Man with collar and glass eyes:
 22½in (57cm) at auction   **$1,760**
Ladies with fancy hairdos, at auction:
 Molded hat, decorated plate, glass eyes, 22½in (57cm)   **$4,840**
 Blonde hair, blue tiara:
  24in (61cm)   **$1,900**
 Blonde hair with blue ribbons:
  11in (28cm)   **$1,045**
 Blonde hair with long waves onto shoulders, molded necklace:
  17in (43cm)   **$3,520**
 Black hair, brush marks around face:
  16in (41cm)   **$1,100**
Head only, decorated shoulder plate, glass eyes: 5in (13cm)   **$850**
Head only, molded blouse with black bow, pierced ears, blonde hair:
 3½in (8cm)   **$325**
All-parian, pink lustre boots, fine quality: 5½in (14cm)   **$250-$275**

18in (46cm) *Dolley Madison* parian. *H & J Foulke, Inc.*

16in (41cm) *Countess Dagmar* parian. *H & J Foulke, Inc.*

Philadelphia Baby

FACTS
J.B. Sheppard & Co., Philadelphia, PA, U.S.A. Ca. 1900. All-cloth.
Mark: None

Philadelphia Baby: All-cloth with treated shoulder-type head, lower arms and legs; painted hair, well-molded facial features, ears; stocking body; very good condition.

18-22in (46-56cm)	**$4,200-$4,500**
Fair, showing wear	**$1,600-$1,800**

Rare style face (see *6th Blue Book*, page 302, for exact doll), at auction
$9,350

Philadelphia Baby, all original. *H & J Foulke, Inc.*

Right: 16½in (42cm) *Bèbè Rabery,* exceptional example. *Connie & Jay Lowe.*

Rabery & Delphieu

FACTS
Rabery & Delphieu of Paris, France.
1856 (founded)-1899, then with S.F.B.J.
Mark: R ⁵⁄₀ D
On back of head:

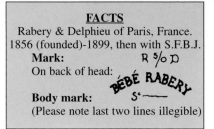

Body mark: ᵇᴱᴮᴱ RABERY Sᶜ——
(Please note last two lines illegible)

Marked R.D. Bébé: Ca. 1880s. Perfect bisque head, lovely wig, paperweight eyes, closed mouth; jointed composition body; beautifully dressed; entire doll in good condition; very good quality bisque, very pretty.

12-14in (31-36cm)	**$2,500-$2,800***
18-19in (46-48cm)	**$2,900-$3,300***
24-25in (61-64cm)	**$3,500-$4,000***
28in (71cm)	**$4,750-$5,000***

Open mouth:
19-22in (48-56cm)	**$1,500-$1,750**

*Allow extra for exceptional modeling and decoration.

Raggedy Ann and Andy

Early Raggedy Ann or **Andy:** Volland Co. 1918-1934. All-cloth with movable arms and legs; brown yarn hair, button eyes, painted features; legs of striped fabric for hose and black for shoes; original clothes; all in good condition.
Mark: "PATENTED SEPT. 7, 1915"

Early hand-painted face Ann
$2,200-$2,500
Single eyelash $3,500
Printed face $1,500-$1,750
Wear, stains, not original clothes
$800-$900

FACTS
Various makers. 1915 to present.
All-cloth
Creator: Johnny B. Gruelle.

Characters: $2,500
Beloved Belindy: $4,000**

**Not enough price samples to compute a reliable range.

Above: 16in (41cm) Volland *Raggedy Ann* with early face. *H & J Foulke, Inc.*

16in (41cm) Volland *Raggedy Andy* with later printed face. *H & J Foulke, Inc.*

Mollye's Raggedy Ann or **Andy:** 1935-1938, manufactured by Mollye's Doll Outfitters. Red hair and printed features; original clothes; all in good condition, bright color.

Mark:
"Raggedy Ann and Raggedy Andy Dolls, Manufactured by Mollye's Doll Outfitters" [printed writing in black on front torso]
18-22in (46-56cm)	
	$1,600-$1,900 each
Mint-in-box, at auction	**$2,800**
30in (76cm) at auction	**$5,200**
Babies:	
14in (36cm) pair	**$4,000-$5,000**

Exposition Doll & Toy Co.: Late 1934 to mid 1935. Very distinctive look.
18in (46cm)	**$5,500-$6,500****

Georgene Raggedy Ann or **Andy:** 1938-1963, manufactured by Georgene Novelties, Inc. Red hair, black button eyes; original clothes; all in good condition, light wear and fading acceptable.

Mark: Various cloth labels sewn in side seam of body.
Black Outline Nose, Ca. 1938-1944:	
19-20in (48-51cm)	**$1,200-$1,500**
32in (81cm)	**$2,500-$2,800**
Asleep/Awake, Black Outline Nose:	
13in (33cm) pair	**$1,800**
Asleep/Awake, plain nose:	
12in (30cm)	**$800**
Face #2, long nose, ca. 1944-1946:	
19in (48cm)	**$1,000-$1,200**
Silsby Label, 1946, bright color:	
15in (38cm)	**$750**
20in (51cm) pair	**$1,250**
22in (56cm) *Andy*, blue striped legs, flowered hat and shirt, at auction	
	$2,850
Small nose, curved sides, bright color, excellent condition:	
15in (38cm)	**$350-$400**
Boxed	**$500-$600**

**Not enough price samples to compute a reliable range.

19-20in (48-51cm)	**$450-$550**
Boxed	**$650-$700**
23in (58cm)	**$550-$650**
49in (124cm) at auction	**$1,800**

Small nose, worn faded, all original:

15in (38cm)	**$200-$250**
19in (48cm)	**$300**

Camel with Wrinkled Knees:

At auction	**$2,638**

Beloved Belindy:

19in (48cm)	**$1,500-$2,000**
Boxed with label, at auction	**$3,800**

Handmade Raggedy Ann or Andy: 1930-1940.

15-19in (38-48cm)	**$185-$225**

Knickerbocker Toy Co. Raggedy Ann or Andy: 1963-1982. Bright color, excellent condition.

Early: 1964. 15in (38cm) boxed with clouds **$300**
Various print dresses:

15in (38cm)	**$150-$175**

19in (48cm)	**$200-$300**

Common print dress:

15in (38cm)	**$65-$85**
19in (48cm)	**$85-$95**
Boxed	**$125**
32-35in (81-86cm) pair	**$300-$400**

Beloved Belindy:

15in (38cm)	**$800-$900**

Camel with Wrinkled Knees:

15in (38cm)	**$300-$350**

Musical: 1966.

15in (38cm) boxed	**$225-$250**

Teach N Play ("Dress Me"), 1971.

18in (46cm)	**$125-$135**

Embraceables, 1973.

7in (18cm) pair	**$50-$65**
Boxed	**$100-$125**

Talking: 1973.

18in (46cm) boxed	**$225**

Hand Puppets: 1973.

9½in (24cm) pair	**$27**

Pajama Bag:

25in (64xm), at auction	**$167.50**

Marionette:

12in (31cm) boxed	**$55-$65**

Georgene Asleep/Awake *Raggedy Ann*, all original. *H & J Foulke, Inc.*

15in (39cm)
Georgene *Raggedy Andy* with Silsby
label, all original
H & J Foulke, Inc.

Applause: 1981-on.
Embroidered eyes:

9in (23cm)	**$15**
12in (31cm)	**$15-$18**
17in (43cm)	**$19-$22**
24in (61cm) pair	**$115**
36in (91cm) pair	**$150**

Classic model, button eyes:

17-20in (43-51cm)	**$25-$28**
25in (63cm)	**$35-$40**
Talking: 16in (41cm) boxed	**$45-$55**
Dance With Me: 45in (115cm)	**$35-$45**
Musical: 6½in (17cm)	**$55-$60**

1992 75th Anniversary Ann or **Andy:**

19in (48cm) boxed	**$75-$85**

1993 Molly-E Baby Raggedy Ann:

13in (33cm)	**$80-$90**

1994 Raggedy Ann or **Andy:**

13in (33cm) boxed	**$80-$90**
Camel with Wrinkled Knees	**$110**

1995 Raggedy Ann, U.S. Patent:

17in (43cm)	**$125**

1997 Stamp Doll:

17in (43cm) boxed	**$55-$65**

1998 Stars & Stripes:

17in (43cm) boxed	**$75-$85**

1998 Rags: 18in (46cm)   **$75**

Hasbro, Inc.: 1983-on.

12in (31cm), boxed	**$15-$18**
18in (46cm), boxed	**$22-$25**
24in (61cm)	**$35**

Baby:

9in (23cm) pair, boxed	**$38-$42**

80th Anniversary Ann:

18in (46cm) boxed	**$30-$35**

1996 Anniversary pair:

11in (28cm) boxed	**$35-$45**

Playskool: 1989-on.

1992 Boxed pair: 9in (23cm)	**$35**

1990 Christmas Ann & Andy pair:

12in (31cm) pair	**$25**

1989 Baby Ann or **Andy:**

10in (25cm)	**$10-$15**

1991 Dress Me Raggedy Ann:

14in (35cm) boxed	**$30-$35**

Alexander:

1993 Mop Top Wendy & Billy:

pair	**$90-$100**

Recknagel

R.A. Child: Ca. 1890s-World War I. Perfect marked bisque head, good wig, set or sleep eyes, open mouth; jointed composition or wooden body; some dolls with molded painted shoes and socks; all in good condition.

1907, 1909, 1914:

8-9in (20-23cm) five-piece body
$125-$135

16-18in (41-46cm) **$275-$300**

24in (61cm) **$400-$425**

R.A. Character Baby: 1909-World War I. Perfect bisque head, painted or glass eyes; cloth baby body or composition bent-limb baby body; nicely dressed; all in good condition.

#121, 126, 127, 1924 infants:

8-9in (20-23cm) long **$200-$225**

#23 character babies:

7-8in (18-20cm) **$250-$275**

#22, 28, and **44** bonnet babies:

8-9in (20-23cm) **$475-$525**

11-12in (28-31cm) **$600-$650**

Character children:

6-8in (15-20cm) composition body
$275-$300

18in (46cm) smiling face, at auction
$1,700

#31 Max and **#32 Moritz,** molded hair, painted features:

8in (20cm) **$650-$700**

#45 and **46,** googlies:

7in (18cm) **$400-$450**

#43, 44, googlies with molded hats:

7in (18cm) **$500**

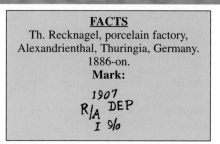

FACTS
Th. Recknagel, porcelain factory, Alexandrienthal, Thuringia, Germany. 1886-on.
Mark:

7in (18cm) R.A. character girl. *H & J Foulke, Inc.*

Grace Corry Rockwell

Grace Corry Rockwell Child: 1926-1928. **Pretty Peggy,** George Borgfeldt & Co. Perfect bisque head with molded hair or wig, sleep eyes, closed mouth; cloth body with composition limbs; appropriate vintage clothes; all in excellent condition.

Mark:
> Copr. By
> Grace C. Rockwell
> Germany

14in (36cm)	**$5,000**
16in (41cm)	**$6,600**

FACTS
Designer: Grace Corry Rockwell 1920s.

Grace Corry Child: 1927. **Little Brother** and **Little Sister,** Averill Mfg. Co. Smiling composition face, molded hair, sometimes covered with a wig, painted eyes, closed mouth; cloth body with composition limbs; appropriate or original clothes, some with Madame Hendren labels; all in very good condition.

Marks:

Head:	Body:
©	Genuine
By	Madame Hendren
Grace Corry	Doll

14in (36cm) **$450-$550**

14in (36cm) Rockwell child with bisque head. *H & J Foulke, Inc.*

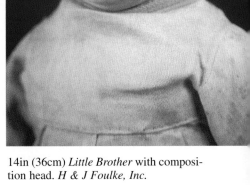

14in (36cm) *Little Brother* with composition head. *H & J Foulke, Inc.*

Rollinson Doll

S.F.B.J.

FACTS
Utley Doll Co., Holyoke, MA, U.S.A.
1916-on.
Designer: Gertrude F. Rollinson
Mark: Stamp in shape of a diamond
with a doll in center, around border:
"Rollinson Doll Holyoke, Mass."

Marked Rollinson Doll: All molded
cloth with painted head and limbs;
painted hair or human hair wig, painted
features (sometimes teeth also);
dressed; all in good condition.
Chase-type with painted hair:

18-22in (46-51cm)	**$800-$1,200**

Child with wig:

16in (41cm)	**$800-$1,200**
26in (66cm)	**$1,500-$2,000**

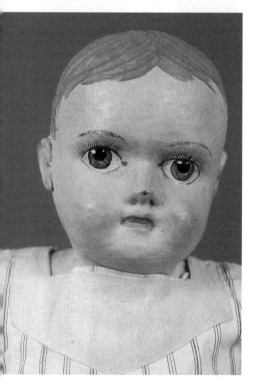

Rollinson with molded and painted hair.
Nancy A. Smith.

FACTS
Société Française de Fabrication de
Bébés & Jouets, Paris, France.
1899-on.
Mark:

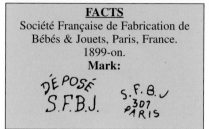

Child Doll: 1899-on. Perfect bisque
head, good French wig, set or sleep
eyes, open mouth, pierced ears; jointed
composition body; nicely dressed; all
in good condition.
Jumeau-type, paperweight eyes (no
mold number), 1899-1910:

14-16in (36-41cm)	**$900-$1,000**
21-23in (53-58cm)	**$1,400-$1,600**
27-28in (64-69cm)	**$1,800-$2,200**

#301, (some stamped "Tête Jumeau"
on labeled Jumeau body):

8in (20cm)	**$650**
10in (25cm)	**$675-$775**
12-14in (31-36cm)	**$500-$600**
18-21in (46-53cm)	**$725-$800**
28-30in (71-76cm)	**$1,000-$1,200**
37in (94cm)	**$2,200-$2,500**
11in (28cm) original box and trousseau	**$2,750**
22in (56cm) lady body	**$1,000**

#60, end of World War I on:

7½in (19cm) with Jumeau tag	**$425-$450**
12-14in (31-36cm)	**$425-$475**
19-21in (48-53cm)	**$550-$650**
28in (71cm)	**$800-$900**

Walking, kissing and flirting:

22in (56cm)	**$1,600-$1,800**

Papier-mâché head **#60,** fully-jointed
body:

17in (43cm)	**$250-$300**
22in (56cm)	**$350-$400**
18in (46cm) child in original sailor outfit, like new	**$1,400**

Bleuette #60 or **301:**

10½-11in (27-29cm)	**$2,000-$2,400**

Character Dolls: 1910-on. Perfect bisque head, wig, molded, sometimes flocked hair on mold numbers **237**, **266**, **227** and **235**, sleep eyes; composition body; nicely dressed; all in good condition.

Mark:

#226:
17-19in (43-48cm)   **$1,700-$1,900**
#227: 17in (43cm)   **$1,850-$1,900**
#229: 16in (41cm)   **$2,000-$2,200**
#230, (sometimes Jumeau):
12-14in (30-36cm)   **$850-$950**
20-23in (51-58cm)   **$1,400-$1,600**

11in (28cm) 301 *Bleuette. H & J Foulke, Inc.*

13in (33cm) 230 child. *H & J Foulke, Inc.*

14in (36cm) 226 character child. *H & J Foulke, Inc.*

#233:
16in (41cm)	**$3,300-$3,500**
20in (51cm)	**$4,200-$4,400**

#234: 15in (38cm) baby   **$2,500**
#235: 16in (41cm) child **$1,850-$1,900**
#236, baby:
12-13in (31-33cm)	**$700-$800**
15-17in (38-43cm)	**$900-$1,100**
20-22in (51-56cm)	**$1,400-$1,500**
25in (64cm)	**$1,700-$1,800**

Toddler:
15-16in (38-41cm)	**$1,250-$1,350**
24in (61cm)	**$1,950-$2,000**

#237:
18-19in (46-48cm)	**$2,600-$3,200**
All-original boy, at auction	**$4,000**

#238, child:
17-18in (43-46cm)	**$2,200-$2,500**
Lady: 18-19in (46-48cm)	**$3,000**

#239: 13in (33cm) Poulbot, all original
$8,250
#242, nursing baby:
13-14in (33-35cm)	**$3,250****

#245 Googly: See page 92.
#246: 16½in (42cm)   **$3,100****

#247, toddler:
12-14in (31-36cm)	**$1,700-$1,900**
20in (51cm)	**$2,250-$2,750**

Baby: 8in (20cm) in original presentation
basket, at auction   **$2,700**
#248:
10-12in (25-30cm)	**$7,500-$8,500****

#250:
19-20in (48-51cm)	**$3,250-$3,500**

#251, toddler:
8in (20cm)	**$1,600**
14-15in (36-38cm)	**$1,300-$1,500**
21-23in (53-58cm)	**$1,900-$2,200**

#252, baby:
7-8in (18-20cm)	**$1,600-$2,000**
12in (31cm)	**$3,200**

Toddler:
8in (20cm)	**$3,500-$3,800**
13in (33cm)	**$4,800-$5,500**
20in (51cm)	**$6,500-$7,500**

Boxed set: 12in (30cm) baby with three
character heads (233, 235, 237)
$7,500-$8,500**

**Not enough price samples to compute a
reliable range.

![15in (38cm) 235 character child]

15in (38cm) 235 character child. *H & J
Foulke, Inc.*

15½in (39cm) 236 character child. *H & J
Foulke, Inc.*

Bruno Schmidt

Marked B.S.W. Child Doll: Ca. 1898-on. Bisque head, good wig, sleep eyes, open mouth; jointed composition child body; dressed; all in good condition.

    18-20in (46-51cm)   **$400-$450***
    24-26in (61-66cm)   **$500-$550***

Marked B.S.W. Character Dolls: Bisque socket head, glass eyes; jointed composition body; dressed; all in good condition.

#2048, 2094, 2096, (so-called "**Tommy Tucker**"), molded hair, open mouth:

    13-14in (33-36cm)   **$700-$800**
    19-21in (48-53cm)   **$950-$1,100**
    25-26in (64-66cm)   **$1,300-$1,500**

#2042, (molded hair, painted eyes):

    16in (41cm) toddler   **$2,200****

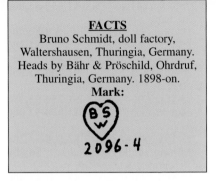

FACTS
Bruno Schmidt, doll factory, Waltershausen, Thuringia, Germany. Heads by Bähr & Pröschild, Ohrdruf, Thuringia, Germany. 1898-on.
Mark:

*Allow $50 to $100 for flirty eyes.
**Not enough price samples to compute a reliable range.

22in (56cm) 2096 child with open mouth. *H & J Foulke, Inc.*

#2048, (closed mouth) toddler:
  16-18in (41-46cm) **$2,500-$2,600**
#2072:
  19in (48cm) toddler **$3,000**
#2033, (so-called **"Wendy"**) (**537**):
  12-13in (30-33cm) **$12,500**
  15-17in (38-43cm) **$16,000-$20,000**
  20in (51cm) **$30,000**
#2023 (539):
  24in (61cm) at auction **$3,000****
#2025 (529), closed mouth, wigged:
  22in (56cm) **$6,500-$7,000****
#2097, #692, character baby, open mouth:
  13-14in (33-36cm) **$400-$425**
  18in (46cm) **$475-$525**
  24in (61cm) **$750**
#2097, toddler:
  17in (43cm) **$950-$1,050**
#425, all-bisque baby:
  5½-6in (13-15cm) **$300-$350**
#426, all-bisque toddler:
  9½in (24cm) **$1,200****

**Not enough price samples to compute a reliable range.

22in (56cm) BSW child with flirty eyes. *H & J Foulke, Inc.*

Franz Schmidt

FACTS
Franz Schmidt & Co., doll factory, Georgenthal near Waltershausen, Thuringia, Germany. Heads by Simon & Halbig, Gräfenhain, Thuringia, Germany. 1890-on.

Marked S & C Child Doll: Ca. 1890-on. Perfect bisque socket head, good wig, sleep eyes, open mouth; jointed composition child body; dressed; all in good condition. Some are Mold **#293** or **269**.
  6-7in (15-18cm) five-piece body
  $350-$400
  11in (28cm) **$550-$600**
  16-18in (41-46cm) **$350-$400**
  22-24in (56-61cm) **$450-$500**
  29-30in (74-76cm) **$750-$850**
  Flapper: 20in (51cm), flirty eyes
  $550-$600
  42in (107cm) **$3,000-$3,200**
  Shoulder head, kid body:
  24-26in (61-66cm) **$400-$450**
Mark: *S & C*
  SIMON & HALBIG
  28

Marked F.S. & Co. Character Baby: Ca. 1910. Perfect bisque character head, good wig, sleep eyes, open mouth, may have open nostrils; jointed bent-limb composition body; suitably dressed; all in good condition.

#1271, 1272, 1295, 1296, 1297, 1310:
Baby:
  12-14in (31-36cm) **$400-$425**
  20-21in (51-53cm) **$550-$650**
  26-27in (66-69cm) **$950-$1,100**
Toddler:
  7-8in (18-20cm) **$850-$950**
  13-15in (33-38cm) **$750-$850**
  19-21in (48-53cm) **$1,000-$1,200**
  26-27in (66-69cm) **$1,500-$1,750**
#1255: 24in (61cm) baby at auction
  $2,875

#1266, bald head, painted eyes, closed mouth:

16-17in (41-43cm) **$3,500-$3,900****

#1267, open/closed mouth, painted eyes: 12in (31cm) baby   **$1,450****

#1270: 11in (28cm) baby   **$1,200****

#1286, molded hair with blue ribbon, glass eyes, open smiling mouth:

16in (41cm) toddler   **$4,000****

Mark:

1295
F. S. & Co.
Made in
Germany
30

**Not enough price samples to compute a reliable range.

Left: 11in (28cm) S & C child, fully-jointed body. *H & J Foulke, Inc.*

Below: 21in (53cm) 1295 toddler with pierced nose and flirty eyes. *H & J Foulke, Inc.*

Schmitt

Marked Schmitt Bébé: Ca. 1879. Perfect bisque socket head with skin or good wig, large paperweight eyes, closed mouth, pierced ears; Schmitt-jointed composition body with flat bottom; appropriate clothes; all in good condition.

Long face:
   16-18in (41-46cm) **$13,000-$15,000**
   23-25in (58-64cm) **$20,000-$22,000**
   30in (76cm)   **$25,000-$30,000**
Short face (parted lips):
   11in (28cm)   **$9,500**
   14-16in (36-41cm) **$11,000-$12,500**
   19in (48cm)   **$14,000**
Oval/round face:
   13-14in (33-36cm) **$9,000-$10,000**
   17-18in (43-46cm) **$13,000-$15,000**
Cup and saucer neck:
   17in (43cm)   **$17,000****

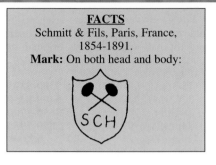

FACTS
Schmitt & Fils, Paris, France, 1854-1891.
Mark: On both head and body:

Open/closed mouth, two rows of teeth:
   24in (61cm)   **$25,000****
Wax-over papier-mâché head:
   16in (41cm)   **$2,200-$2,600****

**Not enough price samples to compute a reliable range.

17in (43cm) bèbè, size 2 with shield mark. *Kay Jensen Antique Dolls.*

Schoenau & Hoffmeister

Child Doll: Perfect bisque head, original or good wig, sleep eyes, open mouth; ball-jointed body; original or good clothes; all in nice condition.

#1906, 1909, 5700, 5800:

14-16in (36-41cm)	**$300-$325**
21-23in (53-58cm)	**$400-$450**
28-30in (71-76cm)	**$650-$700**
33in (84cm)	**$850-$950**
39in (99cm)	**$2,000**

#4000, 4600, 5000, 5500:

15-17in (38-43cm)	**$375-$425**
22in (56cm)	**$450-$550**
26in (66cm)	**$700-$800**
35in (89cm)	**$1,150**

FACTS
Schoenau & Hoffmeister, Porzellanfabrik Burggrub, Burggrub, Bavaria, Germany, porcelain factory, 1901-on. Arthur Schoenau also owned a doll factory. 1884-on.
Trademarks: Hanna, Burggrub Baby, Bébé Carmencita, Viola, Künstlerkopf, Das Lachende Baby.
Mark:

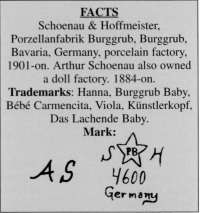

15in (38cm) 4000 child. *H & J Foulke, Inc.*

Right: 23in (58cm) 1909 child with walking body. *H & J Foulke, Inc.*

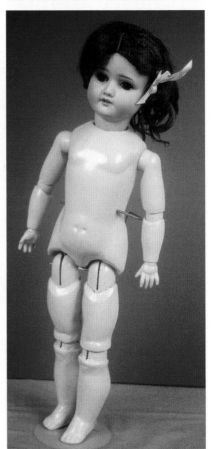

Künstlerkopf:
   24-26in (61-66cm)   **$850-$950****
Shoulder head, kid body:
   18-20in (46-51cm)   **$275-$350**
   13-15in (33-38cm) hinged pink kid
   body   **$425-$475**

Character Baby: 1910-on. Perfect bisque socket head, good wig, sleep eyes, open mouth; composition bent-limb baby body; all in good condition. **#169, 769** "Burggrub Baby" or "Porzellanfabrik Burggrub."
   13-15in (33-38cm)   **$275-$325**
   18-20in (46-51cm)   **$400-$450**
   23-24in (58-61cm)   **$550-$600**
   28in (71cm)   **$750**
   Painted bisque: 14in (36cm) toddler, factory original   **$325-$350**

Hanna:
Baby:
   14-16in (36-41cm)   **$450-$500**
   20-22in (51-56cm)   **$750-$800**

Toddler: 14-16in (36-41cm) **$750-$850**
Brown: See page 55.
OX: 15in (38cm) toddler
                              $1,400-$1,500**
Das Lachende Baby, 1930:
   23-24in (58-61cm) **$2,200-$2,500****

Princess Elizabeth, 1929, chubby five-piece body:
   17in (43cm)   **$1,700-$1,900**
   20-23in (51-58cm)   **$2,000-$2,200**

Pouty Baby: Ca. 1925. Perfect bisque solid dome head with painted hair, tiny sleep eyes, closed pouty mouth; cloth body with composition arms and legs; dressed; all in good condition.
   11-12in (28-31cm)   **$600-$700**

**Not enough price samples to compute a reliable range.

21in (53cm)
Princess Elizabeth.

Schoenhut

Salesman's Cutaway Sample
$800-$1,000
Original Stand **$75-$100**
Original Shoes: very good condition
$200-$250
Character: 1911-1930. Wooden head and spring-jointed body, marked head and/or body; original or appropriate wig, brown or blue intaglio eyes, open/closed mouth with painted teeth or closed mouth; original or suitable clothing; original paint may have a few scuffs.

14-21in (36-53cm):
Excellent condition **$1,900-$2,200***
Very good, some wear
$1,200-$1,400*
Fading, wear, crazing **$750-$900**
Smiling face, exceptional and all-original condition, at auction **$3,300**

*Allow extra for rare faces and exceptional original condition.

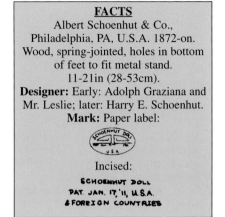

FACTS
Albert Schoenhut & Co., Philadelphia, PA, U.S.A. 1872-on. Wood, spring-jointed, holes in bottom of feet to fit metal stand. 11-21in (28-53cm).
Designer: Early: Adolph Graziana and Mr. Leslie; later: Harry E. Schoenhut.
Mark: Paper label:

Incised:

SCHOENHUT DOLL
PAT. JAN. 17, '11, U.S.A.
& FOREIGN COUNTRIES

Character with carved hair: Ca. 1911-1930. Wooden head with carved hair, comb marks, possibly a ribbon or bow, intaglio eyes, mouth usually closed; spring-jointed wooden body;

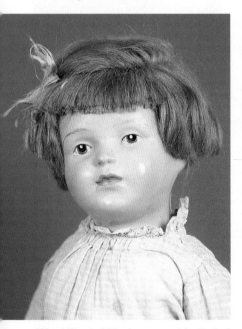

19in (48cm) 308 character girl. *H & J Foulke, Inc.*

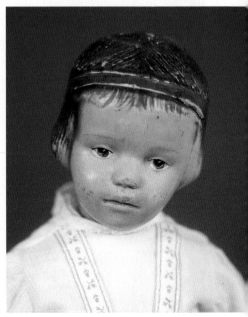

14in (36cm) 105 character girl with carved hair. *H & J Foulke, Inc.*

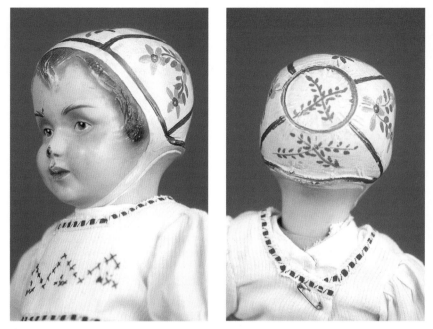

16in (41cm) girl with carved bonnet, very rare model. *H & J Foulke, Inc.*

original or suitable clothes; original paint may have a few scuffs.

14-21in (36-53cm):

Excellent condition	**$2,800-$3,100**
Very good, some wear	**$1,600-$1,800**
Fading, wear, crazing	**$900-$1,100**
Early style	**$5,000-$8,000**

Tootsie Wootsie: 15in (38cm) at auction **$4,900**

Snickelfritz: 15in (38cm) with moderate wear **$3,800****

Carved Hat: **$6,500-$7,500**

Mannekin Man:

20in (51cm) **$2,500****

Baby Face: Ca. 1913-1930. Wooden head and fully-jointed toddler or bent-limb baby body, marked head and/or body; painted hair or mohair wig, painted eyes, open or closed mouth; suitably dressed; original paint; all in good condition, with some wear.

Mark:

Baby:

12in (31cm)	**$450-$500**
15-16in (38-41cm)	**$650-$700**

Toddler:

11in (28cm)	**$600-$700**
14in (36cm)	**$650-$750**
16-17in (41-43cm)	**$750**

Mama Doll: 1924-1927. Wood head and hands, cloth body:

14-17in (36-43cm) **$750-$850****

Walker: Ca. 1919-1930. All-wood with "baby face," mohair wig, painted eyes; curved arms, straight legs with "walker" joint at hip; no holes in bottom of feet; original or appropriate clothes; all in good condition; original mint.

13-17in (33-43cm) **$700-$800+**

**Not enough price samples to compute a reliable range.

+Allow $100 additional for original shoes with "wedge" sole.

19in (48cm) 316 *Miss Dolly*, all original.
H & J Foulke, Inc.

Miss Dolly: Ca. 1915-1930. Wooden head and spring-jointed wooden body; original or appropriate mohair wig, decal eyes, open/closed mouth with painted teeth; original paint; original or suitable clothes.
14-21in (36-53cm):
    Excellent condition   **$850-$950**
    Good condition, some wear
                     $650-$750
    Mint, all original   **$1,250**
Sleep Eyes:
    Excellent condition **$1,000-$1,200**
    Mint, all original, at auction **$1,700**

All-Composition: Ca. 1924. Molded blonde curly hair, painted eyes, tiny closed mouth; original or appropriate clothing; in good condition.
Paper label on back:

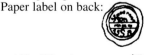

13in (33cm)   **$500-$600****

**Not enough price samples to compute a reliable range.

Simon & Halbig

FACTS
Simon & Halbig, porcelain factory, Gräfenhain, Thuringia, Germany, purchased by Kämmer & Reinhardt in 1920. 1869-on.
Mark:

S 13 H
949

1079-2
DEP
S H
Germany

Shoulder head with molded hair: Ca. 1870s. Perfect bisque shoulder head, painted or glass eyes, closed mouth, molded hair; cloth body, bisque lower arms; appropriately dressed; all in good condition.
Mark: *S 7 H*

on front shoulder plate

13-15in (33-38cm)	**$1,100-$1,200**
17-18in (43-46cm)	**$1,400-$1,600**
23in (58cm)	**$2,200-$2,400**
Swivel neck:	
9in (23cm)	**$1,250**
12in (31cm)	**$1,500**

Fashion Doll (*Poupée*): Ca. 1870s. Perfect bisque socket head on bisque shoulder plate, good mohair wig or molded blonde hair, glass eyes, closed mouth; gusseted kid lady body; appropriately dressed; all in good condition. No marks. (For face, see *12th Blue Book* page 330.)

15-17in (38-43cm)	**$2,250-$2,750**
Twill over wood body:	
9-10in (23-25cm)	**$3,000-$3,500**
15-16in (38-41cm)	**$4,500-$5,500**

22in (56cm) 929 child with open mouth. *Constance Blain Antiques.*

Child doll with closed mouth: Ca. 1879. Perfect bisque socket head on ball-jointed wood and composition body; good wig, glass set or sleep eyes, closed mouth, pierced ears; dressed; all in good condition. (See *Simon & Halbig Dolls, The Artful Aspect* for photographs of mold numbers not shown here.)

#719:

12in (31cm)	**$3,750**
20-23in (51-58cm)	**$5,500-$6,500**

#749: 20-22in (51-56cm) **$3,800****

#905, 908:

14-17in (36-43cm)	**$3,500-$4,500****

#929:

17-18in (43-46cm)	**$3,800- $4,200****

#939:

14-15in (36-38cm)	**$2,500-$2,700**
26in (66cm)	**$3,700-$4,000**

#949:

14-15in (36-38cm)	**$1,900-$2,300**
22-23in (56-58cm)	**$2,900-$3,100**
27-28in (69-71cm)	**$3,800-$4,200**

#979: 15-16in (38-41cm) **$3,000****

**Not enough price samples to compute a reliable range.

24in (61cm) 949 child. *Connie & Jay Lowe.*

Kid or **Cloth Body:**
#720, 740, 940, 950:

9-10in (23-25cm)	**$550-$650**
16-18in (41-46cm)	**$900-$1,100**
22in (56cm)	**$1,300-$1,500**

#949:

18-21in (46-53cm)	**$1,600-$1,800**

#920:

18-20in (46-51cm)	**$1,800-$2,000**

All-Bisque Child: 1880-on. All-bisque child with swivel neck, pegged shoulders and hips; appropriate mohair wig, glass eyes, open or closed mouth; molded stockings and shoes.

#886, over-the-knee black or blue stockings, low orange or blue stockings; open mouth:

4½in (11cm)	**$750-$800***
5½-6in (14-15cm)	**$1,100-$1,300***
7-7½ (18-19cm)	**$1,600-$2,000***
8½-9in (22-23cm)	**$2,500-$3,200***

21in (53cm) early 1009 child. *H & J Foulke, Inc.*

#886, five-strap boots:

7½in (19cm)	**$2,500-$2,750**

#890, over-the-knee black stockings; open mouth:

3¾in (9cm)	**$500-$550**
5-5½in (13-14cm)	**$725-$825**
7-7½in (18-19cm)	**$1,100-$1,250**

Closed mouth, round face:

6-6½in (15-16cm)	**$1,900-$2,200**
Jointed knees	**$5,500****

Closed mouth, five-strap bootines:

7½-8in (19-21cm)	**$3,600-$4,400****

6in (15cm) all-bisque child with round face. *H & J Foulke, Inc.*

*Allow extra for strap bootines and square cut teeth.

**Not enough price samples to compute a reliable range.

Child doll with open mouth and composition body: Ca. 1889 to 1930s. Perfect bisque head, good wig, sleep or paperweight eyes, open mouth, pierced ears; original ball-jointed composition body (may be French); very pretty

18in (46cm) 1039 child with flirty eyes. *H & J Foulke, Inc.*

13in (33cm) 1139 child, very rare number *H & J Foulke, Inc.*

clothes; all in nice condition. (See *Simon & Halbig Dolls, The Artful Aspect* for photographs of mold numbers not shown here.)

#719, 739, 749, 759, 769, 939, 979:

17-19in (43-45cm)	**$1,900-$2,300**
22-23in (56-58cm)	**$2,500-$3,000**

#719: 23in (58cm) Edison, operating **$4,800**

#905, 908:

14-16in (36-41cm)	**$1,800-$2,000**

#929: 23in (58cm) **$3,800****

#949:

17-18in (43-46cm)	**$1,400-$1,500**
28-30in (71-76cm)	**$2,300-$2,500**

#979: 33in (84cm) at auction **$4,600**

#1009:

15-16in (38-41cm)	**$650-$750**
19-21in (48-53cm)	**$800-$900**
24-25in (61-64cm)	**$1,100-$1,300**

#1039:

10in (25cm) flirty eyes	**$1,250**
16-18in (41-46cm)	**$650-$750***
23-25in (58-64cm)	**$900-$1,000***

#1039, key-wind walking body, (R. & D.): 16-22in (41-56cm) **$1,700-$1,800**
#1039, walking, kissing:

20-22in (51-56cm)	**$950-$1,00**

#1078, 1079:

7-10in (18-26cm) five-piece body **$425-$525**

8in (20cm) fully jointed	**$750-$800**
10-12in (25-31cm)	**$800-$900**
14-15in (36-38cm)	**$500-$550**
17-19in (43-48cm)	**$550-$600**
22-24in (56-61cm)	**$650-$700**
28-30in (71-76cm)	**$800-$1,000**
36in (91cm)	**$1,800-$2,200**
42in (107cm)	**$3,800-$4,200**

#1109:

14in (36cm)	**$850****
18in (46cm)	**$1,100****

#1139: 13in (33cm) **$1,200****

#1248, 1249, Santa:

12in (31cm)	**$850**
15in (38cm)	**$750-$800**
20in (51cm)	**$1,000-$1,100**
26-28in (66-71cm)	**$1,700-$1,900**
31-32in (79-81cm)	**$1,700-$2,000**
38in (96cm)	**$3,200**

*Allow $100 extra for flirty eyes.
**Not enough price samples to compute a reliable range.

22in (56cm) CT child, made for Carl Troutman. *H & J Foulke, Inc.*

#540, 550, 570:
  22-24in (56-61cm)   **$450-$550**
#176, (A. Hülss), Flapper:
  18in (46cm)   **$650-$750**
Baby Blanche: 23in (58cm)   **$600**

Child doll with open mouth and kid body: Ca. 1889 to 1930s. Perfect bisque swivel head on shoulder plate or shoulder head with stationary neck, sleep eyes; well costumed; all in good condition.
#1010, 1040, 1080, 1260:
  17-18in (43-46cm)   **$450-$550**
  21-23in (53-58cm)   **$600-$650**
#1009, 1039:
  17-19in (43-48cm)   **$600-$700**
#1250, 1260: with pink kid body and composition arms:
  14-16in (36-41cm)   **$550-$650**
  22-24in (56-61cm)   **$800-$900**
  29in (74cm)   **$1,000-$1,100**
#949:
  19-21in (48-53cm)   **$1,200-$1,400**
#970: 14in (36cm) at auction   **$1,300**

So-called "Little Women" type: Ca. 1900. Mold number **1160.** Shoulder head with fancy mohair wig, glass set eyes, closed mouth; cloth body with bisque limbs, molded boots; dressed; all in good condition.
  5½-7in (14-18cm)   **$350-$400**
  10-11in (25-28cm)   **$425-$475**
  14in (36cm)   **$625-$675**

Character Child: Ca. 1909. Perfect bisque socket head with wig or molded hair, painted or glass eyes, open or closed mouth, character face; jointed composition body; dressed; all in good condition. (See *Simon & Halbig Dolls, The Artful Aspect* for photographs of mold numbers not shown here.)
#120:
  18-19in (46-48cm)   **$3,200-$3,400**
#150:
  11in (28cm)   **$5,500-$6,000**
  20in (51cm)   **$25,000**
  24in (61cm)   **$30,000**
#151:
  14-15in (36-38cm)   **$5,000-$5,500**
  18in (46cm)   **$7,500**
  24in (61cm)   **$13,000**

#153:
    12in (31cm) **$12,000**
    17in (43cm) **$35,000-$40,000**
#174: 21in (53cm) **$1,750-$1,950****
#600:
    12in (31cm) **$900**
    18-19in (46-48cm) toddler
        $1,400-$1,500

#1279:
    14-17in (36-43cm) **$1,600-$2,000**
    19-21in (48-53cm) **$2,200-$2,500**
    26-27in (66-69cm) **$3,000-$3,500**
    34in (86cm) **$4,500**
#1299: 20in (51cm) **$1,300**
#1339:
    18in (46cm) **$1,000-$1,100****
    28-32 (71-81cm) **$1,900-$2,100****
#1388, 23in (58cm) **$30,000****
#1398, 23in (58cm) **$20,000****
IV, #1448:
    13-14in (33-36cm)
        $16,000-$18,000**
    17-18in (43-46cm) **$24,000****

Character Baby: Ca. 1909 to 1930s. Perfect bisque head, molded hair or wig, sleep or painted eyes, open or open/closed mouth; composition bent-limb baby or toddler body; nicely dressed; all in good condition. (See *Simon & Halbig Dolls, The Artful Aspect* for photographs of mold numbers not shown here.)

#156 (A. Hülss):
  Baby:
    15-17in (38-43cm) **$550-$600**
    23in (58cm) **$800-$850**
  Toddler, five-piece body:
    15in (38cm) **$750-$800**
    29in (73cm) **$2,400****
#1294:
  Baby:
    17-19in (43-48cm) **$500-$550**
    23-25in (58-64cm) **$800-$900**
    28in (71cm) with clockwork eyes
        $2,500**
  Toddler: 20in (51cm) **$1,000-$1,200**

**Not enough price samples to compute a reliable range.

28in (71cm) 1260 shoulder head child. *H & J Foulke, Inc.*

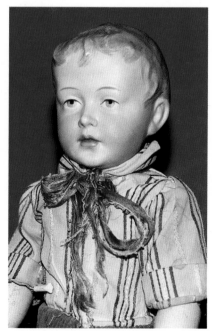

16in (41cm) character boy. *Laraine & Gangolf Freisberg.*

19in (48cm) 1305 character. *Private Collection.*

19in (48cm) 1159 lady. *H & J Foulke, Inc.*

#1428:
Baby:
10-11in (25-28cm)	**$1,000-$1,200**
13-14in (33-36cm)	**$1,200-$1,500**
21in (53cm)	**$2,400-$2,800**

Toddler:
11in (28cm)	**$1,400-$1,600**
15-18in (38-46cm)	**$1,800-$2,200**
24in (61cm)	**$3,500-$3,800**

#1488:
Baby: 20in (51cm)	**$4,000-$4,500**
15in (38cm)	**$3,500-$4,000**

Toddler:
16-18in (41-46cm)	**$4,500-$5,000**

#1489 Erika, baby:
21-22in (53-56cm)	**$3,700-$4,200****

#1498:
Baby: 16in (41cm)	**$2,500****
Toddler: 22in (56cm)	**$4,600****

#172, baby:
14-15in (36-38cm)	**$3,500****

Lady doll: Ca. 1910. Perfect bisque socket head, good wig, sleep eyes, pierced ears; lady body, molded bust, slim arms and legs; dressed; all in good condition.

#1159 (may have an H. Handwerck body):
12in (31cm)	**$1,100-$1,200**
17-18in (43-46cm)	**$1,800**
21-23in (53-58cm)	**$2,200-$2,400**
27in (69cm)	**$2,800-$3,000**

#1468, 1469:
13-15in (33-38cm) naked	**$2,500**
Original clothes	**$3,500**

#1303 lady:
20in (51cm)	**$18,000-$20,000****

#152 lady:
20in (51cm) at auction	**$23,200**

#1308 man:
13in (33cm)	**$8,000-$10,000****

#1307: 21in (53cm)	**$12,500**
#1303 Indian: 21in (53cm)	**$12,000****
#1305: 18in (46cm)	**$12,500**

**Not enough price samples to compute a reliable range.

Snow Babies and Santas

Snow Babies: All-bisque immobile figures with snowsuits and caps of pebbly-textured bisque; painted features; various positions.

Standing: 1½in (4cm)	**$55-$65**
2½in (6cm)	**$150-$160**
4¾in (12cm)	**$400-$450**
Sitting:	
1½in (4cm)	**$50-$60**
3-3½in (8-9cm)	**$250-$300**
Jointed arms and legs:	
3½in (9cm)	**$350-$400**
5¼in (13cm)	**$450-$500**
Shoulder head on cloth body:	
4½in (11cm)	**$185-$210**
10in (25cm)	**$300-$350**
Fine early quality with high hood:	
2in (5cm)	**$185-$210**
With musical instrument: 2in (5cm)	
	$125-$150
Twins: 2in (5cm)	**$150-$160**
Snowman: 2½in (6cm)	**$100-$125**
Snow bear: 1½in (4cm)	**$60-$75**

Action Figures:

Huskies pulling sled with snow baby:	
3in (9cm)	**$300**
Reindeer pulling sled with snow baby: 2in (5cm)	**$275**
Snow baby riding reindeer:	
2½in (6cm)	**$325**
Snow baby riding snow bear:	
3in (9cm)	**$350**
Tumbling snow baby:	
2½in (6cm)	**$175-$185**
Snow baby on sled:	
1½in (4cm)	**$125**
3in (8cm)	**$225**
Three snow babies on sled	**$225**
Snow babies sliding on cellar door:	
2½in (6cm)	**$275-$325**
Snow dog and snowman on sled:	
2in (5cm)	**$275-$325**
Snow Children:	
Seated girl: 1½in (4cm)	**$135**
Boy or girl on sled	**$185-$210**

"No Snows:"

Boy and girl on sled:	
2in (5cm)	**$175**
Elf with teddy: 2in (5cm)	**$195**
Skiing boy: 2½in (6cm)	**$110**
Santas (with or without snow):	
3in (9cm) standing	**$125-$135**
2in (5cm) with toy sack	**$175**
Santa riding snow bear:	
2½in (6cm)	**$350**
Santa in sleigh with reindeer:	
3½in (9cm)	**$300**
Santa on igloo with snow baby:	
2½in (6cm)	**$250**
Santa with bell tower:	
2½in (6cm)	**$350**

3-3/8in (8cm) and 2½in (6cm) snow babies. *H & J Foulke, Inc.*

Steiff

FACTS
Fräulein Margarete Steiff,
Würtemberg, Germany. 1894-on.
Mark: Metal button in ear.

Steiff Doll: Felt, plush or velvet, jointed; seam down middle of face, painted features, button eyes; original clothes; most are character dolls, many have large shoes to enable them to stand; all in excellent condition.

Children (Character Dolls):
11-12in (28-31cm)	**$1,000-$1,250**
16-17in (41-43cm)	**$1,500-$1,650**
Black child: 19in (48cm)	**$2,200**
Adults*:	**$2,000 up**
Gnome: 12in (31cm)	**$700-$900**
Clown: 39in (99cm) at auction	**$7,260**

Schlopsnies: 1922-1925. Celluloid head, cloth body, all original with label:
16in (41cm) at auction	**$3,383**

U.S. Zone Germany:
12in (31cm) child with glass eyes	**$500-$600**

1987/1988 Vinyl Children:
20in (51cm) boxed	**$150-$200**

1986/1987 Limited Edition felt dolls:
Tennis Lady	**$200**
Gentleman	**$175**
Peasant Lady	**$125**

*Fewer women are available than men.

Collector's Note: To bring the prices quoted, Steiff dolls must be clean and have good color. Faded and dirty dolls bring only one-third to one-half of these prices.

Steiff character boy. *Private Collection.*

Jules Steiner

Round face: Ca. 1870s. Perfect very pale bisque socket head, appropriate wig, bulgy paperweight eyes, round face, pierced ears; jointed composition body; dressed; all in good condition.
Mark: None, but sometimes body has a label.
Two rows of pointed teeth:
  16-19in (41-48cm)   **$6,000-$7,000**
Closed mouth:
  18-22in (46-56cm)   **$10,000-$12,000**

Gigoteur: Kicking, crying bébé, mechanical key-wind body with composition arms and lower legs:
  18-20in (46-51cm)   **$2,200-$2,500**
Täufling-type body: Bisque shoulders, hips and lower arms and legs:
  18-21in (46-53cm)   **$6,500**
  Swivel neck   **$7,500**

Marked C or A Series *Bébé Steiner*: 1880s. Perfect socket head, cardboard pate, appropriate wig, sleep eyes with wire mechanism or bulgy paperweight eyes with tinting on upper eyelids, closed mouth, round face, pierced ears with tinted tips; jointed composition body with straight wrists and stubby

FACTS
Jules Nicolas Steiner and successors, Paris, France. 1855-1908.

fingers (sometimes with bisque hands); appropriately dressed; all in good condition. Sizes 4/0 (8in) to 8 (38in). Series "C" more easily found than "A."
Mark: (incised)   S ^{IE} A O
(red script)
J Steiner Gte Sg Dg J Bourgoin S?
(incised)   S ^{IE} C 4
(red stamp)
   J STEINER B. S. G. D. G.

8-10in (20-25cm)	**$6,000-$8,000**
15-16in (38-41cm)	**$6,500-$7,000**
21-24in (53-61cm)	**$9,000-$11,000**
28in (71cm)	**$12,000**
32in (81cm)	**$14,500**
36in (91cm)	**$18,000**
Open mouth:	
16-18in (41-46cm)	**$6,200-$6,800**

18in (46cm) Bourgoin "C" *Bèbè Steiner* with two rows of teeth. *Gloria & Mike Duddlesten.*

14in (36cm) Bourgoin Series "A" *Bèbè Steiner. H & J Foulke, Inc.*

18in (46cm) Figure B *Bébé Steiner* with two rows of teeth. *Kay Jensen Antique Dolls.*

Series F:
　24in (61cm) at auction　**$48,000**
Series G, closed mouth:
　15in (38cm)　**$21,000**
　24-25in (61-64cm) **$27,000-$28,000**

Figure A or **Figure C** *Bébé Steiner*:
Ca. 1887-on. Perfect bisque socket
head, cardboard pate, appropriate wig,
paperweight eyes, closed mouth,
pierced ears; jointed composition body;
appropriately dressed; all in good condition. Figure "A" more easily found
than "C."
Mark: (incised) J. STEINER
　　　B^TE S.G.D.G.
　　　　PARIS
　　　　Fl^RE A 15

Body and/or head may be stamped:
　　"Le Petit Parisien
　　BÉBÉ STEINER
　　MEDAILLE d'OR
　　PARIS 1889"
or paper label of doll carrying flag
Mark: head (incised):
1892 on A -19
PARIS

(red stamp):
　　"LE PARISIEN"
　　body (purple stamp):
　"BÉBÉ 'LE PARISIEN'
　　MEDAILLE D'OR
　　　PARIS"

8-10in (20-25cm) five-piece body
　　　　$3,300-$4,000
8-10in (20-25cm) fully-jointed
　　　　$4,300-$5,000
15-16in (38-41cm)　**$4,500-$4,750**
22-24in (56-61cm)　**$5,300-$5,800**
28-30in (71-76cm)　**$6,500-$7,000**
35in (89cm)　　　　**$8,500**

Figure A, open mouth:
　17in (43cm)　　　　**$2,500**
　22in (56cm)　　　　**$2,900**
　23-25in (58-64cm) *Le Petit Pas* with
　key wind body　**$4,500-$5,000**

Figure B, open mouth with two rows of
teeth:
　16in (41cm)　　**$3,500-$3,700**
　23-25in (58-64cm)　**$5,000-$6,000**
　32in (81cm) at auction　**$7,000**

12in (31cm) Figure A *Bébé Steiner.*
Laraine & Gangolf Freisberg.

Swaine & Co.

Swaine Character Babies: Ca. 1910-on. Perfect bisque head; composition baby body with bent limbs; dressed; all in good condition. (See previous *Blue Books* for photographs of specific models.)

Incised Lori, molded hair, glass eyes, open/closed mouth:

21-24in (53-61cm)	**$2,000-$2,200**

#232, (open-mouth **Lori**):

8½in (21cm)	**$500-$550**
12-14in (31-36cm)	**$800-$1,000**
20-22in (51-56cm)	**$1,200-$1,400**

DIP (wig, glass eyes, closed mouth):

8½–9½in (21-24cm)	**$650-$700**
11in (28cm)	**$750-$800**
14-16in (36-41cm)	**$1,100-$1,200**
14in (36cm) toddler	**$1,500**

DV (molded hair, glass eyes, open/closed mouth):

13in (33cm)	**$1,000-$1,100**
16in (41cm)	**$1,250-$1,300**

12in (31cm) 232 character baby. *H & J Foulke, Inc.*

FACTS

Swaine & Co., porcelain factory, Hüttensteinach, Sonneberg, Thuringia, Germany. Ca. 1910-on for doll heads. **Mark:** Stamped in green:

DI (molded hair, intaglio eyes, open/closed mouth):

12-13in (31-33cm)	**$700-$750**

B.P., B.O. (smiling character):

16-18in (41-46cm)	**$5,000-$5,500****

F.P.: 8-9in (20-23cm) **$800-$900****

A.P. (wig, painted eyes, closed mouth):

15in (38cm) at auction	**$5,200**

Blonde Molded Curly Hair Boy (intaglio eyes, closed mouth):

17in (43cm) at auction	**$1,900****

**Not enough price samples to compute a reliable range.

Thuillier

Marked A.T. Child: Perfect bisque head, cork pate, good or appropriate old wig, paperweight eyes, pierced ears, closed mouth; body of wood, kid or composition; appropriate old clothes, excellent quality; in good condition.

Early face, soft features and decoration:
12-13in (31-33cm) **$30,000-$35,000**
16-18in (41-46cm) **$40,000-$45,000**
24in (61cm) **$55,000-$60,000**

Later face, heavier features and decoration:
16-18in (41-46cm) **$23,000-$25,000**
26in (66cm) **$32,000-$35,000**

Open mouth, two rows of teeth:
20-22in (51-56cm) **$9,000-$12,000**
36in (91cm) **$25,000**

FACTS
A. Thuillier, Paris, France. Some heads by F. Gaultier. 1875-1893.
Mark:

A. 8 . T.

Approximate size chart:
1 = 9in (23cm)
3 = 12in (31cm)
7 = 15½in (39cm)
9 = 18in (46cm)
12 = 22-23in (56-58cm)
15 = 36-37in (91-93cm)

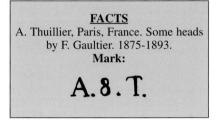

28in (71cm)
A 11 T.
Private Collection.

Unis

Unis Child Doll: Perfect bisque head, good wig, sleep eyes, open mouth; wood and composition jointed body; pretty clothes; all in nice condition.

#301 or **60** (fully-jointed body):

8-10in (20-25cm)	**$425-$475**
15-17in (38-43cm)	**$500-$550**
23-25in (58-64cm)	**$700-$725**
28in (71cm)	**$900-$1,000**

Five-piece body:

5in (13cm) painted eyes	**$160-$185**
6½in (17cm) glass eyes	**$275-$300**
11-13in (28-33cm)	**$300-$350**

Black or brown bisque:

11-13in (28-33cm)	**$325-$375**
Bleuette: 11in (28cm)	**$1,600-$2,000**

Princess: See page 109.

FACTS

Société Française de Fabrication de Bébés et Jouets. (S.F.B.J.) of Paris and Montreuil-sous-Bois, France. 1922 on.

Mark:

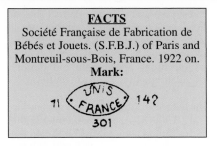

#251 character toddler:

14-15in (36-38cm)	**$1,300-$1,500**

Composition head **#301** or **#60**:

11-13in (28-33cm)	**$150-$175**
16-18in (41-46cm)	**$300-$350**

Composition head **#251** or **#247** toddler:

22in (56cm)	**$650-$750**

16in (41cm) Unis girl with composition head, all-original Brittany costume. *H & J Foulke, Inc.*

Izannah Walker

Izannah Walker Doll: Stockinette, pressed head, features and hair painted with oils, applied ears; treated limbs; muslin body; appropriate clothes; in very good condition.

Pre-patent dolls:

17-19in (43-48cm)	**$18,000-$22,000**
Fair condition	**$8,500-$9,500**
Very worn	**$3,000-$4,000**

1873 patent dolls, molded ears:

18in (46cm)	**$4,000-$6,000**

FACTS
Izannah Walker, Central Falls, RI, U.S.A. 1873, but probably made as early as 1840s.
Mark: Later dolls are marked:

Patented Nov. 4th 1873

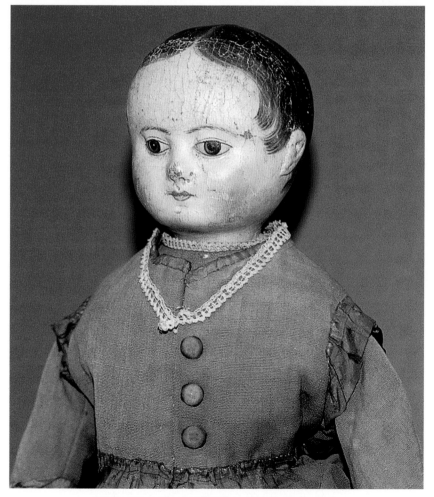

16½in (42cm) Izannah Walker. *Private Collection.*

Wax Dolls (Poured)

Wax (Reinforced)

English Poured Wax Doll:

Various firms in London, such as Peck, Montanari, Pierotti, Meech, Marsh, Morrell, Cremer and Edwards. 1850s-early 1900s. Head, lower arms and legs of wax; cloth body; sometimes stamped with maker or store; set-in hair, glass eyes; lovely elaborate original clothes or very well dressed; all in very good condition.

Baby:
17-19in (43-48cm)
    $1,250-$1,650
23-24in (58-61cm)
    $1,900-$2,200

Child:
6in (15cm) all original
    $650-$750
17-18in (43-46cm)
    $1,700-$2,000

Baby or child, lackluster ordinary face:
20-22in (51-56cm)
    $800-$1,000

Man or Lady:
19-22in (48-56cm)
    $2,500-$3,000

French Fashion Lady: Ca. 1930. Wax head, couturier outfit:
13in (33cm)   **$400-$600**

French Fashion Lady: Ca. 1917. Lafitte-Desirat, all original:
14in (36cm)   **$1,200**
Ca. 1930. Wax head, couturier outfit,
12in (33cm) **$400-$600**

Mechanical Baby in satin-lined wood box, musical:
12in (31cm)   **$350-$450**

FACTS
Various firms in Germany. 1860-1890.
Mark: None.

Reinforced Poured Wax Doll: Poured wax shoulder head lined on the inside with plaster composition, glass eyes (may sleep), closed mouth, open crown, pate, curly mohair or human hair wig nailed on (may be partially inset into the wax around the face); muslin body with wax-over-composition lower limbs (feet may have molded boots); appropriate clothes; all in good condition, but showing some nicks and scrapes.

Child or baby:
11in (28cm)   **$250-$275**
14-16in (36-41cm)   **$375-$425**
19-21in (48-53cm)   **$550-$600**
Lady: 19-22in (48-56cm)   **$800-$1,000**

Socket head on ball-jointed composition body (Kestner-type):
13in (33cm)   **$700-$800**
19in (48cm)   **$1,200-$1,300**

19in (48cm) reinforced wax. *Floyd Jones.*

Wax-Over-Composition

English Slit-head Wax: Ca. 1830-1860. Round face, human hair wig, glass eyes (may open and close by a wire), faintly smiling; all in fair condition, showing wear.

18-22in (46-56cm)	**$900-$1,100**
28-30in (71-76cm)	**$1,500-$1,800**

Molded Hair Doll: Ca. 1860-on. German wax-over-composition shoulder head; nice old clothes; all in good condition, good quality.

14-16in (36-41cm)	**$325-$375**
22-25in (56-64cm)	**$550-$650**

Alice hairdo: 16in (41cm) early model, squeaker torso **$650-$750**

Wax-over Doll with Wig: Ca. 1860s to 1900. German. Original clothing or suitably dressed; entire doll in nice condition.

Standard quality:

11-12in (28-31cm)	**$225-$250**
16-18in (41-46cm)	**$300-$350**
22-24in (56-61cm)	**$400-$450**

Superior quality (heavily waxed):

16-18in (41-46cm)	**$425-$475**
25-26in (64-66cm)	**$675-$775**

"Blinking" eye doll, eyes open and close with bellows in torso:

16in (41cm) all original **$1,000**

Molded Bonnet Wax-over Doll: Ca. 1860-1880. German. Nice old clothes; all in good condition.

16-17in (41-43cm), common model **$450-$500**

13½in (35cm) baby with bonnet and real curls **$750-$800**

20-24in (51-61cm) lady with real curls and unusual hat **$2,000-$3,000**

Double-Faced Doll: 1880-on. Fritz Bartenstein. One face crying, one laughing, rotating on a vertical axis by pulling a string, one face hidden by a hood. Body stamped "Bartenstein."

15-16in (38-41cm) **$850**

8in (20cm) wax-over child with Alice hairdo and täufling body. *Kay Jensen Antique Dolls.*

14½in (37cm) Bartenstein double-faced wax baby. *H & J Foulke, Inc.*

Norah Wellings

Wellings Doll: All-fabric, stitch-joint-ed shoulders and hips; molded fabric face (also of papier-mâché, sometimes stockinette covered), painted features; all in excellent condition. Most commonly found are sailors, Canadian Mounties, Scots and Black Islanders.

Characters (floppy limbs):

8-10in (20-25cm)	**$75-$100**
13-14in (33-36cm)	**$135-$175**
Glass eyes:16-19in (41-48cm) black	**$250-$300**

Children:

12-13in (31-33cm)	**$350-$400**
16-18in (41-46cm)	**$550-$575**
23in (58cm)	**$800-$900**
11½in (29cm) chubby toddler	**$300-$350**
Glass eyes:	
16-18in (41-46cm)	**$650-$700**

FACTS
Victoria Toy Works,
Wellington, Shropshire, England,
for Norah Wellings.
1926-ca. 1960.
Designer: Norah Wellings
Mark: On tag on foot:
"Made in England by Norah Wellings."

Boudoir Doll:

22-24in (56-61cm)	**$300-$400**
Old Couple:	
26in (66cm)	**$1,200-$1,500 pair**
Bobby: 16in (41cm) glass eyes	**$800**
Harry the Hawk: 10in (25cm)	**$200**
Nightdress Case	**$300-$400**
Baby: 11in (28cm)	**$350-$400**
Rabbit: 9in (23cm)	**$350**

13in (33cm) American Indian. *H & J Foulke, Inc.*

15in (38cm) black character. *H & J Foulke, Inc.*

Martha Wellington

Wellington Baby: All stockinette with oil painted head and lower limbs, distinctive buttocks with rounded cheeks; needle-sculpted features, painted eyes and hair; appropriate old clothes.

22-24in (56-61cm)
Excellent condition
$12,000-$14,000**
Fair to good condition
$6,500-$7,500**

**Not enough price samples to compute a reliable range.

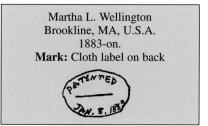

Martha L. Wellington
Brookline, MA, U.S.A.
1883-on.
Mark: Cloth label on back

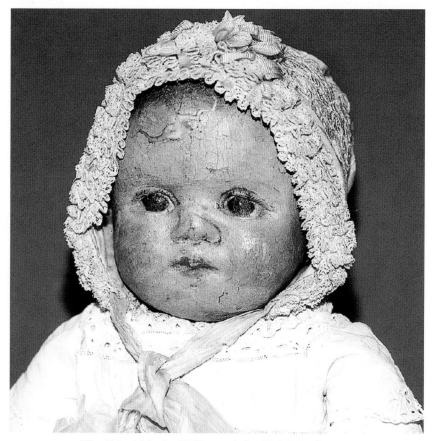

22in (56cm) Martha Wellington baby. *H & J Foulke, Inc.*

Wood, American
(Springfield Dolls)

Joel Ellis Wooden Doll: Co-operative Manufacturing Co., Springfield, Vermont. 1873-1874. All-wood with mortise and tenon joints; carved hair painted black (a few blondes), painted eyes; metal hands and feet painted black (a few bright blue). Marked only with a black paper band around waist with 1873 patent date. Fair condition, most have paint chips on the face.

12in (31cm)	**$1,200-$1,500**
15in (38cm)	**$1,800-$2,000**

Martin, Sanders & Johnson Wooden Doll: 1879-1885. Jointed Doll Co., Springfield, Vermont. Composition head over wood core (usually blonde); fully-jointed wood body; metal hands and feet painted blue. Marked only with a black paper band around waist with "Improved Jointed Doll" and patent dates ('79, '80 and '82). Fair condition.

12in (31cm)	**$850-$950**

Mason & Taylor Wooden Doll: 1879-1885. D.M. Smith Co., Springfield, Vermont. Composition head over wood core (usually blonde); fully-jointed wood body; early dolls had wooden spoon-type hands; blue metal feet. Fair condition.

12in (31cm)	**$850-$950**
Very good, at auction	**$1,575**

15in (38cm) Joel Ellis doll. *Private Collection.*

Wood, English

William & Mary Period: Ca. 1690. Carved wooden face, painted eyes, tiny lines comprising eyebrows and eyelashes, rouged cheeks, flax or hair wig; wood body, cloth arms, carved wood hands (fork shaped), wood-jointed legs; appropriate clothes; all in fair condition.

12-17in (31-43cm)	**$40,000**

Queen Anne Period: Ca. early 1700s. Carved wooden face, dark glass eyes (sometimes painted), dotted eyebrows and eyelashes; jointed wood body, cloth upper arms; appropriate clothes; all in fair condition.

18in (46cm)	**$18,500**
24in (61cm)	**$25,000**

Georgian Period: Mid to late 1700s. Round wooden head with gesso covering, inset glass eyes (later sometimes blue), dotted eyelashes and eyebrows, flax or hair wig; jointed wood body with pointed torso; appropriate clothes; all in fair condition.

12-13in (31-33cm)	**$2,500-$3,200**
16-18in (41-46cm)	**$4,500-$5,000**
24in (61cm)	**$6,000**

Early 19th Century: Wooden head, gessoed, painted eyes, flax or hair wig; pointed torso; old clothes (dress usually longer than legs); all in fair condition.

13in (33cm)	**$1,300-$1,600**
16-21in (41-53cm)	**$2,000-$3,000**

13in (33cm) Queen Anne-type, ca. 1750, some restoration. *Private Collection.*

Wood, German
(Peg-Woodens)

Early to Mid 19th Century: Delicately carved head, varnished, carved and painted hair and features, with a yellow tuck comb in hair, painted spit curls, sometimes earrings; mortise and tenon peg joints; old clothes; all in fair condition.

4in (10cm)	**$450-$550**
6-7in (15-18cm)	**$650-$750**
12-13in (31-33cm)	**$1,350-$1,450**
17-18in (43-46cm)	**$1,800-$2,000**
31in (79cm) carved bun and long curls, at auction	**$13,500**

Fortune tellers:

17-20in (43-51cm)	**$2,500-$3,000**

Shell dolls:

8½in (28cm)	**$1,500-$1,600 pair**

Peddler with lovely old wares:

8in (20cm)	**$2,400**

Late 19th Century: Wooden head with painted hair, carving not so elaborate as previously, sometimes earrings, spit curls; dressed; all in good condition.

1in (2½cm)	**$100-$125**
4in (10cm)	**$125-$135**
7-8in (18-20cm)	**$175-$225**

FACTS

Craftsmen of the Grödner Tal, Austria, and Sonneberg, Germany, such as Insam & Prinoth (1820-1830), Gorden Tirol and Nürnberg verlagers of peg-wooden dolls and wood doll heads. Late 18th to 20th century.

Mark: None.

12in (31cm)	**$350-$375**
16in (41cm)	**$450-$500**
21in (53cm)	**$1,000-$1,100**

Turned red torso:

10in (25cm)	**$150-$200**

Wood shoulder head, carved bun hairdo, cloth body, wood limbs:

9in (23cm) all original	**$350-$400**
17in (43cm)	**$500-$550**
24in (61cm)	**$800-$900**

Early 20th Century: Turned wood head, carved nose, painted hair; peg-jointed; painted white lower legs, painted black shoes.

11-12in (28-31cm)	**$60-$80**

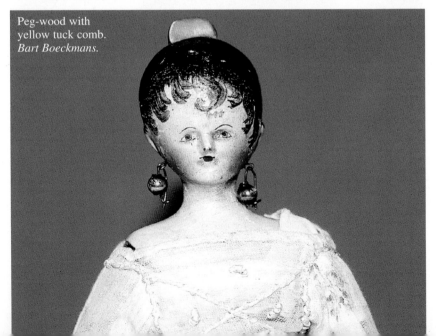

Peg-wood with yellow tuck comb. *Bart Boeckmans.*

Wood, German
(20th Century)

Wood, Swiss

FACTS
Various companies, such as Rudolf Schneider and Schilling, Sonneberg, Thuringia, Germany. 1901-1914. For French trade.
Mark: Usually none; sometimes Schilling "winged angel" trademark.

FACTS
Various craftsmen, Brienz, Switzerland. 20th century.
Mark: Usually a paper label on wrist or clothes.

"Bébé Tout en Bois" (Doll All of Wood): All of wood, fully-jointed; wig, inset glass eyes, open mouth with teeth; appropriate clothes; all in fair to good condition.

Child:

13in (33cm)	**$425-$475**
17-19in (43-48cm)	**$650-$750**
22-24in (56-61cm)	**$950**
18in (46cm) mint, all original	**$1,100**
Baby: 16½in (42cm)	**$400-$500**

Swiss Linden Wood Doll: Wooden head with hand-carved features and hair with good detail (males sometimes have carved hats); all-carved wood-jointed body; original regional attire; excellent condition.

9-10in (23-25cm)	**$275-$375**
12in (31cm)	**$450-$550**
15in (38cm)	**$750-$850**
17-18in (43-46cm)	**$1,000-$1,200**
12in (31cm) boy with carved hat	**$600-$650**
13in (33cm) wood and cloth babies	**$450**

11in (28cm) *Tout en Bois. Private Collection.*

13in (33cm) Swiss wood baby with cloth body, wood lower arms and legs. *H & J Foulke, Inc.*

WPA

WPA Milwaukee Cloth Doll: Molded and painted stockinette head with painted eyes, yarn hair; cloth body with uniquely jointed legs; original clothes; all in very good condition.
Mark: "#7040, Milwaukee, Wis."

22in (56cm)	**$900-$1,200**
Black	**$1,200-$1,500**

FACTS
Various artists under the sponsorship of the United States Federal Works Progress Administration (later Works Projects Administration). 1935-1943.

22in (56cm) Milwaukee cloth doll. *H & J Foulke, Inc.*

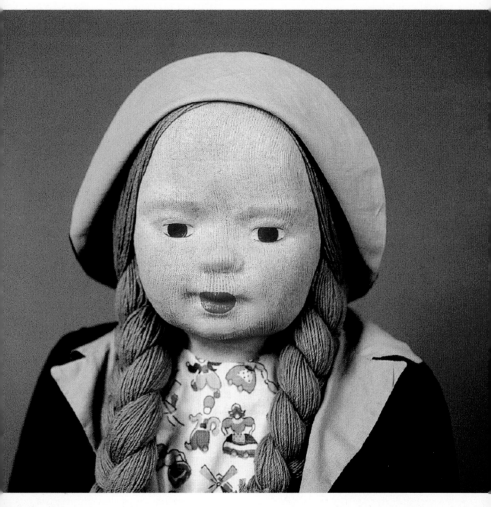

Modern & Collectible Dolls

Dolls in this section are listed alphabetically by manufacturer, by material or sometimes by trade name. Dolls are arranged in chronological order by date within a main entry.

Unless otherwise indicated, values given in this section are retail prices for clean dolls in excellent overall condition, with good complexion color, perfect hair in original set and original unfaded clothing, including underwear, shoes and socks. Dolls in crisp mint condition will bring 25 to 50 percent more. Dirty and faded dolls that have been heavily played with are worth 10 to 30 percent of these values.

15in (38cm) *Puzzy* and 14in (36cm) *Sizzy* composition characters. *Anya Lowe Collection.*

Madame Alexander
Alexander Doll Company

CLOTH DOLLS: Original tagged clothing.

Characters: Ca. 1933-1940. All-cloth with molded felt or flocked mask face, painted eyes to the side. **Little Women, David Copperfield, Oliver Twist, Edith, Babbie, Alice** and others.

16in (41cm) only:

Fair	$200-$300
Good	$350-$450
Excellent	$750-$850

Alice:

9-20in (48-51cm) good	**$400-$500**

Kamkins-type: (hard felt face), very good condition:

20in (51cm)	**$650-$750****

Tiny Twinkle:

15in (38cm) excellent	**$800****

Bunny Belle:

12in (31cm) excellent	**$750**

Cloth Baby: Ca. 1936.

13in (33cm) very good	**$300-$350**
17in (43cm) very good	**$475-$525**
24in (61cm)	**$625**

Cloth Dionne Quintuplet: Ca. 1935.

17in (43cm) very good	**$850-$900****
24in (61cm) very good	**$1,200-$1,300****

**Not enough samples to compute a reliable range.

10in (25cm) cloth *Little Shaver,* all original, 2000-2001. *H & J Foulke, Inc.*

Left: 15in (38cm) *Tiny Twinkle. Rosemary Kanizer.*

Susie Q. & Bobby Q.: Ca. 1938.
12in (31cm) excellent with purse or
book strap **$700-$750**
15in (38cm) excellent pair, at auction
$3,000
Little Shaver: 1942. Yarn hair, very
good condition:
7in (18cm) **$475-$500**
10-12in (25-31cm) **$450-$500**
20in (51cm) **$750**
Little Shaver: 2000-2001.
10in (25cm) **$45-$50**
Poodles: 16in (41cm) **$325-$375**
Funny: 1963-1977.
18in (46cm) **$50-$60**
Muffin: 1963-1977.
14in (36cm) **$75-$85**

Dionne Quintuplet toddler in original
box, all original. *H & J Foulke, Inc.*

COMPOSITION DOLLS: All in
original tagged clothing; excellent
condition, with bright color and perfect
hair; faint crazing acceptable.
Dionne Quintuplets: 1935. (Each
Quint has her own color for clothing:
Yvonne - pink; **Annette** - yellow;
Cecile - green; **Emelie** - lavender;
Marie - blue):
7-8in (18-20cm) **$275-$325**
Matched set **$2,200-$2,500**
In bed **$2,600-$2,750**
In basket with extra outfits
$3,350-$3,750
With five pieces of wooden
Dionne furniture **$3,750**
10-11in (25-28cm) baby **$350-$375**
11-12in (28-31cm) toddler
$400-$450
14in (36cm) toddler **$500-$550**
16in (41cm) baby with cloth
body **$450**
20in (51cm) toddler **$700-$750**
23-24in (58-61cm) baby with cloth
body **$650-$750**
Pins, each **$90-$100**
Tagged dress and bonnet **$150**

Small dolls: 1935-1945.
7-9in (18-23cm):
Foreign Countries: **$175-$225**
Storybook Characters:
$250-$300
Special Outfits: **$400-$500**
Birthday Dolls: **$325-$375**
Bride and Bridesmaids:
$225-$250 each
Little Women: **$275 each**

Little Colonel: 1935.
8½in (22cm) **$600-$700**
13in (33cm) **$650-$700**
Unnamed Girl: Ca. 1935. Dimples,
sleep eyes, 13in (33cm) **$400-$450**
Nurse (for *Dionne Quintuplets*): Ca.
1935. 13in (33cm) **$900-$1,100**
Betty: Ca. 1935. Painted or sleep eyes,
wigged or molded hair:
13in (33cm) **$425-$475**
19in (48cm) **$700-$750**
Baby Jane: 1935.
16in (41cm) **$900-$1,000**
Topsy Turvy: Ca. 1936.
7½in (19cm) **$210-$235**

Dr. DaFoe: 1936.
  14in (36cm)   **$1,600-$1,700**
Three Little Pigs: 1938-1939.
  12-13in (31-33cm)   **$750-$800**

Marionettes: 1935. Character faces,
  10-12in (25-30cm):
    Tony Sarg: **$250-$275**
    Disney: **$350-$400**

Babies: 1936-on. **Little Genius, Baby McGuffey, Precious, Butch, Bitsey;** composition head, hands and legs, cloth bodies.
  11-12in (28-31cm)   **$225-$275**
  16-18in (41-46cm)   **$350-$400**
  24in (61cm)   **$500-$550**

Princess Elizabeth Face: Original tagged clothes; all in excellent condition.
Princess Elizabeth: 1937.
  13in (33cm) closed mouth **$400-$500**
  16-18in (41-46cm)   **$550-$650**
  22-24in (56-61cm)   **$750-$850**
  27in (69cm)   **$950-$1,000**
  8in (20cm) *Dionne* head   **$600**

McGuffey Ana: 1937. Braids:
  9in (23cm) painted eyes   **$425-$475**
  11in (28cm) closed mouth
                             $475-$525
  15-16in (38-41cm)   **$525-$625**
  20-22in (51-56cm)   **$750-$850**
Snow White: 1937. Closed mouth, black hair:
  13in (33cm)   **$500-$550**
  16-18in (41-46cm)   **$700-$750**
Flora McFlimsey: 1938.
  13in (33cm)   **$550-$650**
  15in (38cm)   **$700-$800**
  22in (56cm)   **$1,000-$1,100**
Kate Greenaway: 1938.
  13in (33cm)   **$600-$650**
  16-18in (41-46cm)   **$800-$850**

Wendy Ann Face: Original tagged clothes; all in excellent condition.
Wendy Ann: 1936.
  9in (23cm) painted eyes   **$350-$375**
  14in (36cm) swivel waist **$450-$550**
  21in (53cm)   **$800-$900**
  14in (36cm) molded hair **$600-$650**

14in (36cm) *Dr. DaFoe*, all original. *H & J Foulke, Inc.*

7in (18cm) *Carmen*, all original. *H & J Foulke, Inc.*

17in (43cm) *Little Genius*, all original. *H & J Foulke, Inc.*

12in (31cm) *Butch*, all original. *H & J Foulke, Inc.*

11in (28cm) tagged Alexander girl, all original, possibly *Kate Greenaway*. *H & J Foulke, Inc.*

11in (28cm) *McGuffey Ana*, all original. *H & J Foulke, Inc.*

Scarlett O'Hara: 1937. Black hair, blue or green eyes:

11in (28cm)	**$950**
14in (36cm)	**$950-$1,000**
18in (46cm)	**$1,450**
21in (53cm)	**$1,850**

Madelaine du Bain: 1938. 14in (36cm)
$750-$850

Miss America: 1939.

14in (36cm)	**$900-$1,000**

Bride & Bridesmaids: 1940.

14in (36cm)	**$400-$450**
18in (46cm)	**$600-$650**
21in (53cm)	**$750-$850**

Portraits: 1940s.

21in (53cm)	**$2,500-$4,500***

Sleeping Beauty, Cinderella: Ca. 1941. 14in (36cm) **$550-$650**

Carmen (Miranda): 1942. Black hair:

9in (23cm) painted eyes	**$350-$375**
14-15in (36-38cm)	**$500-$600**
21in (53cm)	**$1,200-$1,400**

Fairy Princess or Fairy Queen: 1942.

14in (36cm)	**$650-$700**
18in (46cm)	**$750-$800**

Armed Forces Dolls: 1942.

WAAC, WAVE, WAAF, Soldier, Marine: 14in (36cm) **$900-$1,000**

Mommy & Me: Late 1940s.

14in (36cm) and 7in (18cm)
$1,500-$1,600 set

*Depending on rarity.

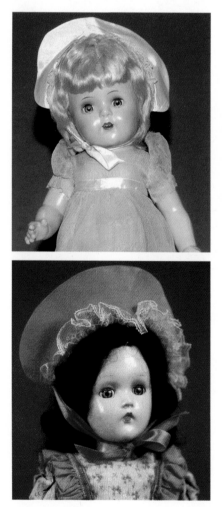

Left: 14in 36cm) tagged Alexander girl, all original. *Rosemary Kanizer.*

14in (36cm) *Alice-in-Wonderland*, all original. *H & J Foulke, Inc.*

Left: 14in (36cm) *Scarlett* or *Southern Belle*, all original. *H & J Foulke, Inc.*

Special Faces: Original tagged clothes; all in excellent condition.

Jane Withers: 1937.

13in (33cm) closed mouth	**$1,100-$1,300**
15-16in (38-41cm)	**$1,250-$1,350**
21in (53cm)	**$1,650-$1,850**

Sonja Henie: 1939.

14in (36cm) swivel waist	**$800-$900**
15in (38cm) gift set, boxed	**$3,200**
18in (46cm)	**$900,-$1,000**
21in (53cm)	**$1,200-$1,400**

Jeannie Walker: 1941.

13-14in (33-36cm)	**$850**
18in (46cm)	**$1,200**
13in (33cm) boxed	**$1,500**
14in (36cm) non-walker	**$550-$650**

Special Girl: 1942. Cloth body:

22in (56cm)	**$550-$650****

Margaret Face: Original tagged clothes; all in excellent condition with perfect hair and pretty coloring.

Margaret O'Brien: 1946. With dark braided wig:

14in (36cm)	**$900-$1,000**
18in (46cm)	**$1,350-$1,500**

Karen Ballerina: 1946. With blonde wig in coiled braids:

14in (36cm)	**$850-$950**
18in (46cm)	**$1,250**
21in (53cm)	**$1,650-$1,850**

Alice-in-Wonderland: 1947.

14in (36cm)	**$525-$575**
18in (46cm)	**$650-$750**
21in (53cm)	**$1,000**

**Not enough price samples to compute reliable range.

Left: 14in (36cm) *Bride,* all original. *H & J Foulke, Inc.*

14in (36cm) *Margaret O'Brien,* all original. *H & J Foulke, Inc.*

Left: 15in (38cm) *Sonja Henie,* all original. *H & J Foulke, Inc.*

HARD PLASTIC DOLLS: 1948-on. Original tagged clothes; excellent condition with bright color and perfect hair.

Margaret Face: 1948-1956.

> Collector's Note: Dolls in crisp and mint "like new" condition will bring higher prices.

Alice-in-Wonderland: 1949-1952.
| 14in (36cm) | **$700-$800** |

Babs: 1948-1949.
| 14in (36cm) | **$900-$1,000** |
| 18in (46cm) | **$1,200** |

Bride: 1948.
| 14in (36cm) | **$700-$800** |
| 20in (51cm) | **$1,200-$1,400** |

Bride: 1950. Pink gown:
| 14in (36cm) | **$1,000** |
| 18in (46cm) | **$1,200** |

14in (36cm) *Cinderella,* all original. *H & J Foulke, Inc.*

Cinderella: 1950.
Ball gown:
14in (36cm)	**$850**
18in (46cm)	**$1,250**
"Poor" dress: 14in (36cm)	**$650**

Cynthia (black): 1952-1953.
| 14in (36cm) | **$1,000** |
| 18in (46cm) | **$1,300-$1,500** |

Fairy Queen: 1947-1948.
| 14in (36cm) | **$750** |
| 18in (46cm) | **$950** |

Fashions of the Century: 1954.
18in (46cm) at auction **$3,000-$3,500**

Glamour Girls: 1953.
| 18in (46cm) | **$1,600-$1,800** |

Godey Ladies: 1950.
| 14in (36cm) | **$1,400-$1,600** |
| Groom: 18in (46cm) | **$800-$850** |

Margaret O'Brien: 1948.
| 14in (36cm) | **$1,000-$1,100** |
| 18in (46cm) | **$1,300-$1,500** |

Margaret Rose: 1948-1953.
14in (36cm)	**$750-$800**
18in (46cm)	**$850-$900**
18in (46cm) **Beaux Arts Series,** 1953	**$1,650-$1,850**

Mary Martin: 1950. Sailor suit:
| 14in (36cm) | **$850** |
| 18in (46cm) | **$1,000** |

McGuffey Ana: 1949.
| 14in (36cm) | **$1,100-$1,200** |
| 18in (46cm) | **$1,300-$1,400** |

Nina Ballerina: 1949-1951. Blonde:
14in (36cm)	**$850**
18in (46cm)	**$1,100**
21in (53cm)	**$1,600**

Peggy Bride: Ca. 1950.
| 20in (51cm) | **$1,200-$1,500** |

Prince Charming: 1950.
| 14in (36cm) | **$775** |
| 18in (46cm) | **$875** |

Prince Philip: Ca. 1950.
| 18in (46cm) | **$800-$850** |

Queen Elizabeth II: 1953.
| 18in (46cm) with long velvet cape | **$1,600-$1,800** |
| No cape | **$1,000-$1,200** |

Snow White: 1952.
| 14in (36cm) | **$800-$900** |
| 18in (46cm) | **$1,200** |

Story Princess: 1954-1956.
| 14in (36cm) | **$650-$700** |
| 18in (46cm) | **$750-$850** |

14in (36cm) *Snow White*, all original. *Rosemary Kanizer.*

Wendy-Ann: 1947-1948.
   14in (36cm)   **$750-$800**
   18in (46cm)   **$900-$1,000**
Wendy Bride: 1950.
   14in (36cm)   **$700-$750**
   18in (46cm)   **$900-$1,000**
Wendy (from **Peter Pan** set): 1953.
   14in (36cm)   **$550-$650**

Maggie Face: 1948-1956.

> Collector's Note: Dolls in crisp and mint "like new" condition will bring higher prices.

Alice-in-Wonderland: 1949-1952.
   14in (36cm)   **$700-$800**
   18in (46cm)   **$900-$1,000**
Annabelle: 1952.
   15in (38cm)   **$700-$800**
   18in (46cm)   **$900-$1,000**
Arlene Dahl: 1950-1951. 20in (57cm)
fair condition, at auction   **$3,327**
Glamour Girls: 1953.
   18in (46cm)   **$1,500-$1,800**
Godey Man: 1950. 14in (36cm) **$1,200**
John Powers Models:
   14in (36cm)   **$2,000**

14in (36cm) *Alice-in-Wonderland,* all original. *Rosemary Kanizer.*

Kathy: 1951.

14in (36cm)	$800-$850
18in (46cm)	$900-$1,000

Margot Ballerina: 1953.

14in (36cm)	$800-$850
18in (46cm)	$900-$1,000

Maggie: 1948-1953.

14in (36cm)	$750-$850
17in (43cm)	$900
20in (51cm)	$1,000-$1,100

Me and My Shadow: 1954.

18in (46cm)	$1,600-$2,000

Peter Pan: 1953.

15in (38cm)	$750-$850

Polly Pigtails: 1949.

14in (36cm)	$700-$800
17in (43cm)	$800-$900

Rosamund Bridesmaid: 1953.

15in (38cm)	$750-$850
18in (46cm)	$900-$1,000

Little Women: 1948-1956.
Floss hair, 1948-1950:

14-15in (36-38cm)	$475-$525 each
Amy, loop curls	$525-$550
Dynel hair	$375-$425 each

Little Men (Nat, Stuffy, Tommy Bangs): 1952. $900-$1,000

Babies (Baby Genius, Bitsey, Butch): 1948-1951. Cloth body, hard plastic or vinyl limbs.

12in (31cm)	$250-$300
16-18in (41-46cm)	$400-$450

Winnie and Binnie: 1953-1955.

15in (38cm)	$450-$550
18in (46cm)	$600-$650
25in (64cm)	$500-$600
Skating outfit	
15in (38cm)	$700-$800

Mary Ellen: 31in (79cm) $650-$750

Sweet Violet:

18in (46cm) fully-jointed body	
	$1,000-$1,250

Victoria (black, green-and-white dress): 15in (38cm) $600-$650

Flower Girl:

15in (38cm)	$650
18in (46cm)	$1,050

14in (36cm) *Binnie Walker,* all original. *Rosemary Kanizer.*

24in (61cm) *Winnie Walker,* all original. *H & J Foulke, Inc.*

21in (53cm) *Cissy Bride,* all original. *Rosemary Kanizer.*

8in (20cm) *Wendy,* all original. *Rosemary Kanizer.*

Cissy: 1955-1959. 21in (53cm):
Street clothes **$550-$650**
Basic underwear, shoes, stockings
$400
Cocktail dresses **$650-$750**
Ball gowns **$950-$1,250**
Queen: **$1,000-$1,200**
Bride: **$1,200 up**

Alexander-Kins: 1953-to present. All-hard plastic; original tagged clothes; all in excellent condition with perfect hair and rosy cheeks.

> Collector's Note: A played-with doll having a partial or faded costume will bring 25 percent of quoted prices.

Wendy, Wendy Ann or Wendy-Kin: 7½-8in (19-20cm):
1953. Straight-leg non-walker
$450-$650
Nude **$300**
1954-1955. Straight-leg walker
$400-$600
Nude **$275**
1956-1964. Bent-knee walker
$350-$550

Nude **$185**
1965-1972. Bent-knee non-walker
$275-$475
Nude **$90**

Wendy: basic (panties, shoes and socks), boxed **$350-$450**
Quizkin: 1953. **$550-$650**
Wendy in Special Outfits:
Agatha: 1953. **$1,000-$1,200**
American Girl: 1962-1963. **$350**
Amish Boy or Amish Girl: 1966-1969. **$350**
Aunt Pitty Pat: 1957. **$1,600**
Baby Clown: 1955. **$1,000-$1,200**
Bible Characters: **$7,000-$10,000**
Billy or Bobby: 1955-1963.
$450-$500
Bride: 1955-1960. **$350-$450**
Bridesmaid (pink): 1955. **$900**
Cherry Twin: 1957.
$1,000-$1,200 each
Cousin Grace: 1957. Boxed **$1,600**
Cousin Marie: 1963. **$900**
Cowboy or Cowgirl: 1967-1970.
$300-$350

8in (20cm) *Wendy Sewing Basket,* all original. *Rosemary Kanizer.*

Davy Crockett Boy or Girl: 1955.
$600-$700
Easter Wendy: 1953. $1,000
Edith: 1958. $650-$700
Groom: 1956-1963. $400-$450
Guardian Angel: 1954. $700-$800
Hiawatha: 1967-1969. $350
Little Madeline: 1953. $775
Little Southern Girl: 1953.
$850-$950
Little Victoria: 1954. $1,200-$1,300
Maypole Dance: 1954. Boxed $550
McGuffey Ana: 1964-1965. $350
Miss USA: 1966-1968. Boxed $425
My Shadow: 1954. $1,500
Nurse: 1956-1965. $450-$500
Parlour Maid: 1956. $1,000
Pocahontas: 1967-1969. $350
Prince Charles: 1957. $700-$800
Princess Anne: 1957. $700-$800
Priscilla or Colonial Girl:
1962-1970. $300
Scarlett: 1965-1972. $350-$400
Southern Belle: 1963. $450-$500
Wendy Sewing Basket: 1965-1966.
$2,500

Wendy Dude Ranch: 1955. $600
Wendy in Easter Egg: 1965. $1,700
Wendy Ice Skater: 1956. $450
Wendy Loves to Waltz: 1955. $625
Wendy in Riding Habit: 1965.
Boxed $450-$550
Wendy Loves Being Loved: 1992.
Boxed set $150
Wendy Being Just Like Mommy:
1993. With baby carriage $110

International Costumes:
Bent-knee walker $125-$150
1965-1972. Bent-knee non-walker
$75-$85
Korea, Africa, Hawaii, Vietnam,
Eskimo, Morocco, Ecuador, Bolivia
$250-$300
1973-1976. Straight-leg, rosy cheeks
$50-$60
1982-1987. Straight-leg, pinched lips
$40-$45
1988-on. Current face $40-$50
Storybook, Ballerinas & Brides:
Bent-knee non-walker $75-$100
1973-1976. Straight-leg, rosy cheeks
$60-$70

1982-1987. Straight-leg, pinched lips
$40-$45
1988-on. Current face   **$45-$55**
Little Women, set of five:
1955. Straight-leg walker   **$1,500**
1956-1964. Bent-knee walker **$1,200**
Bent-knee non-walker   **$650-$750**
Straight legs   **$300-$350**
1994 FAO Schwarz movie outfits
$600

Exclusive and Special Editions:
Enchanted Doll House: 1980-1981.
$250-$275
Wendy: 1989. MADC exclusive
$175
Navajo Woman: 1994.
MADC Convention   **$300-$350**
Bobbie Sox: 1990. Disney
$175-$200
David & Diana: 1989.
FAO Schwarz set   **$175-$200**
Mouseketeer: 1991. Disney
$200-$225
Easter Bunny: 1991. Child at Heart
$300-$350
Cowboy: 1987. MADC Convention
$400-$450
Little Miss Magnin: 1992. I.
Magnin with tea set and teddy
bear   **$175-$200**
Tippi Ballerina: 1988.
CU Gathering   **$350-$400**
Little Emperor: 1992.
UFDC Luncheon   **$400-$450**
Anne of Green Gables: 1994. Trunk
set, Neiman-Marcus   **$225-$275**
Sailor Boy: 1990. UFDC **$700-$750**
Wendy Shops FAO: 1993.
FAO Schwarz   **$100-$125**

Little Genius: 1956-1962. Baby with
short curly wig, 8in (20cm):
Basic or simple outfit   **$200-$225**
Fancy outfit   **$275**
Christening outfit   **$350**
Lissy Face: 1956-1958.
Lissy: 12in (31cm)   **$400-$500**
Boxed with trousseau,1957   **$1,500**
F.A.O. Schwarz exclusive   **$950**

8in (20cm) *Colonial Girl,* all original. *H & J Foulke, Inc.*

8in (20cm) *Betsy Ross,* all original. *H & J Foulke, Inc.*

Bridesmaid: 1956-1957.   **$600**
Kelly: 1959.   **$400-$500**
Little Women: 1957-1969. Jointed
elbows and knees   **$250-$300**
Southern Belle: 1963.
     $1,200-$1,400
McGuffey Ana: 1963.
     $1,600-$1,800
Katie: 1962.   **$800-$1,000**
Scarlett: 1963.   **$1,200-$1,400**
Tommy: 1962.   **$800-$1,000**
Cinderella: 1966.   **$850**
   Boxed set   **$1,250**
Laurie: 1967.   **$400**
Pamela: 1962-1963.
   Boxed with wigs   **$1,000**
   Suitcase gift set   **$1,500**
Columbian Sailor: 1993. UFDC
     $175-$200

8in (20cm) *Welcome Home (Desert Storm),* 1991, all original with flag. *H & J Foulke, Inc.*

Elise: 1957-1964. 16½in (42cm):
   Basic undergarment, shoes, stockings
     $250-$275
   Street clothes   **$400-$425**
   Ball gowns   **$650-$850**
   Bride: **$425-$475**
   Sleeping Beauty: Disney **$600-$700**
   Bridesmaid   **$500-$550**
   Ballerina   **$550**

Cissette Face: 1957-1973.
   Cissette: 1957-1963. 10in (25cm):
      Basic doll, mint-in-box **$350-$400**
      Day dresses   **$375-$425**
      Cocktail dresses   **$500-$600**
      Evening gowns   **$650-$800**
   Queen: 1957-1963.   **$400-$450**
   Gold Ballerina: 1959.   **$450-$500**
   Denmark: 1962.   **$500-$600**
   Gibson Girl: **$700-$800**
   Jacqueline: 1962.   **$750-$850**
   Margot: 1961.   **$500-$600**
   Klondike Kate: 1962. **$1,250-$1,500**
   Sleeping Beauty: 1959-1960.
     $375-$425
   Mardi Gras: 1992. Spiegel **$90-$125**
   Diamond Lil: 1993. MADC
     $250-$300
   Lady Hamilton #975: 1957. **$1,200**
   Cinderella: 1989. Disney **$650-$750**
   Miss Unity: 1991. UFDC **$350-$400**
   Portrettes: 1968-1973.
      Godey: 1968-1970.   **$300-$350**
      Scarlett: 1968-1973.   **$300-$350**
      Renoir: 1968-1970.   **$325-$375**
      Agatha: 1968.   **$350-$375**
      Southern Belle: 1968-1973.
     $300-$350
      Melinda: 1968-1970.   **$300-$350**
      Jenny Lind: 1969.   **$500-$550**
      Melanie: 1969-1970.   **$375-$400**
      Queen: 1972-1973.   **$250-$350**

Shari Lewis: 1959.
   14in (36cm)   **$550-$650**
   21in (53cm)   **$750-$850**

Maggie Mixup: 1960-1961.
   16½in (42cm)   **$400-$450**
   8in (20cm)   **$450-$550**
   8in (20cm) angel   **$750-$850**
   Little Lady: **$350**
   Little Lady Gift Set: **$1,000**

VINYL DOLLS. Original tagged clothing; excellent never-played-with condition, bright color.

Miss Flora McFlimsey: 1953.
15in (38cm)	**$450-$500**

Kathy, Kathy Cry Dolly, Kathy Tears: 1954-1962.
15in (38cm)	**$85-$95**
18-19in (46-48cm)	**$110-$125**

Kelly Face: 1958-1965. 15in (38cm).
Kelly:	**$275-$325**
Pollyana:	**$275-$325**
Marybel: Complete case	**$300-$350**
Edith:	**$325-$375**
Elise: 1964.	**$325-$375**
Riding outfit	**$425-$475**

Betty: 1960. Smiling face, walker,
30in (76cm)	**$300-$350**

Timmy Toddler: 1960-1961.
23in (58cm)	**$125-$150**

Chatterbox: 1961. Battery-operated talker, 24in (61cm) **$200-$225**

Mimi: 1961.
30in (76cm) fully-jointed	**$400-$500**

Jacqueline: 1961-1962.
21in (53cm) suit	**$650-$700**
Riding habit	**$700-$750**
Gown	**$800-$900**

Caroline: 1961-1962.
15in (38cm)	**$300-$400**
Riding habit	**$375-$425**

Smarty Face: 1962-1965. 12in (31cm).
Smarty: 1962-1963.	**$200-$225**
With baby	**$300-$325**
Brother:	**$200-$225**
Katie (black): 1965.	**$275-$300**

Portraits: 1962-current. 21in (53cm).

Scarlett:
Cotton print, 1968.	**$800-$900**
Green velvet or taffeta, 1975-1982.	
	$250-$300
Satin print, 1978.	**$400-$500**
Red gown, 1989.	**$300-$400**
Melanie: 1967-1974.	**$300-$400**
Queen: 1968.	**$600-$700**
Godey: 1969.	**$400-$450**
Bride: 1969.	**$550-$600**
Mimi: 1971.	**$400-$450**
Gainsborough: 1973.	**$300-$350**

Madame Alexander: 1984-1990.
	$200-$225

Sarah Bernhardt: 1987. **$200-$250**

Marie Antoinette: 1987-1988.
	$200-$250

Melinda: 1963.
14in (36cm)	**$250-$300**

10in (25cm) *Jacqueline*, all original. *Rosemary Kanizer.*

15in (38cm) *Miss Flora McFlimsey*, all original. *H & J Foulke, Inc.*

17in (43cm) *Maggie,* all original. *Doodlebug Dolls.*

21in (53cm) *Coco Portrait,* all original. *Private Collection.*

Janie Face: 1964-1990. 12in (31cm):

Janie: 1964-1966.	**$175-$200**
Lucinda: 1969-1970.	**$200-$225**
Rozy: 1969.	**$200-$225**
Suzy: 1970.	**$200-$225**
Muffin: 1989-1990.	**$40-$50**

Brenda Starr: 1964.

12in (31cm)	**$225-$250**
Yolanda: 1965.	**$225-$250**

Patty: 1965. 18in (46cm)   **$250-$275**

Polly Face: 1965-1971. 17in (43cm).

Polly: 1965	**$200-$225**
Mary Ellen Playmate:	**$225**
Leslie (black): 1965-1971.	
	$250-$275

Mary Ann Face: 1965-current.
14in (36cm).

Mary Ann: 1965.	**$150-$175**
Orphant Annie: 1965-1966.	**$200**
Gidget: 1966.	**$200-$225**
Little Granny: 1966.	**$125-$150**
Riley's Little Annie: 1967.	**$175**
Renoir Girl: 1967-1971.	**$125-$150**
Disney Snow White: 1967-1977.	
	$300-$350
Easter Girl: 1968.	**$550-$600**
Scarlett: 1968. Flowered gown.	
	$350-$400
Madame: 1967-1975.	**$150-$175**
Jenny Lind & Cat: 1969-1971.	**$225**
Gone with the Wind: 1969-1986.	
	$75-$95
Jenny Lind: 1970.	**$200-$225**
Grandma Jane: 1970.	**$150-$175**
Goldilocks: 1978-1982.	**$65-$75**
Bonnie Blue: 1989.	**$100-$110**
Discontinued dolls: 1982-1995,	
	$50-$90

Anne of Green Gables Trunk Set:
1992-1994.   **$200-$250**

Babies: 1963-present. Cloth and vinyl.

Littlest Kitten: 1963. 8in (20cm).	
Basic or simple outfit	**$200-$225**
Fancy outfit	**$250-$275**
Sugar Tears: 1964.	
14in (36cm)	**$75-$100**
Fischer Quints: 1964.	
7in (18cm) set	**$300-$350**
Baby Ellen (black): 1965-1972.	
14in (36cm)	**$100-$110**
Sweet Tears: 1965-1982.	
14in (36cm)	**$55-$65**
Layette sets	**$125-$175**

Little Bitsey: 1967-1968.
  9in (23cm)   **$110-$130**
Victoria: 1967-1989.
  20in (51cm)   **$65-$75**
So Big: 1968-1975.
  22in (56cm)   **$125-$150**
Mary Cassatt Baby: 1969-1970.
  20in (51cm)   **$175-$200**
Pussy Cat (black): 1970-1984.
  14in (36cm)   **$60**
  20in (51cm)   **$90-$100**
Happy: 1970.
  20in (51cm)   **$200-$225**
Smiley: 1971.
  20in (51cm)   **$200-$225**
Baby McGuffey: 1971-1976.
  20in (51cm)   **$175-$200**
Baby Lynn: 1973-1976.
  20in (51cm)   **$100-$125**
Baby Brother: 1977-1979.
  20in (51cm)   **$75-$85**
Mommy's Pet: 1977-1986.
  20in (51cm)   **$75-$100**
Mary Mine: 1977-1989. **$125-$150**
Sound of Music: 1965-1970. Small set.
  Friedrich: 8in (20cm)   **$125**
  Gretl: 8in (20cm)   **$125**
  Marta: 8in (20cm)   **$125**
  Brigitta: 10in (25cm)   **$150**
  Louisa: 10in (25cm)   **$150**
  Liesl: 10in (25cm)   **$150**
  Maria: 12in (31cm)   **$175**
Sound of Music: 1971-1973. Large set (allow 100 percent more for sailor outfits).
  Friedrich: 11in (28cm)   **$125-$150**
  Gretl: 11in (28cm)   **$125**

Marta: 11in (28cm)   **$125**
Brigitta: 14in (36cm)   **$100-$125**
Louisa: 14in (36cm)   **$100-$125**
Liesl: 14in (36cm)   **$100-$125**
Maria: 17in (43cm)   **$225-$275**
Kurt: 11in (28cm) sailor suit **$250**
Coco: 1966. Right leg bent slightly at knee.
  21in (53cm)   **$1,800-$2,000**
  Portrait Dolls: 1966. **$1,800-$2,200**
  Scarlett #2061: White gown **$2,500**
Elise Face: 1966-1991. Redesigned vinyl face, 17in (43cm).
  Elise Portrait: 1972-1973.
                             $125-$150
  Ballerinas   **$75-$85**
  Brides   **$65-$75**
  Formals   **$65-$75**
  Marlo: 1967.   **$550-$650**
  Maggie: 1972-1973.   **$150-$175**
Peter Pan Set: 1969.
  Peter Pan: 14in (36cm) **$200-$225**
  Wendy: 14in (36cm)   **$200-$225**
  Michael: 11in (28cm)   **$250**
  Tinker Bell: 10in (25cm) **$300-$350**
Nancy Drew Face: 1967-1994. 12in (31cm).
  Nancy Drew: 1967.   **$200-$225**
  Renoir Child: 1967.   **$100-$125**
  Pamela: 1969. Boxed set, with wigs
                             $550-$650
  Poor Cinderella: 1967. **$100-$125**
  Little Women: 1969-1989. **$50-$65**
  Romantic Couples   **$75 pair**
  Discontinued dolls   **$30-$35**
First Ladies: 1976-1989. 14in (36cm)
                             $50-$75 each

14in (36cm) *Anne of Green Gables* Trunk Set. *H & J Foulke, Inc.*

American Character

Marked Petite or American Character Mama Dolls: 1923-on. Composition/cloth; original clothes; all in good condition.

16-18in (41-46cm)	**$225-$265**
24in (61cm)	**$325-$375**

Baby Petite: 12in (31cm) **$175-$200**

Puggy: 1928. All-composition, frowning face; original clothes; all in good condition, 12in (31cm) **$525-$575**

Marked Petite Girl Dolls: 1930s. All-composition; original clothes; all in good condition with nice coloring and perfect hair.

16-18in (41-46cm)	**$275-$325**
24in (61cm)	**$350-$375**
Petite Toddler:	
13in (33cm)	**$200-$225**

12in (31cm) *Puggy. H & J Foulke, Inc.*

FACTS
American Character Doll Co.,
New York, NY, U.S.A.
1919-on.
Trademark: Petite.

Sally: 1930. All-composition; painted eyes, molded hair or wigged with sleep eyes; original clothes; all in good condition with nice coloring.

12in (31cm)	**$175-$200**
16in (41cm)	**$275-$300**

Sally-Joy: 1930. Composition, cloth.

18in (46cm)	**$325-$350**
21in (53cm)	**$350-$375**

Carol Ann Beery: 1935. All-composition "Two-Some Doll" with special crown braid, matching playsuit and dress.

13in (33cm)	**$500-$600**
16½in (42cm)	**$700-$800**

11½in (29cm) *Tiny Tears*, all original and boxed. *H & J Foulke, Inc.*

Toodles: 1956. Hard rubber baby, drink-and-wet baby; original clothes; excellent condition.
   18-20in (46-56cm)   **$250-$300**

Toodles Toddler: 1960. Vinyl and hard plastic, "Peek-a-Boo" eyes; original clothes.
   24in (61cm)   **$275-$300**
   30in (76cm)   **$350-$375**

Tiny Tears: 1950s. Hard plastic head with tear ducts; drink-and-wet baby; original clothes; excellent condition.
Rubber body:
   13in (33cm)   **$200-$250**
   18in (46cm)   **$300-$350**
Original box and accessories:
   13in (33cm)   **$400-$500**
   18in (46cm)   **$750**
All-vinyl, 1963:
   12in (31cm)   **$75-$95**
   15in (38cm)   **$100-$125**
   Boxed with accessories   **$250**
Clothing and Accessories:
   Pink piqué dress and bonnet **$45-$50**
   Romper suit   **$30-$35**
   Plastic cradle   **$50-$60**
   Bottle   **$30-$40**
   Shoes   **$18-$22**
   Bubble pipe   **$20-$25**
   Bracelet   **$30**

10in (25cm) *Toni*, all original. H & J Foulke, Inc.

Sweet Sue: 1953. All-hard plastic or hard plastic and vinyl, some with walking mechanism, some fully-jointed including elbows, knees and ankles; original clothes; all in excellent condition, with perfect hair and pretty coloring.

14in (36cm)	**$275-$325**
18-21in (46-53cm)	**$325-$350**
24in (61cm)	**$325-$375**

Annie Oakley: 1955.

14in (36cm)	**$450**

Alice-in-Wonderland:

18in (46cm)	**$550**

Sweet Sue Sophisticate: Vinyl head.

20in (51cm)	**$275-$325**

Toni: 1958. Vinyl head, all original.

10½in (26cm)	**$190-$210**
20in (51cm)	**$275-$325**

Ricky, Jr.: 1955. All-vinyl, all original.

14in (36cm)	**$110-$125**
21in (53cm)	**$200-$225**

Eloise: Ca. 1955. All-cloth; yellow yarn hair; original clothing; in excellent condition. Designed by Bette Gould from the fictional little girl "Eloise" who lived at the Plaza Hotel in New York City.

21in (53cm)	**$450-$500**

Whimsies: 1960. Characters; original clothing; excellent condition. **Hedda Get Bedda (three faces), Wheeler the Dealer, Lena the Cleaner, Polly the Lolly, Bessie the Bashful Bride, Dixie the Pixie** and others:

19-21in (48-53cm)	**$125-$150**
Mint-in-box with tag	**$225**

Little Miss Echo: 1962. Recorded voice; original clothing, excellent condition.

30in (76cm) boxed	**$250-$300**
Out of box	**$150**

Tressy: 1963-1965. Growing hair:

12½in (32cm) boxed	**$125-$150**
Doll only	**$70-$80**
Black	**$400**

Pre-teen Tressy: 1963. Growing hair.

14in (36cm) boxed	**$100-$125**
Cricket: 1965. Boxed	**$100-$125**
Mary Make-up: 1965. Boxed	
	$100-$125

Arranbee

FACTS
Arranbee Doll Co.,
New York, NY, U.S.A.
1922-1960.
Mark: "ARRANBEE" or "R & B."

My Dream Baby: 1924. Bisque head, cloth body:

15-16in (38-41cm)	**$325-$350**

Storybook Dolls: 1930s. All-composition; original storybook costumes; all in excellent condition, with perfect hair and pretty coloring.

9-10in (23-25cm)	**$175-$195**
Boxed	**$275**

Bottletot: 1926. All-composition; molded celluloid bottle in hand; appropriate clothes; all in good condition,

13in (33cm)	**$175-$195**

Nancy: 1930. All-composition; original clothes; all in good condition, with pretty coloring.

12in (31cm) molded hair, painted eyes	**$200-$225**
12in (31cm) with trousseau in wardrobe trunk	**$400-$450**
16in (41cm) sleep eyes, wig, open mouth	**$350-$375**

Debu'Teen and **Nancy Lee:** 1938-on. All-composition; original clothes; all in good condition with perfect hair and pretty coloring.

11in (28cm)	**$275-$325**
14in (36cm)	**$350-$375**
18in (46)	**$425-$475**
21in (53cm)	**$500**
Skating Doll: 18in (46cm)	**$500**
Brother: 14in (36cm)	**$350-$375**
WAC: 18in (46cm)	**$500-$550**

Little Angel Baby: 1940s. Composition, cloth; original clothes; all in good condition.

16-18in (41-46cm)	**$300-$350**
Hard plastic: 18in (46cm)	**$350**

Nanette and **Nancy Lee:** 1950s. All-hard plastic; original clothes; all in excellent condition, with rosy cheeks.

14in (36cm)	**$400-$450**
17in (43cm)	**$500-$550**
20in (51cm) Skater	**$650**
Cinderella:	
14in (36cm)	**$500-$600**

Littlest Angel: 1956. All-hard plastic, jointed knees, walker; original clothes; all in excellent condition.

10-11in (25-28cm)	**$150-$175**
Boxed	**$250-$300**
Boxed outfits	**$45-$65**

Coty Girl: 1958. All-vinyl, fashion body, high-heeled feet.

10½in (27cm) boxed	**$175-$200**

18in (46cm) *Angel Baby,* all original. *H & J Foulke, Inc.*

17½in (45cm) Bride, all original. *H & J Foulke, Inc.*

14in (36cm) *Nanette,* all original. *H & J Foulke, Inc.*

Artist Dolls, Traditional

Traditional Artists: Many members of NIADA or ODACA. All dolls original and excellent.

Barrie, Mirren: Cloth historical characters, 11½in (30cm) **$110-$125**

Beckett, Bob & June: Carved wooden children **$225-$275**

Blakeley, Halle: High-fired clay lady dolls **$550-$750**

Bringloe, Frances: Carved wooden.
  American Pioneer Children,
   6¼in (16cm) **$600 pair**

Bruyere, Muriel: Biscuit-fired clay.
  Little Vie, 8in (31cm) **$125-$135**

Bullard, Helen: Carved wood.
  Holly, Barbry Allen **$165-$195**

Hitty: **$350**
  American Family Series: (16 dolls) **$300 each**

Clear, Emma: Porcelain, china and bisque shoulder head dolls **$350-$500**
  Danny **$450**
  George & Martha Washington **$500-$600 pair**
  Gibson Girl **$350-$400**

DeNunez, Marianne:
  Bru Jne:
   10in (25cm) **$300**
   19in (49cm) **$350**

Flather, Gwen:
  Katharine Hepburn:
   13½in (34cm) **$295**

Carol Nordell's *Ballerina. H & J Foulke, Inc.*

Right: Ann Parker's *Queen Elizabeth. H & J Foulke, Inc.*

Florian, Gertrude:
Ceramic dressed ladies   **$300**
Mother and Baby   **$400**
Heizer, Dorothy: Cloth sculpture.
Fashion Pair of 1770s   **$2,800**
Queens:
10-13in (25-33cm) **$1,100-$1,500**
Mary, Mary: 16in (41cm)   **$3,100**
Hale, Patti:
Carved wood heads   **$200-$300**
Hitty: All-wood   **$300**
Kane, Maggie Head: porcelain.
Gypsy Mother   **$400-$450**
Ling, Tita: Philippines, carved wood.
12in (30cm)   **$650**
Nordell, Carol:
Porcelain ballerinas   **$125**
Oldenburg, Maryanne:
Porcelain children   **$200-$250**
Park, Irma: Wax-over-porcelain.
Miniature vignettes   **$265**
Parker, Ann: Historical characters
$275-$300
Redmond, Kathy:
Embellished porcelain shoulder heads:
 Victoria Set: Four dolls   **$1,500**
 Henry VIII   **$600**
 Henry's Wives   **$450 each**
 Elizabeth I & Edward $250 each
 Medieval Ladies   **$450**
 Children   **$350-$400**
Saucier, Madeline: Cloth.
15in (38cm)   **$450**
Shreve Island Plantation: Flat wood, painted underwear.
 Julie Ann: 3¾in (9cm)   **$45-$50**
Smith, Sherman: Carved wood.
5-6in (13-15cm)   **$300**
Pinocchio: 7½in (19cm) **$350-$400**
Hitty   **$350**
Miss Unity: 12½in (31cm)   **$550**
Sorensen, Lewis: Wax.
 Father Christmas   **$1,000-$1,200**
 Toymaker   **$700-$800**
 Gibson Girls: **$350-$375**
Thompson, Martha: Porcelain.
 Princess Caroline, Prince Charles,
 Princess Anne   **$800-$900 each**
 Little Women   **$600-$700**
 Betsy   **$800-$900**
 McKim Child: (not bisque)   **$800**
 Royal Ladies   **$1,500 up**
 The Eisenhowers   **$2,300 pair**

Fawn Zeller *Angela. H & J Foulke, Inc.*

Tuttle, Eunice:
Miniature porcelain children
$450-$550
 Angel Baby   **$375-$400**
Vargas: Black wax characters   **$400**
Walters, Beverly: Porcelain.
Miniature fashions   **$500 up**
Wilson, Lita: Porcelain.
 Carolyn & John Kennedy
$165 pair
Wyffels, Berdine: Porcelain.
6in (15cm) girl, glass eyes   **$195**
Zeller, Fawn: Porcelain.
 One-of-a-kind dolls   **$2,000 up**
 Angela, Jeanie   **$600-$650**
 Jackie Kennedy   **$800**
 Polly Piedmont: 1965. **$600-$800**
 Polly II: 1989, U.S. Historical Society   **$200-$225**

Artist Dolls, UFDC

U.F.D.C. National & Regional Souvenir Dolls: Created by doll artists in limited editions and distributed to convention attendees as souvenirs. Before 1982, most dolls were given as kits; after 1982, most dolls were fully made up and dressed. Except as noted, dolls have porcelain heads, arms and legs; cloth bodies. A few are all-porcelain.

Alice in Wonderland: Yolanda Bello, 1990 Region 10, complete doll **$165**
Alice Roosevelt: Kathy Redmond, 1990 National, complete doll **$150-$165**
   Eleanor, companion doll **$225-$250**
Baby Stuart: Pat Robinson; 1996 National, complete doll **$135-$165**
Bo-Peep: Fred Laughon, 1989 Region 15, carved wood with staff and sheep **$85**

Charity: Fred Laughon, 1995 National, peg-wooden **$100-$125**
Cookie: Linda Steele, 1987 Regional, complete doll **$200-$225**
Crystal Faerie: Kazue Moroi and Lita Wilson, 1983 Midwest Regional, complete doll **$85**
Emma: Rappahannock Rags, 1993 National, cloth **$95**
Father Christmas: Beverly Walters, 1980 National, (kit) fully made up **$400**
Gibson Girl Bathing Beauty: Phyllis Wright, 1993 Regional, with bathing costume and beach chair **$85**
Janette: Fawn Zeller, 1991 National, complete doll, undressed **$300-$350**
Kate: Anili, 1986 National, all-cloth, with original box **$165-$185**
Ken-Tuck: Janet Masteller, 1972 Regional, (kit) fully made up **$65-$75**
Laurel: Lita Wilson and Muriel Kramer, 1985 Regional, fully made up **$75-$85**

6in (15cm) sitting *Cookie,* Linda Steele, 1987 Region 13 Conference. *H & J Foulke, Inc.*

15in (38cm) *Kate,* Anili, 1986 National Convention doll. *H & J Foulke, Inc.*

Li'l Apple: Faith Wick, 1979 National, fully made up with romper suit **$50**
  Apple Lil: Companion doll   **$75**
Lindbergh: Faith Wick, 1981 National, complete doll   **$85**
Lissette: Cathy Hansen, 1998 National, all-bisque doll with trunk   **$330**
Little Miss Sunshine: Diana Lence Crosby, 1974 National, (kit) fully made up   **$65-$75**
Louise: Marilyn Stauber, 1997 National, complete doll   **$135**
Mary: Linda Steele, 1987 National, complete doll   **$90-$100**
  Lewis: Companion doll **$125-$150**
Miami Miss: Fawn Zeller, 1961 National, (kit) fully made up
                                    $200-$250
  Dressed   **$300-$350**
Nellie Bly: Muriel Kramer, 1985 Pittsburgh Regional, complete doll
                                      $85-$95
Osceola: X. Kontis, 1954 National, composition, all original   **$150**
PaPitt: X. Kontis, 1953 National, composition, all original   **$150**
Portrait of a Young Girl: Jeanne Singer, 1986 Rochester Regional, complete doll   **$150-$175**
Precious Lady: Maori Kazue, 1992 National, fully made up   **$65-$75**
Princess Kimimi: Lita Wilson, 1977 Ohio Regional, (kit) fully made up
                                      $85-$95
Queen Victoria: Virginia Orenyo, 1994 National, complete doll
                                    $135-$150
Rose O'Neill: Lita Wilson, 1982 National, complete doll   **$100-$125**
Scarlett: Beverly Walters, 1976 Regional, half-doll, fully made up
                                          $135
Scarlett: Lita Wilson and Muriel Kramer, 1989 Florida Regional, half-doll, fully made up   **$125-$135**
Sunshine: Lucille Gerrard, 1983 National, complete doll   **$55-$65**
  Wain: Companion doll   **$75-$80**
Tammy: Jeanne Singer, 1989 Western New York Doll Club, complete doll
                                           $85
Trick or Treat: Dana Martindale, 1991 Regional, complete doll with "Nose"   **$125**

Artist Dolls,
Commercial

Commercial Doll Artists: Prices are for a factory perfect doll, never-played-with, including all accessories, wrist tag, certificate and box, if any.

Good-Krüger, Julie:
Vinyl:
  Children: 21in (53cm)   **$75-$125**
  A Trip to Grandma's: 1994. Doll, suitcase, clothes and accessories, 16in (41cm)   **$150**

Gunzel, Hildegard:
Wax-over-porcelain:
  28-31in (71-79cm)   **$1,200-$1,500**
Vinyl:
  For Alexander Doll Co., 1990-1993:
    17in (43cm)   **$50**
    27in (69cm)   **$125**
  Large Girls: **$400-$600**
  Lamponi: 22in (56cm) **$320-$360**
  Piccolina II: 1998.
    25in (63cm)   **$300-$350**
  Gunzel Kids: 1992.
    13in (33cm)   **$35-$40**
Porcelain:
  Melody and Friend: 1992.
    25in (63cm)   **$200**
  Girls from Dreams Collection:
    1995. 14in (36cm)   **$50-$60**

Hartmann, Sonja:
  Children, vinyl   **$125-$175**

Heath, Philip:
  World of Children Collection
                                    $300-$400
    Nkike I: 1996.   **$850**
    Lisa I: 1995.   **$750**
    Jerteh: 1995.   **$750**
    Desiree: 1999. 33½in (85cm) **$700**

Heller, Karin:
All-cloth:
  Children   **$200-$250**
Iacono, Maggie:
All-cloth:
  Children, fully-jointed **$500-$650**

Kish, Helen:
   Ballerinas: 12in (33cm)   **$95-$105**
   Little Drummer Boy: Expo East,
      10in (25cm)   **$275**
   Kristina: Fully-jointed   **$200**
   Margot: 1996.   **$200**
Lawton, Wendy:
   Little Colonel: 1990.
      13in (33cm)   **$255**
   Marigold Garden: 1992.
      14in (36cm)   **$190**
   Scarlet Ribbons: 1993.
      10in (25cm)   **$190**
   Patricia & Her Patsy: 1993.   **$375**
   Bessy & Her Bye-Lo: 1995.   **$250**
   Travel Doll: 1997. 9in (23cm)   **$695**

Marcella & Her Raggedy Family:
   1998. 16in (41cm)   **$550**
Marcella & Raggedy Ann:
   13in (33cm)   **$300**
   Storybook Collection   **$40-$50**
Middleton, Lee:
Vinyl:
   Honey Love and other babies and
   toddlers   **$65-$85**
   Bubba Chubbs: 22in (56cm)   **$195**
Roche, Lynne & Michael:
Porcelain and wood:
   Children:
      20-22in (51-56cm)   **$750-$1,000**
   Tiny Sophy: 12in (31cm)   **$500**

Black Baby, Julie Good-Krüger. *H & J Foulke, Inc.*

Margaret, Robert Tonner, porcelain, limited edition of 50. *Rae-Ellen Koenig.*

Schrott, Rotraut, for Gadco:
  Martina: 1988.
    Porcelain, 28in (71cm) **$300-$400**
    Vinyl   **$150-$200**
  Marlene: 1990.
    Porcelain, 28in (71cm) **$300-$400**
    Vinyl   **$150-$200**
  Puyi: 1989. 26in (66cm)   **$150**
  Suzi: 1989. 28in (71cm)   **$150**
  Trixie: 1992. 28in (71cm) **$200**
  Jasmine: 1991. 28in (71cm) **$200**
Spanos, FayZah:
  Vinyl:
    Babies   **$50-$100**
    Children   **$125-$150**
Tonner, Robert:
  Models: 19in (48cm)   **$175-$200**
    Sydney: Collectors United, 2002
                               $400
    Tyler: Galeries Lafayette, Paris,
    2003   **$400**
    Ellen: Expo East, 1998   **$425**
    Tyler: "Blush," Paris, 2003
                           $275-$350
  Ann Estelle:
    10in (25cm)   **$60-$75**
    18in (46cm)   **$100**
  Titanic Trunk Set: FAO Schwarz
  exclusive   **$900**
Treffeisen, Ruth:
  Porcelain children:
    25-30in (64-76cm) **$1,200-$1,500**
  Vinyl children   **$250-$350**
Turner, Virginia:
  Vinyl:
    Large children:
    30-32in (76-81cm)   **$150-$175**
    Small children:
    21in (53cm)   **$75-$85**
Woods, Robin:
  Vinyl:
    Camelot Collection:
    14in (36cm)   **$50-$100**
    Let's Play Dolls (Alexander Doll
    Co.):
    13in (33cm) trunk set **$100-$125**
    Dancer's Recital: trunk and wardrobe
                         $100-$125
    Children:
    8in (21cm)   **$25-$30**
    12-14in (31-36cm)   **$50-$75**

Ashton-Drake Galleries

Prices are for dolls in mint condition with certificates and boxes.

Designer – Yolanda Bello:
  Picture Perfect Babies:
    Jason: (1st)   **$150-$200**
    Heather: (2nd)   **$45-$50**
    Jennifer: (3rd)   **$50-$60**
    Matthew: (1987) (4th) **$40-$50**
    Amanda: (1988)   **$45-$50**
    Sarah: (1989)   **$35-$40**
    Jessica: (1989)   **$35-$40**
    Lisa: (1990)   **$40-$45**
    Michael: (1990)   **$45-$50**
    Emily: (1991)   **$35-$40**
    Danielle: (1991)   **$35-$40**
  Playtime Babies:
    Lindsey: (1994)   **$25-$30**
    Shawna: (1994)   **$25-$30**
    Todd: (1994)   **$25-$30**
  Lullaby Babies: **$25-$30**
  Moments to Remember:
    Jill: (1993)   **$35-$40**
    Justin: (1991)   **$65-$75**
  Magical Moments of Summer:
    Whitney: (1995)   **$30-$35**
    Dana: (1996)   **$30-$35**
  Heaven Scent Babies:
    Megan Rose: (1994)   **$30-$35**
    Sweet Carnation   **$30-$35**

Designer – Wendy Lawton:
  Little Women: Set of five:
    16in (41cm)   **$250-$300**
  Mary Had a Little Lamb: 1994.
                           $25-$30
  Little Bo-Peep: 1994.
    15in (38cm)   **$25-$30**
  Little Miss Muffet: 1995.
    14in (36cm)   **$25-$30**

Designer – Joan Ibarolle:
  Little House on the Prairie:
  1992-1995.
    Children   **$85-$115 each**
    Ma & Pa   **$150-$175 each**

*Mary, Mary.
Sidney Jeffrey
Collection.*

Designer – Dianna Effner:
  **Heroines from the Fairy Tale
  Forest: 16in (41cm):
    Goldilocks, Cinderella, Snow
    White, Red Riding Hood,
    Rapunzel $35-$40**
  **What Little Girls Are Made Of:
    15in (38cm):
    Sunshine & Lollipops (1997),
    Peaches & Cream, Christmas &
    Candy Canes: (1999) $30-$35**
  **Mother Goose Series:
    14in (36cm):
    Mary, Mary (1991), Girl with
    curl (1992), Curly Locks (1993),
    Snips & Snails (1993) $30-$35**
  **Classic Collection: Hillary, (1995)
    15in (38cm) $40-$45**
  **Babies: Sugar Plum, (1994)
    8in (20cm) $40-$45**

Designer – Julie Good-Krüger:
  **Amish Blessings: Rebeccah,
    Rachael, Adam $40-$50 each**

Fire's Out. Sidney Jeffrey Collection.

Designer – Jenny Lundy:
   Simple Pleasures, Special Days,
   Amish Children: Molly (1999),
   Gretchen (1998)   **$50-$60 each**

Designer – Mary Tretter:
   Wizard of Oz: Dorothy,
   Scarecrow, Cowardly Lion,
   Tinman   **$25-$35 each**

Designer – Brigette Duval:
   Fairy Tale Princesses:
   18in (46cm)   **$40-$50 each**

Designer – Titus Tomescu:
   From This Day Forward: (Brides)
   1994.   **$60-$70**
   Barely Yours: (Babies).
      Snug as a Bug: **$60-$70**
      Cute as a Button: 1993. **$60-$70**
      Pretty as a Picture: 1996.   **$60**
      Good as Gold: 1997.   **$65**
   Snow Babies: **$40**

For Walt Disney:
   Snow White: **$40-$50**
   Dopey: **$40-$50**
   Disney Babies   **$40-$50**
   Disney World Girl: 2001.
   16in (41cm)   **$35-$45**

Designer – Mel Odom:
   Gene:
      Premiere: 1996   **$250-$350**
      Holiday Magic: 1996. First
      Christmas, outfit only **$150-$175**
      Atlantic City 1996 Convention
      Package: Bathing outfit and all
      handouts given at the convention
          $900-$1,100
      My Favorite Witch: 1997
      Convention doll   **$1,000**
      Broadway Medley: 1998
      Convention doll   **$200-$225**
      King's Daughter: **$125-$150**
      Mood Music: 1999 Convention
      Package   **$150-$175**
      Toast at Twelve: 2000
      Convention doll   **$200**
      Belle of the Ball: 2001
      Convention doll   **$175-$200**

Barbie®

BARBIE® is a registered trademark of Mattel, Inc.

> ### FACTS
> Mattel, Inc., Hawthorne, CA, U.S.A.
> 1959 to present. Hard plastic and vinyl.
> 11½–12in (29-31cm).
> **Mark:** 1959-1962: "Barbie TM/Pats.
> Pend./© MCMLVIII/by/Mattel, Inc."
> 1963-1968: "Midge TM/©
> 1962/Barbie®/© 1958/by/Mattel, Inc."
> 1964-1966: "© 1958/Mattel, Inc./U.S.
> Patented/U.S. Pat. Pend."
> 1966-1969: "© 1966/Mattel, Inc./U.S.
> Patented/U.S. Pat. Pend./
> Made in Japan."

Pricing Note: Condition is extremely important in pricing BARBIE® dolls. Mint condition means the doll has never been played with, coloring is beautiful, hair is perfect, all accessories are present. Rule of thumb dictates that to price out-of-original-box dolls and accessories, deduct 50 percent; for lightly played-with items, deduct an additional 25 percent.

#1 BARBIE®: 1959. Vinyl, solid body; very light complexion, white irises, pointed eyebrows, gold hoop earrings, ponytail; black and white striped bathing suit; holes in feet to fit stand; mint condition.
   11½in (29cm) boxed
          $6,000-$6,800*
   Doll only, no box or accessories:
      Mint   **$2,800-$3,200**
      Very good   **$2,00-$2,200**
      Stand   **$1,500**
      Shoes, spikes   **$75-$95**
      Shoes, closed toe   **$35-$45**
      Hoop earrings   **$75**

#2 BARBIE®: 1959-1960. Vinyl, solid body; very light complexion; same as above, but no holes in feet; some wore pearl earrings; mint condition. Made three months only.
   11½in (29cm) boxed
          $6,000-$7,000*
   Doll only, no box or accessories,
   very good   **$2,800-$3,400**

*Brunette harder to find than blonde.

#3 BARBIE®: 1960. Vinyl, solid body; very light complexion; same as #2, but with blue irises and curved eyebrows; no holes in feet; mint condition.

11½in (29cm) boxed	**$1,200-$1,400**
Doll only, mint	**$600-$800**

#4 BARBIE®: 1960. Vinyl; same as #3, but with solid body of flesh-toned vinyl; mint condition.

11½in (29cm) boxed	**$500-$600**
Doll only, mint	**$250-$300**

#5 BARBIE®: 1961. Vinyl; same as #4; ponytail hairdo of firm Saran; mint condition.

11½in (29cm) boxed	**$325-$425**
Doll only, mint	**$225-$275**

Other **BARBIES®:** All prices are for mint-in-box dolls unless otherwise noted.
Bubble Cut **BARBIE®:** 1961 on.

	$250-$300*
Doll only, mint	**$100-$150**
Bubble side part: Doll only, mint	
	$275-$300

*Allow 25 percent extra for platinum or white ginger hair.

#5 Ponytail BARBIE®, boxed. McMasters Harris Premier Doll Auctions.

Bubble Cut BARBIE®, boxed. McMasters Harris Premier Doll Auctions.

Swirl Ponytail BARBIE®, boxed. McMasters Harris Premier Doll Auctions.

Fashion Queen BARBIE®: 1963.
$400-$500
Doll only with three wigs $125-$135
Miss BARBIE®: 1964. $1,100-$1,300
Swirl Ponytail BARBIE®: 1964.
$550-$650*
Doll only, mint $250-$350*

Bendable Leg BARBIE®: 1965 and 1966.
  American Girl, center part, mint-in-box $1,500-$2,400
  Side part $3,500-$4,500
Color Magic BARBIE®: 1966.
  Brunette $1,600-$2,200
  Blonde $1,200-$1,800
  Midnight to ruby red $1,600
  Doll only, mint:
    Brunette $1,000-$1,200
    Blonde $650-$850
Twist 'N Turn BARBIE®: 1967.
$375-$425
  Trade-In box, mint $700-$750
  Doll only $225-$250
Talking BARBIE®: 1970. $225-$250
Living BARBIE®: 1970. $200-$225
Live Action BARBIE®: 1970.
$200-$250
Hair Happenin's BARBIE®: 1971.
$1,200
Montgomery Ward BARBIE®: 1972.
$250-$300
Growin' Pretty Hair: 1971-1972.
$325-$375
Quick Curl: 1972. $75-$95

Gift Sets, mint-in-box:
  Fashion Queen BARBIE® & Ken: 1964. $2,800-$3,200
  Wedding Party: 1964. $3,000
  On Parade (BARBIE®, Ken and Midge): 1964. $2,500-$3,200
  Silver Blue: 1967. $2,500-$3,200
  Tennis BARBIE® & Ken
$2,600-$3,200

Outfits: All never-removed-from-package. Deduct 50 percent for *complete* but out-of-package outfits.

Roman Holiday	$3,000 up
Gay Parisienne	$2,000 up
Easter Parade	$2,500 up
Shimmering Magic	$1,400 up

Here Comes the Bride	$950 up
Pan Am Stewardess	$4,000 up
BARBIE® Baby Sits	$200-$300
Dogs & Duds	$150-$175
Enchanted Evening	$250-$300
1600 Series and Jacqueline Kennedy-style outfits	$450 up
Dinner at 8	$200-$250
Commuter Set	$1,250-$1,500
Picnic Set	$300-$350
Midnight Blue	$700-$800
Silken Flame	$125-$150
Senior Prom	$250-$300
Plantation Belle	$300-$350
Open Road	$275-$350
Registered Nurse	$200-$250

Accessories, Mint-in-package:
  BARBIE® doll's First Car $250-$300
  BARBIE® doll's First Dreamhouse
$125-$150
  Fashion Shop $250-$300
  Little Theatre $400-$500
  Cases $40 up
  BARBIE® doll's bed $100
  Ken's Hot Rod Roadster $200

*Allow 25 percent extra for platinum or white ginger hair.

Color Magic Barbie®, boxed. McMasters Harris Premier Doll Auctions.

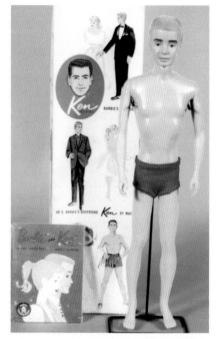

Redesigned *Barbie®*, boxed. *McMasters Harris Premier Doll Auctions.*

Ken, with flocked hair, boxed. *McMasters Harris Premier Doll Auctions.*

Left: *Ken,* with bendable legs, boxed. *McMasters Harris Premier Doll Auctions.*

Right: *Allan,* with bendable legs, boxed. *McMasters Harris Premier Doll Auctions.*

Other Dolls: All prices are for mint-in-box dolls unless otherwise noted.

Ken #1: 1961.	**$175-$225**
Bendable legs	**$300-$325**
Dressed boxed doll	**$275 up**
Midge: 1963.	**$175-$195**
1966, Bendable legs	**$450-$550**
Allan: 1964-1966.	
Bendable legs	**$150-$200**
Straight legs	**$100-$125**
Skipper: 1964. Straight legs, mint-in-box	**$150-$175**
Dramatic New Living Skipper	
	$125-$150
Bendable Legs	**$175-$200**
Ricky: 1965.	**$150-$200**
Scooter: 1965. Straight legs	
	$150-$200
Francie: 1966-1967.	
Doll only, bendable legs, mint	
	$175-$210
Straight legs	**$175-$210**
Twist 'N Turn	**$260-$285**
Black: 1967, mint-in-package	
	$1,500-$1,900
Doll only, mint	**$850**
"No Bangs," 1970.	**$1,500**
Doll only, mint	**$900-$1,100**
Growin' Pretty Hair	**$250-$275**
Hair Happenin's: 1970.	**$225-$275**
Casey: 1967.	**$250-$300**
Twiggy: 1967.	**$325-$375**
Christie: 1968-1972. (Black)	
Twist 'N Turn	**$300-$350**
Stacey: 1968-1971.	
Twist 'N Turn	**$300-$350**
Talking	**$300-$350**
P.J.: 1969-1971.	
Twist 'N Turn	**$225-$275**
Live Action on Stage	**$215**
Truly Scrumptious: 1969.	**$425-$475**
Doll only, mint	**$275-$300**
Julia: 1969.	**$225-$275**
Talking	**$150-$200**
Tutti: 1967-1970.	**$200-$225**
Chris: 1967-1970.	**$200-$225**
Todd: 1967-1970.	**$200-$225**
Pretty Pairs:	
Angie 'N Tangie	**$250-$300**
Nan 'N Fran	**$225-$250**
Lori 'N Rori	**$250-$275**

Above: *Ken,* Cinderella Little Theatre Costume Dressed Doll Box. *Rosemary Kanizer.*

Twist 'N Turn *Francie* with bendable legs. *McMasters Harris Premier Doll Auctions.*

Bob Mackie BARBIE® Dolls:

1990 Gold	$300-$400
1991 Platinum	$250-$300
1991 Starlight Splendor (black)	
	$250-$300
1992 Empress Bride	$500-$550
1992 Neptune Fantasy	$335-$385
1993 Masquerade Ball	$200
1994 Queen of Hearts	$150-$175
1995 Goddess of the Sun	$125-$150
1996 Moon Goddess	$125
1997 Madame du BARBIE®	
	$150-$200

Jewel Essence Collection: Five dolls
$275-$300

Christmas BARBIE® Dolls

1988, English language box	
	$325-$375
1989	$100-$150
1990	$100-$150
1991	$75-$125
1992	$50-$75
1993	$50-$75
1994	$50
1995	$25
1996	$25
1997	$25
1998	$25

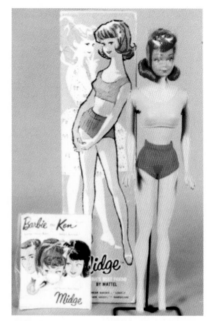

Midge, boxed. *McMasters Harris Premier Doll Auctions.*

Air Force *Ken*, 1990, boxed. *H & J Foulke, Inc.*

Left: *Rapunzel*, 1995 Children's Series, boxed. *H & J Foulke, Inc.*

Exclusive Store Specials:
1990 Winter Fantasy (FAO Schwarz)
$65-$75
1993 Little Debbie, First **$30-$40**
1993 Rockettes (FAO Schwarz) **$95**
1994 Nicole Miller (Bloomingdales)
$40-$45
1994 Victorian Elegance (Hallmark)
$40-$45
1994 Silver Screen (FAO Schwarz)
$65-$75
1994 Tooth Fairy (WalMart) **$15**
1995 Shopping Chic (Speigel)
$50-$60
1995 Jeweled Splendor
(FAO Schwarz) **$85-$95**
1995 Circus Star (FAO Schwarz)
$40-$50
1995 Donna Karan (Bloomingdales)
$40-$50
1995 Royal Enchantment
(J.C. Penney) **$20**
1995 Statue of Liberty
(FAO Schwarz) **$75-$100**
1997 Pink Ice (Toys R Us) **$55-$65**

Timeless Creations (now BARBIE®
Collectibles):
Stars and Stripes Collection:
1990 Air Force BARBIE® **$30**
1991 Navy BARBIE® **$40**
1992 Marine BARBIE® **$30-$40**
1992 Marine Gift Set **$75-$85**
1993 Army Gift Set **$40**
1994 Air Force Gift Set **$40**
Classique Collection:
1992 Benefit Ball **$65**
1993 Opening Night **$50**
1993 City Style **$40**
1994 Uptown Chic **$40**
1994 Evening Extravaganza **$45**
1994 Evening Extravaganza
(black) **$55**
1995 Midnight Gala **$45**
Nostalgia Series:
1994 35th Anniversary **$35-$40**
1994 Gift Set **$100-$125**
1994 Solo in the Spotlight **$30**
1995 Busy Gal **$45**
1996 Enchanted Evening **$30**
1996 Poodle Parade **$30**
1997 Fashion Luncheon **$40-$50**
Scarlett Series, 1994 & 1995:
Green Velvet **$60**
Red Velvet **$60**
Barbecue **$60**
Honeymoon **$60**

Ken as **Rhett Butler** **$50**
Great Eras:
1993 Gibson Girl **$70**
1993 1920s Flapper **$85**
1994 Egyptian Queen **$70**
1994 Southern Belle **$65**
1995 Medieval Lady **$40**
1996 Grecian Goddess **$50**
1997 Chinese Empress **$45**
Other BARBIE® Dolls:
1986 Blue Rhapsody (porcelain)
$200-$250
1988 Mardi Gras **$50**
1989 Pink Jubilee **$1,300 up**
1990 Wedding Fantasy **$50**
1992 My Size **$90**
1994 Snow Princess **$75-$85**
(brunette) **$285**
1994 Gold Jubilee **$350-$400**
1994 Evergreen Princess **$50**
1994 Evergreen Princess (red hair)
$150
1995 Peppermint Princess **$45**
1995 Starlight Waltz **$60**
1995 Dior, First **$75**
1995 50th Anniversary (porcelain)
$225-$275
1995 Rapunzel **$30**
1996 Pink Splendor **$450-$500**
1996 Jewel Princess **$25-$35**
1996 Jewel Princess (Disney
brunette) **$75-$85**
1996 Escada **$50**
1996 Dior, Second **$60**
1996 Wedding Fantasy Gift Set
$60
1996 BARBIE® Bandstand
Convention Package **$500**
1996 Erté Stardust **$350-$450**
1997 Bill Blass **$55**
1997 Midnight Princess **$45**
1997 Midnight Princess (Disney,
brunette) **$75**
1997 Illusion **$100**
1998 Harley-Davidson BARBIE®,
Second **$65-$75**
1998 Crystal Jubilee **$200**
1998 Rendezvous **$65**
1998 Fabregé Imperial Elegance
(porcelain) **$375**
Silkstone Lingerie BARBIE®:
#1 **$300-$350**
#2 **$275**
#3 **$140**
2003 Chantaine (FAO Schwarz
exclusive) **$400**

Betsy McCall

American Character Doll Co.: 1957. All-hard plastic, jointed knees; molded eyelashes, rooted Saran hair on wig cap; original clothes; excellent with rosy cheeks.

8in (20cm) basic, (undergarment,

shoes and socks)	**$250-$275**
Mint-in-box, basic	**$375-$425**
In dresses	**$250-$300**
In gowns	**$300-$400**
Mint-in-box, pink dress and hat,	
at auction	**$766**
Mint-in-blister pack, at auction	
	$575

Clothes, clean and in very good condition:

Dresses	**$30-$65**
Shoes and socks	**$35-$40**
Boxed outfits	**$100-$125**

American Character: 1960. All-vinyl, slender limbs; lashed sleep eyes; original clothes; excellent condition.

14in (36cm)	**$350-$375**
20in (51cm)	**$450-$500**
30in (76cm)	**$550-$600**
36in (91cm)	**$650-$750**

Boxed, all original:

14in (36cm)	**$700-$775**
20in (51cm)	**$900-$1,000**

Jointed at wrists, waist, knees and ankles:

22in (56cm)	**$400-$450**
30in (76cm)	**$625-$675**

8in (20cm) Rothschild *Betsy McCall*, all original. *H & J Foulke, Inc.*

Left: 11½in (29cm) Uneeda *Betsy McCall*, boxed. *Rosemary Kanizer.*

Ideal Novelty & Toy Co.: 1948. Vinyl head, hard plastic body; original clothes; excellent condition

14in (36cm)	**$250-$300**
Mint-in-box	**$725**

Ideal Novelty & Toy Co.: 1959. All-vinyl; original clothes; excellent condition.
Betsy McCall:
36in (91cm)   **$550-$650**
Sandy McCall:
38in (96cm)   **$500-$600**

Uneeda: 1959-1961.
All-vinyl, 11½in (29cm) **$125-$135**
Boxed   **$275-$300**

Horsman: 1974.
All-vinyl:
29in (73cm) boxed   **$225-$275**
Beauty Box:
13in (33cm) boxed   **$50-$60**

Tomy: 1984. Porcelain/cloth, all original and boxed, Four Seasons:
16in (41cm)   **$40-$50**

Rothschild: 1986. Hard vinyl:
8in (20cm), all original   **$25-$30**

Tonner, Robert: 1997. All original, boxed and mint.
Porcelain, first model, signed,
13in (33cm)   **$225**
2002 Betsy McCall Convention:
14in (36cm)   **$95**
2002 Collectors United Convention Gift Set, 8in (20cm)   **$165**
Betsy McCall Goes to the Movies: 2002. 8in (20cm) Piedmont Doll Club
$175
Disney Favorite Teddy:
8in (20cm)   **$99**
Hello Portland: 2001.
8in (20cm)   **$90-$100**

27in (69cm) boudoir doll.
H & J Foulke, Inc.

Boudoir Dolls

Boudoir Doll: Head of composition, cloth or other material, painted features, mohair wig; composition or cloth stuffed body, unusually long extremities; usually high-heeled shoes; original clothes elaborately designed and trimmed; all in excellent condition.

Cloth Face, 1920s:
Exceptional quality art doll: silk hair, 28-30in (71-76cm) **$350-$450**
Standard quality: dressed
28-30in (71-76cm)   **$200-$225**
Naked   **$80-$90**
Composition Head:
1920s dressed   **$150-$5175**
Smoker   **$250-$300**
1940s, dressed   **$100-$125**
Lenci: See page 140.
Poured Wax: 22in (56cm)   **$600**
Blossom Doll Co. Wedding Party, all original.
Set of 10 dolls, at auction **$1,300**
Vintage high-heeled shoes   **$50-$60**

Buddy Lee

Burgarella

FACTS
H.D. Lee Co., Inc., garment manufacturers of
Kansas City, MO, U.S.A. 1920-1962.
Mark: "Buddy Lee" embossed on back

FACTS
Gaspare Burgarella, Rome, Italy. Ca. 1925 until World War II.
Designer: Ferdinando Stracuzzi
Mark: Cloth label sewn on clothes "BURGARELLA Made in Italy"

Marked Buddy Lee: Molded hair, painted eyes to side; jointed at shoulders, stiff hips, legs apart; dressed in original Lee clothes; all in very good condition.

Composition, 1920-1948:
13in (33cm) **$450-$550***
Hard Plastic, 1949-1962:
13in (33cm) **$450-$550***

*Allow extra for Coca-Cola and gasoline station uniforms.

Burgarella Child: Excellent quality; all-composition; jointed at neck, shoulders, elbows, hips and knees; human hair or mohair wig, short face with chubby cheeks, dramatic painted eyes, small mouth; all in excellent condition.

All original clothing:
16-18in (41-46cm) **$500-$600**
22in (56cm) **$650-$750**
Sexed boy, all original **$750-$800**

13in (33cm) hard plastic *Buddy Lee*. *Gloria & Mike Duddlesten.*

22in (56cm) Burgarella child, original dress. *Dorothy Hunt, Sweetbriar.*

Cameo Doll Company

Kewpie: 1913. See page 125.
Bundie: 1918-1925. All-composition,
11in (28cm) **$300****
Scootles: 1925. Designed by Rose
O'Neill. All-composition; appropriate
clothes; all in very good condition.

    7-8in (18-20cm) **$450-$500**
    12-13in (31-33cm) **$450-$500**
    15-16in (38-41cm) **$550-$600**
    20in (51cm) **$900-$1,100**
    Sleep eyes:
      12in (31cm) **$700-$750**
      20in (51cm) **$1,250-$1,500**
    Black: 13-14in (33-36cm)**$650-$750**
    All-bisque (Japan):
      4½in (11cm) **$325-$375**
      6-7in (15-18cm) **$500-$550**
Baby Bo Kaye: 1925. See page 40.

Wood Segmented Characters:
Designed by Joseph L. Kallus.
Composition head, segmented wood
body; undressed; all in very good condition.
    Margie: 1929.
      10in (25cm) **$225-$250**
      15in (38cm) **$400-$450**
      17in (43cm) **$550**

FACTS
Cameo Doll Company,
New York, NY, later
Port Allegany, PA, U.S.A.
Original owner: Joseph L. Kallus.
1922-on.

Pinkie: 1930. 10in (25cm)**$250-$275**
Joy: 1932.
    10in (25cm) **$250-$275**
    15in (38cm) **$375-$400**
Betty Boop: 1932.
    12in (31cm) **$650-$750**
    With molded bathing suit and
composition legs; wearing a cotton
print dress **$750-$850****
Pop-Eye: 1935. 14in (36cm) **$700****
Hotpoint Man: 16in (41cm) **$800****
RCA Radiotron: 16in (41cm) **$800****
Bandy: General Electric:
    18in (46cm) **$800****
Pete the Pup: 9in (23cm) **$400-$425**

**Not enough price samples to compute a
reliable range.

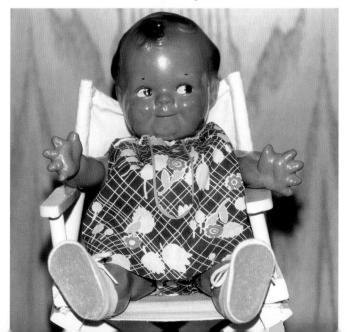

13in (33cm)
black composi-
tion *Scootles.*
*Private
Collection.*

15in (38cm) *Joy*, replaced dress. *H & J Foulke, Inc.*

12in (31cm) *Betty Boop. George Bassett.*

Giggles: 1946. Designed by Rose O'Neill. All-composition; original romper; all in very good condition.

14in (36cm)	**$450-$500**
Boxed	**$650-$750**

Little Annie Rooney: 1925. Designed by Jack Collins. Composition; painted eyes, yarn wig; all original.

16in (41cm)	**$650-$700****

Baby Blossom: 1927. Composition and cloth, 19-20in (48-51cm) **$550-$650****

Champ: 1942. Composition, molded hair, freckles, all original.

16in (41cm)	**$500-$600****

Vinyl Dolls:
   Miss Peep: 1957. All original.

16-18in (41-46cm)	**$75-$85**
Boxed	**$125-$135**

Newborn Miss Peep: 1962.

14in (36cm) boxed	**$65**

Baby Mine: 1961. All original.

20in (51cm) boxed	**$175-$225**

Margie: 1958. All original.

17in (43cm) boxed	**$175-$225****

Scootles: All original.

1964, 14in (36cm)	**$165-$185**
19-20in (48-51cm) sleeping eyes	**$350**
1973 Ltd. Ed. (Maxines),	
16in (41cm)	**$200-$225**
1980s, (Jesco), all original.	
12in (31cm)	**$40-$50**
16in (31cm)	**$65-$75**
1997 **Lee Middleton Stamp Doll:**	
12in (31cm)	**$35-$40**

**Not enough price samples to compute a reliable range.

Campbell Kids

E.I. Horsman Co.: 1910-1914. Designed by Grace G. Drayton. Composition head, molded and painted bobbed hair; original cloth body; appropriate or original clothes; all in good condition.

Mark: On head:

E.I.H. © 1910

Cloth label on sleeve:

> The Campbell Kids
> Trademark by
> Joseph Campbell.
> Mfg. by E.I. Horsman Co

10-13in (25-33cm)	**$250-$300**
16in (41cm)	**$375-$425**

American Character & E.I. Horsman Co.: 1923. Designed by Grace G. Drayton, sometimes called *Dolly Dingle*. All-composition; molded bobbed hair, painted eyes to side; original clothes; all in good condition.

12in (31cm)	**$550-$650****

E.I. Horsman Co.: 1948. All-composition; molded bobbed hair, painted eyes to side, watermelon mouth; original clothes; all in good condition.

12-13in (31-33cm)	**$450-$475**
With Campbell Soup outfit and label	**$600-$650**

All-Vinyl: 1950 on. Original clothes, bright color, unplayed-with condition.

8in (20cm)	**$25-$30**
Boxed	**$45**
16in (28cm)	**$40-$45**

All-Cloth, Knickerbocker: 1973.

12in (31cm) boxed	**$38-$42**

Porcelain: 1997. Soup Can box.

11½in (29cm)	**$35**

1990s Horsman Reproductions:

1948. 12½in (32cm)	**$50 pair**
1910. 10in (25cm)	**$20**

12in (31cm) 1948 *Campbell Kid*, all original with label. *Nancy A. Smith.*

**Not enough price samples to compute a reliable range.

Dewees Cochran

Composition
(American)

Dewees Cochran Doll: Latex with jointed neck, shoulders and hips; human hair wig, painted eyes, character face; dressed; all in good condition.
Cindy: 1947-1948.
15-16in (38-41cm) **$750-$850**
Grow-up Dolls: 1952-1958. **Stormy, Angel, Bunnie, J.J.** and **Peter Ponsett** each at ages 5, 7, 11, 16 and 20
$1,600-$2,000
Look-Alike Dolls: (six different faces)
$1,600-$2,000
Individual Portrait:
Children **$1,800 up**
Baby: 9in (23cm) **$1,500****
American Children: See page 258.

Condition: Unless otherwise noted, all dolls should be all original with perfect hair, good coloring, original clothes; light crazing acceptable.

All-Composition Child Doll: 1912-1920. Various firms, such as Bester Doll Co., New Era Novelty Co., New Toy Mfg. Co., Superior Doll Mfg. Co., Artcraft Toy Product Co., Colonial Toy Mfg. Co. Ball-jointed composition body; appropriate clothes; all in good condition. These are patterned after German bisque-headed dolls.
22-24in (56-61cm) **$250-$275**
Character baby, all-composition:
19in (48cm) **$200-$250**

Early Composition Character Doll: Ca. 1912. Composition head with molded hair or wig and painted features; cloth body; appropriate clothes.
12-15in (31-38cm) **$150-$175**
18-20in (46-51cm) **$225-$275**
24-26in (61-66cm) **$325-$350**
Two-face toddler:
14in (36cm) **$275-$300**

Molded Loop Dolls: Ca. 1930s. Composition head with molded bobbed hair and loop for tying on a ribbon; quality is generally mediocre.
12-15in (31-38cm) **$125-$150**

Patsy-type Girl: Ca. 1930s. All-composition with molded bobbed hair; of good quality.
9-10in (23-25cm) **$125-$150**
14-16in (36-41cm) **$250**
20in (51cm) **$300**

**Not enough price samples to compute a reliable range.

Dewees Cochran *Angel with Baby.*
Nancy A. Smith Collection.

Mama Dolls: Ca. 1920-on. Composition head with hair wig; composition lower limbs, cloth body.

16-18in (41-46cm)	**$200-$225**
20-22in (51-56cm)	**$300-$325**
24-26in (61-66cm)	**$350-$400**

Babies and Infants: Ca. 1920 on. Composition head with molded hair; composition lower arms, cloth body (may have composition lower legs).

14-16in (36-41cm)	**$150-$200**
18-20in (46-51cm)	**$225-$275**

Dionne-type Doll: Ca. 1935. All-composition with molded hair or wig; of good quality.

7-8in (18-20cm) baby	**$135**
13in (33cm) toddler	**$225**
18-20in (46-51cm) toddler	
	$300-$325

Alexander-type Girl: Ca. 1935. All-composition; of good quality.

13in (33cm)	**$225-$250**
16-18in (41-46cm)	**$300-$350**
22in (56cm)	**$350-$400**

Shirley Temple-type Girl: Ca. 1935-on. All-composition; of good quality.

16-18in (41-46cm)	**$400-$500**

Storybook or International Costume Doll: Ca. 1940. All-composition.

11in (28cm)

Excellent quality	**$150**
Standard quality	**$65-$75**

Miscellaneous Specific Dolls:
Carmen (Miranda): Eegee.

14in (36cm)	**$225**
20in (51cm)	**$350**

Cat, Rabbit or Pig head: Naked.

10-11in (25-28cm)	**$300-$400**

David: Bible Doll Co. of America.

11in (28cm) boxed	**$285**

Famlee: 1921. Boxed with six heads and six costumes **$1,000**

Grace G. Drayton:

14in (36cm)	**$400-$500**

15in (38cm) early unmarked character boy. *H & J Foulke, Inc.*

12in (31cm) unmarked *Patsy*-type girl, all original. *H & J Foulke, Inc.*

17in (43cm) unmarked mama doll, all original. *H & J Foulke, Inc.*

Right: 15in (38cm) girl with molded hair loop. *H & J Foulke, Inc.*

21in (53cm) unmarked mama doll. *Kathy & Terri's Dolls.*

Hedwig/DiAngeli:
  Elin, Hannah, Lydia, Suzanne:
    14in (36cm)   **$625-$675**
Indian child: 1940s.
    8in (21cm) boxed   **$60**
Jackie Robinson:
    13½in (34cm)   **$700-$800**
Jerry Mahoney: Juro Novelty:
    24in (61cm)   **$275-$325**
Kewpie-type characters:
    12in (31cm)   **$65-$75**
Little Miss Movie: Eegee:
    27in (69cm)   **$700-$800**
Lone Ranger: With hat, holster and
gun, 16in (41cm)   **$750-$800**
Miss Curity: 18in (46cm)   **$450-$500**
Monica: 1941-195. Inset human hair:
    17-18in (43-46cm)   **$450-$550**

P.D. Smith: 22in (56cm)   **$2,600****
Paris Doll Co. Peggy:
    28in (71cm) walker   **$300-$350**
Puzzy: 1948. H. of P.:
    15in (38cm)   **$350-$400**
Royal "Spirit of America:"
    15in (38cm) with original box and
    outfits   **$300-$350**
Santa Claus: 19in (48cm)   **$350-$400**
Sizzy: 1948. H. of P.:
    14in (36cm)   **$250-$300**
Sterling Doll Co. Sports Dolls:
    29in (74cm) all original   **$300-$350**
Trudy: 1946. Three faces:
    14in (36cm), all original   **$225-$250**

**Not enough price samples to compute a reliable range.

15in (38cm) unmarked nurse. *H & J Foulke, Inc.*

Right: 14in (36cm) Hedwig/DiAngeli *Suzanne*, all original. *H & J Foulke, Inc.*

Above: 14in (36cm) *Sizzy* and 15in (38cm) *Puzzy*, all original. *Anya Lowe Collection.*

Below: 14in (36cm) *Trudy*, all original. *H & J Foulke, Inc.*

Black Composition Dolls: Ca. 1930. Original or appropriate clothes; some have three yarn tufts of hair on either side and one on top of the head; all in good condition.

"Topsy" Baby:	
10-12in (25-31cm)	**$140-$165**
16in (41cm)	**$250-$275**
Toddler: 15-16in (38-41cm)	**$300-$350**
Girl: 17in (43cm)	**$350-$400**
1910 character:	
13½in (34cm)	**$300-$350**
Patsy-type:	
13-14in (33-36cm)	**$250-$300**
Tony Sarg Mammy with Baby:	
17in (43cm)	**$1,000-$1,100**
Alexander's Ragtime Kids:	
13in (33cm)	**$950 pair**

Ming Ming Baby: 1930. Quan-Quan Co., Los Angeles and San Francisco, California. Ca. 1930. All-composition baby; original Oriental costume of colorful taffeta with braid trim; feet painted black or white for shoes.

10-12in (25-31cm)	**$200-$225**

Composition (German)

All-Composition Child Doll: Socket head with good wig, sleep (sometimes flirty) eyes, open mouth with teeth; jointed composition body; appropriate clothes; all in good condition; of excellent quality.

12-14in (31-36cm)	**$175-$200**
18-20in (46-51cm)	**$300-$325**
22in (56cm)	**$350-$400**

Character face:

18-20in (46-51cm)	**$425-$525**

Double-Face Googly:

14in (36cm)	**$425-$475**

Black Composition Doll: All-composition; molded hair or wig, glass eyes (sometimes flirty); appropriate clothes; all in good condition.

11in (28cm)	**$300-$350**
16-18in (41-46cm)	**$600-$650**

Dora Petzoldt Child: 1919 on. Molded composition (sometimes cloth) head, closed mouth, pensive character face, painted eyes, mohair wig; cloth body, sometimes with long arms and legs; original clothing; all in very good condition.

19-22in (48-56cm)	**$850-$950**
Moderate wear, re-dressed	**$400-$450**

Character Baby: Composition head with good wig, sleep eyes, open mouth with teeth; bent-limb composition baby body or hard-stuffed cloth body; appropriate clothes; all in good condition; of excellent quality.

All-composition baby:

16-18in (41-46cm)	**$275-$325**

Cloth body:

18-20in (46-51cm)	**$250-$300**

All-composition toddler:

16-18in (41-46cm)	**$375-$425**

FACTS
Various German firms such as König & Wernicke, Kämmer & Reinhardt and others.
Ca. 1920s on.

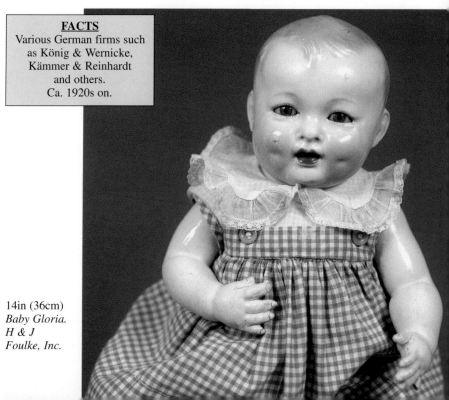

14in (36cm)
Baby Gloria.
H & J
Foulke, Inc.

Composition
(Japanese)

Cosmopolitan

FACTS
Unidentified Japanese Companies,
1920-1940.
Mark: "Japan" incised or
stamped on back torso.

FACTS
Cosmopolitan Doll & Toy Corp.,
Jackson Heights, NY, U.S.A.

Japanese Composition Doll: All-composition with molded hair, painted features; original rayon panties with "Japan" stamp or naked; all in excellent condition.

Dionne Quintuplets:

Baby: 7in (18cm)	**$165-$185**
Baby: 9in (23cm)	**$250-$300***
Toddler: 7½in (19cm)	**$165-$185**
9in (23cm)	**$250-$300**

Choir Boy: With book molded in hands, 10in (25cm) **$135-$150**

Toddler:

8in (20cm), all original **$125-$135**

Shirley Temple: See page 302.

Ginger: 1954 on. All-hard plastic walker; sleep eyes; original clothes; excellent condition with good color and perfect hair.

Unmarked, 8in (20cm)	**$150-$175**
Mint-in-box	**$225**
Roundup, Mouseketeer or **Davy Crockett**	**$225-$250**
Disneyland Costumes	**$300-$350**
Girl Scout or **Brownie**	**$175-$225**
Boxed outfits	**$40-$60**
Vinyl head, all original	**$50-$60**

**Not enough price samples to compute a reliable range.

Cosmopolitan *Ginger*
and *Miss Ginger. Kathy &
Terri's Dolls.*

Miss Ginger: 1957 on. Vinyl head; hard plastic body with adult figure, high-heeled feet; original clothes; excellent condition.
Mark: "GINGER" on head.

10½in (27cm)	**$190-$210**
Dresses	**$20-$30**
Boxed outfits	**$75-$80**

Little Miss Ginger: 1958 on. Vinyl head; rigid vinyl body, adult figure with high-heeled feet; original clothes; excellent condition; eyes not askew.
Mark: "GINGER" on head.

8in (20cm)	**$75-$85**
Shoes	**$20**
Dresses	**$20-$30**
Boxed outfits	**$65-$75**

Deluxe Reading

Bride Dolls: 1958. All-vinyl, fashion doll; complete original bride clothes.

24-29in (61-74cm)	**$65-$75**

Candy: 1962. All-vinyl fashion doll, three extra costumes, hats and accessories; boxed.

20in (51cm)	**$150-$200**

Penny Brite: 1963. All-vinyl child doll, with accessories and wardrobe sold separately.

8in (20cm) original dress	**$25-$30**
Boxed doll	**$40-$45**
Boxed outfit	**$20-$40**
Beauty Salon	**$45**
Kitchen Set	**$45**

Dawn: 1969 on. Topper. All-vinyl play doll with accessories, wardrobe and friends.

6in (15cm)	**$30-$40**
Boxed doll	**$65-$75**
Boxed or packaged outfit	**$40-$60**
Angie: Boxed	**$95**
Kip Majorette:	**$65-$75**
Gary:	**$55-$65**

Suzy Homemaker: 1964. Vinyl and hard plastic, jointed knees:

21in (53cm)	**$55-$65**

Cosmopolitan *Little Miss Ginger.* *Rosemary Kanizer.*

Right: 8in (20cm) Deluxe Reading *Penny Brite*, all original. *H & J Foulke, Inc.*

EFFanBEE

FACTS
EFFanBEE Doll Co.,
New York, NY, U.S.A. 1912-on.
Marks: Various, but nearly always
marked "EFFanBEE" on torso or head,
sometimes with doll's name.
Wore a metal heart-shaped bracelet;
later a gold paper heart label.

Effanbee   EFFANBEE DURABLE DOLLS

Original Metal Heart Necklace or Bracelet with chain	**$45-$50**
Metal Pinback Button	**$65-$75**

COMPOSITION DOLLS

Early Characters: Composition character face, molded painted hair; cloth stuffed body; appropriate clothes; in good condition. Some marked "Deco." 12-16in (30-41cm).

Baby Grumpy: 1912. Molds 172, 174 or 176	**$375-$425**
Miss Coquette, Naughty Marietta: 1912.	**$400-$425**
Pouting Bess: 1915. 162 or 166	**$350-$375**
Billy Boy: 1915.	**$350-$375**
Whistling Jim: 1916.	**$350-$375**
Harmonica Joe: 1924.	**$400-$450**
Katie Kroose: 1918.	**$400-$450**
Buds: 1915-1918.	
7in (18cm)	**$175-$195**
Black	**$200-$225**
Aunt Dinah: 1915. 16in (41cm)	**$600**
Johnny Tu-Face: 1912.	**$400-$450**
Betty Bounce: 1913.	**$350-$400**
Baby Huggins: 1915.	**$300**
Oriental Baby: 1914.	**$350**

12in (31cm) *Baby* Grumpy, all original. *H & J Foulke, Inc.*

19in (48cm) *Mary Ann. H & J Foulke, Inc.*

Shoulder Head Dolls: Composition shoulder head; cloth torso, composition arms and legs; original clothes; all in good condition.

Baby Grumpy: 1925-1939.
12in (31cm) white	**$300-$325**
Black	**$375-$400**

Pennsylvania Dutch Dolls: 1936-1940. All original and excellent **$225**

Baby Dainty: 1912-1922.
15in (38cm)	**$250-$275**

Patsy: 1925.
15in (38cm)	**$350-$400**

Rosemary, 1925; **Marilee,** 1924; and other name dolls:
14in (36cm)	**$275-$300**
17in (43cm)	**$350-$400**
25in (64cm)	**$450-$550**
30in (76cm)	**$650-$750**

Mary Ann: 1928.
19-20in (48-51cm)	**$375-$425**
All-composition	**$450-$500**

Mary Lee: 1928.
16-17in (41-43cm)	**$325-$375**
All-composition	**$375-$425**

Mae Starr, Phonograph doll: 1928.
30in (76cm)	**$650-$750**

Babies: Composition head, light crazing acceptable; perfect hair and good coloring; cloth body; original clothes; all in good condition.

Bubbles: 1924.

Mark: 19 © 24   EFFANBEE
EFFANBEE DOLLS WALK-TALK SLEEP MADE IN USA   BUBBLES COPYR 1924 MADE IN U.S.A.

16-18in (41-46cm)	**$400-$450**
20-22in (51-56cm)	**$500-$550**
25-26in (63-66cm)	**$650-$750**
29in (51cm) re-dressed	**$325-$350**
Baby Evelyn: 18in (46cm)	**$250-$275**

Lovums: 1928.

Mark: EFFANBEE
LOVUMS ©
PAT NO. 1,283,558

16-18in (41-46cm)	**$350-$400**
22-24in (56-61cm)	**$500-$550**
28in (71cm)	**$650-$700**

14in (36cm) shoulder head Patsy. H & J Foulke, Inc.

Mickey, Baby Bright Eyes, Tommy Tucker, Katie: 1939-1949.

16-18in (41-46cm)	**$425-$450**
22-24in (56-61cm)	**$500-$600**
Twins in Boxed Set:	
14in (36cm)	**$900-$1,000**

Sweetie Pie: 1942.

16-18in (41-46cm)	**$375-$425**
22-24in (56-61cm)	**$475-$525**
Boxed, with layette:	
23in (58cm)	**$750**

Baby Effanbee: 1925.

12in (31cm)	**$160-$180**

Lambkin: 1930s.

16in (41cm)	**$450-$475**
Boxed, with pillow	**$650-$700**

Sugar Baby: 1936. Caracul wig.

16-18in (41-46cm)	**$375-$425**

Babyette: 1943. Eyes closed, boxed with pillow, 13in (33cm)　**$550-$600**

Pat-O-Pat: 1925. Clap hands.

13in (33cm)	**$150-$165**

Patsy Family: 1928-on. All-composition; original or appropriate old clothes; may have some light crazing.

Marks:

Bracelet

EFFANBEE PATSY JR. DOLL

EFFANBEE PATSY DOLL

EFFANBEE PATSY BABY KIN

Wee Patsy: 6in (15cm)	**$475-$500**
Boxed	**$550-$600**
Boxed with extra outfits	**$750-$850**
Sewing set, boxed	**$650**
Storybook Doll, all original	**$600**
Black maid	**$1,000**
Baby Tinyette: 7in (18cm)	**$350-$375**
Quintuplets: set of five, boxed, all original	**$2,500**

Tinyette Toddler:	
8in (20cm)	**$350-$375**
Boxed trousseau set	**$1,200**
Patsy Babyette:	
9in (23cm)	**$350-$375**
Patsyette:	
9in (23cm)	**$350-$375**
Boxed wardrobe set	**$750**
Brown	**$650**
Hawaiian	**$650**
George and Martha Washington	
	$650 pair

18in (46cm) *Mickey. Rosemary Kanizer.*

Patsy Baby:	
11in (28cm)	**$350-$400**
Brown	**$650-$750**
In three-tiered trunk with accessories	
	$1,300
Patsy Jr., Patsy Kins, Patricia Kin:	
11in (28cm)	**$425-$475**
Brown	**$800-$900**
Movie **Anne Shirley:** Red wig:	
	$600-$700
Patsy:	
14in (36cm)	**$550-$650**
1946, unmarked	**$400-$450**
Boxed	**$550**
Brother: boxed	**$950**
Patricia:	
15in (38cm)	**$475-$525**
Movie **Anne Shirley:** Red wig	**$700**
Patsy Joan:	
16in (41cm)	**$475-$525**
Boxed, fur coat and hat	**$850**
1946 (different mold)	**$425-$475**
Brown	**$675**
Patsy Ann:	
19in (48cm)	**$525-$575**
Brown	**$1,250**
Boxed, early wig, fur coat and hat	
	$1,250

14in (36cm) *Patsy* with wig, all original.
H & J Foulke, Inc.

6in (15cm) *Wee Patsy,*
all original. *H & J
Foulke, Inc.*

9in (23cm) *Patsyette*
wardrobe set, all
original. *H & J
Foulke, Inc.*

Patsy Lou: 22in (56cm)   **$550-$600**
Patsy Ruth: 26in (66cm)
                  $1,500-$1,600
Patsy Mae: 30in (76cm) **$1,500-$1,600**

Skippy: 1929. 14in (36cm):
Soldier, Sailor	**$425-$475**
Boy's Suit	**$650**
West Point Cadet, at auction	**$1,700**
Cowboy	**$1,000**
Aviator	**$2,100**
Fireman	**$2,100**
Re-dressed	**$350**
Brown	**$850**

W.C. Fields: 1930. Composition head, hands and feet; cloth body; original clothes.
    19in (48cm) at auction   **$1,425**

Dy-Dee Baby: 1933-on.
Mark:

> **"EFF-AN-BEE**
> **DY-DEE BABY**
> **US PAT.-1-857-485**
> **ENGLAND-880-060**
> **FRANCE-723-980**
> **GERMANY-585-647**
> **OTHER PAT PENDING"**

Hard rubber head with applied rubber ears, soft rubber body; appropriate old clothes; good condition.
9in (23cm)	**$275-$300**
11in (28cm)	**$200-$225**
13in (33cm)	**$200-$225**
15in (38cm)	**$250-$275**
20in (51cm)	**$375-$400**
24in (61cm)	**$450**

With box and layette:
13in (33cm)	**$525**
15in (38cm)	**$575**

Carded five-piece nursery set with Dy-Dee booklet   **$150**
Dy-Dee pajamas   **$32**
Bottle, bubble pipe   **$25**
Book: **Dy-Dee Dolls Days**   **$95**

Hard plastic head with applied ears, soft rubber body; appropriate old clothes; good condition.
11in (28cm)	**$150-$175**
15in (38cm)	**$225-$250**
20-21in (51-53cm)	**$325-$350**

16in (41cm) *Patsy Joan. H & J Foulke, Inc.*

All-Composition Children: 1933-on. Original clothes; all in very good condition; nice coloring and perfect hair.
Anne Shirley, 1935-1940; **Little Lady,** 1940-1949.
14-15in (36-38cm)	**$225-$250**
17-18in (43-46cm)	**$250-$275**
21in (53cm)	**$350-$400**
27in (69cm)	**$500-$550**

    Boxed, in fancy dress with parasol, at auction   **$715**
WAAC outfit: 14in (36cm)   **$650**
Little Eva: 15in (38cm)   **$1,400**
Honey: 1949.
    21in (53cm)   **$450-$500**

American Children: 1936-1939. Dewees Cochran.
Closed mouth, 19-21in (48-53cm) marked "American Children" head on "Anne Shirley" body:
    Peggy Lou and others: Painted eyes
                  $2,200

14in (36cm) *Skippy. H & J Foulke, Inc.*

21in (53cm) *Dy-Dee Baby. H & J Foulke, Inc.*

17in (43cm) *Little Lady. H & J Foulke, Inc.*

Gloria Ann and others: Sleep eyes
$2,000
17in (43cm) girl, sleep eyes **$1,800**
17in (43cm) boy, unmarked, painted
eyes **$1,800****
Open mouth, unmarked:
Barbara Joan:
15in (38cm) **$700-$750**
Ice Queen (skater) **$750**
Barbara Ann: 17in (43cm)
$750-$800
Barbara Lou: 21in (53cm)
$900-$950

Suzette: 1939. Painted eyes,
11½in(29cm) **$325-$350**
Suzanne: 1940. 14in (36cm) **$325-$350**
Portrait Dolls: 1940. Ballerina, Bo-
Peep, Gibson Girl, bride, groom, dancing couple, colonial.
11in (28cm) **$275-$300**
Candy Kid: 1946. Toddler, molded
hair.
12in (31cm) **$350-$400**
Boxed **$600**
Betty Brite: 1933, caracul wig.
6½in (42cm) ⌐ **$325-$375**

**Not enough price samples to compute a
reliable range.

Betty Bounce: 1933. "Lovums" head,
caracul wig, 19in (48cm) **$375-$425**
Butin-Nose, 1939:
9in (23cm) **$275-$300**
Oriental **$500**
Brother and Sister: 1943. Yarn hair,
16in (41cm) and 12in (31cm)
$250-$300 each

Charlie McCarthy: 1937. Strings at
back of head to operate mouth; original
clothes; all in very good condition.
17-20in (43-51cm) **$650-$750**
Mint-in-box with button **$850-$950**

Historical Dolls: 1939. All-composition. Three each of 30 dolls portraying
the history of American fashion, 1492-
1939. "American Children" heads with
elaborate human hair wigs and painted
eyes; elaborate original costumes using
velvets, satins, silks and brocades; all in
excellent condition.

Mark: On head:
"EFFaNBEE AMERICAN
CHILDREN"
21in (53cm) **$1,500-$1,800**
Historical Doll Replicas: 1939.
14in (36cm) **$500-$600**
Boxed **$700-$750**

17in (43cm) *American Child* boy, all
original. *H & J Foulke, Inc.*

17in 43cm) *American Child,* all original.
Rhoda Shoemaker Collection.

15in (38cm) *American Child*, so-called "Ice Queen." *H & J Foulke, Inc.*

12in (31cm) *Candy Kid*, boxed and all original. *H & J Foulke, Inc.*

14in (36cm) *Historical Replica*, all original. *H & J Foulke, Inc.*

14in (36cm) *Historical Replica*, all original. *H & J Foulke, Inc.*

HARD PLASTIC DOLLS

Howdy Doody: 1949-1950. Hard plastic or composition head and hands; molded hair, sleep eyes; cloth body; original clothes; all in excellent condition.

19-23in (48-58cm)	**$300-$400**
Mint-in-box	**$525-$575**

Noma, the Electronic Doll: 1950. Battery operated talking mechanism.

28in (71cm)	**$325-$375**
Boxed	**$500**

21in (53cm) composition *Honey,* all original. *H & J Foulke, Inc.*

Honey: 1949-1955. All-hard plastic; original clothes; all in excellent condition. Later dolls have walking mechanism.

Mark: "EFFANBEE"

14in (36cm)	**$250-$275**
18in (46cm)	**$325-$350**
24in (61cm)	**$400**
In Schiaparelli outfits: 18in (46cm)	
	$500
Prince Charming:	**$500-$600**
Cinderella:	**$500-$600**
Alice:	**$400-$450**
Tintair Honey:	
14in (36cm)	**$400**
In original box with accessories	
	$600-$650
18in (46cm)	**$550**

VINYL DOLLS: All original and excellent condition.
Mickey: 1956.
  10-11in (25-28cm)   **$90-$100**
Champagne Lady: 1959.
  19in (48cm)   **$250-$300**
Fluffy*: 1957 on.
  8in (20cm)   **$35-$40**
  11in (28cm)   **$40-$50**
  Boxed Outfits   **$20-$25**
Patsy Ann: 1960 on.
  15in (38cm)   **$100-$125**
Suzette*: 1962. 15in (38cm) **$75-$100**
Melodie: 1953-1956. Battery operated singing talking doll, all original.
  27in (69cm)   **$325-$375**
Mary Jane: 1959 on.
  32in (81cm)   **$225-$275**
  Nurse   **$275-$325**
Little Lady: 1958. 19in (48cm)   **$200**
Fashion Lady: Ca. 1958.
  19in (48cm)   **$250**
Most Happy Family: 1958. (Mother, Sister, Brother, Baby), boxed.
  8-21in (20-53cm)   **$250-$300**
Alyssa: Ca. 1960. 23in (58cm)   **$225**
Bud: Ca. 1960.
  24in (61cm)   **$200-$225**
Happy Boy: 1961.
  10½in (27cm)   **$50-$60**
Half Pint: 1966 on.
  11in (28cm) toddler   **$25-$35**
Boudoir Lady: 1961.
  30in (76cm) boxed   **$275**
Dy-Dee Darlin': 1971.
  18in (46cm)   **$75-$100**
Baby Lisa: 1980, designed by Astry Campbell, in basket with accessories,
  11in (28cm)   **$60**
Disney Dolls: 1977. 14in (36cm) **$175**
  Alice in Wonderland
  Cinderella
  Snow White
  Sleeping Beauty
  Cinderella & Prince Charming
    Set: 1985. 12in (31cm)   **$65**
Hagara, Jan: 1984. 15in (38cm):
  Christina with teddy   **$85**
  Laurel   **$65**
Hibel, Edna: 1984.
  Flower Girl of Brittany   **$45**
  Contessa Isabella   **$45**

Suzie Sunshine: 1961-1979. Designed by Eugenia Dukas:
  18in (46cm) boxed   **$50-$60**
Sugar Pie: 1962-1964.
  18in (46cm) boxed   **$65-$70**

*For Girl Scouts, see page 269.

10in (25cm) *Mickey Boy Scout. H & J Foulke, Inc.*

Effanbee Club Limited Edition Dolls:

1975 Precious Baby	**$150-$175**
1976 Patsy	**$150-$175**
1977 Dewees Cochran	**$60-$70**
1978 Crowning Glory	**$35-$40**
1979 Skippy	**$150-$175**
1980 Susan B. Anthony	**$35-$40**
1981 Girl with Watering Can (Renoir)	**$65-$75**
1982 Princess Diana	**$100-$125**
1983 Sherlock Holmes	**$50-$55**
1984 Bubbles	**$40-$45**
1985 Red Boy	**$35-$40**
1986 China Head	**$20-$25**

Legend Series, Mint-in-box:

W.C. Fields: 1980.	**$125**
John Wayne: (cowboy), 1981.	**$150**
John Wayne: (cavalry), 1982.	**$150**
Mae West: 1982.	**$125**
Groucho Marx: 1983.	**$75**
Judy Garland: 1984.	**$95**
Lucille Ball: 1985.	**$100**
Liberace: 1986.	**$250**
James Gagney: 1987.	**$45**
Humphrey Bogart: 1988.	**$45**
George Burns: 1996.	**$45**
Gracie Allen: 1996.	**$45**
Carol Channing: 1998.	**$40**

Presidents, Mint-in-box:

Abraham Lincoln: 1983.	**$50**
George Washington: 1983.	**$50**
Teddy Roosevelt: 1984.	**$65**
Franklin D. Roosevelt: 1985.	**$45**
Andrew Jackson: 1989.	**$45**

Personalities: Mint-in-box.

Mark Twain: 1984.	**$60**
Louis Armstrong: 1984-1985.	**$75**
Sir Winston Churchill: 1984.	**$50**
Eleanor Roosevelt: 1985.	**$45**
Babe Ruth: 1985.	**$125**

Pride of the South: 1981-1983.
13in (33cm) mint-in-box   **$35**
Grande Dames: 1976-1983.
15in (38cm) mint-in-box   **$35-$40**
Gigi: 1979-1980.
11in (28cm) mint-in-box   **$25**
International & Storybook: 1976 on.
11in (28cm) mint-in-box   **$10-$20**

Wizard of Oz: 1994. Six-doll set	**$125**
Mary Poppins: 1985.	**$25-$30**
Heidi: 1984.	**$25-$30**
Peter Pan: 1994. Three-doll set	**$50**

17in (43cm) *Lady in Orange*, all original. *Emma Vann.*

Freundlich

General Douglas MacArthur: Ca. 1942. All-composition portrait doll; molded hat, original khaki uniform; all in good condition.
Mark: Cardboard tag:
   "General MacArthur"
   18in (46cm)   **$400-$450**

Military Dolls: Ca. 1942. All-composition with molded hats, original clothes; **Soldier, Sailor, WAAC** and **WAVE;** all in good condition.
   15in (38cm)   **$225-$275**

Baby Sandy: 1939-1942. All-composition; appropriate clothes; all in good condition.
   8in (20cm)   **$200-$225**
   12in (31cm)   **$300-$350**
   14-15in (36-38cm)   **$450-$500**
   20in (51cm) boxed   **$850**
   Baby Sandy Doll Button, at auction
                                  $90

Other Composition Dolls:
Orphan Annie & Sandy: 1936.
   12in (30cm) pair with tags **$600-$650**
Three Little Pigs and Wolf:
   Boxed set   **$800-$1,000**

| **FACTS** |
| Freundlich Novelty Corp., |
| New York, NY, U.S.A. |
| 1923-on. |

Red Ridinghood, Wolf & Grandmother Set: 1934. All original,
   9in (23cm)   **$800-$900**
Dionne Quints and Nurse Set:
   All original   **$650-$750**
Dummy Dolls: 1938. Clown, Dan, Davy Crockett and others.
   14-18in (36-46cm)   **$100-$150**
Goo Goo Eva and others: 1937.
   20in (51cm)   **$90-$110**
Goo Goo Topsy: 1937. Black,
   20in (51cm)   **$110-$135**
Pig Baby: 9in (23cm)   **$400**
Animal Head Dolls: Cat, Rabbit, Pig or Wolf.
   10-11in (25-28cm), naked **$300-$400**

15in (38cm) *WAVE,* all original. *H & J Foulke, Inc.*

18in (46cm) *General MacArthur,* all original. *H & J Foulke, Inc.*

G.I. Joe®

Marked G.I. Joe: Molded and painted hair and features, scar* on right cheek; fully-jointed body; complete original outfit; all in perfect condition. Dolls less than perfect sell for considerably less.

*All **G.I. Joe** dolls have a scar on the right cheek except **Foreign** dolls and the **Nurse.**

FACTS
Hasbro (Hassenfeld Brothers, Inc.) Pawtucket, RI, U.S.A. 1964-1979. Hard plastic and vinyl. 12in (31cm) fully-jointed.
Mark: "G.I. Joe®." After 1967, added: "Copyright 1964
Pat. No. 3,277,602
By Hasbro
Patent Pending
Made in U.S.A."

Action Soldier: All original, boxed
$285-$300
Action Sailor: (painted hair), boxed
$400-$450
Action Marine: Boxed   **$350**
Action Pilot: Boxed   **$500-$550**
Action Soldier Black: (painted hair), boxed   **$1,500**

Naked Dolls:
  Action Soldier: (painted hair)   **$75**
  Adventure Team: (flocked hair**)
    $60

  Adventure Team: (flocked hair and beard**)   **$60**
  Black Action Soldier: (painted hair)

    $450
Action Soldiers of the World (painted hair, no scars):
German Soldier:
  Boxed, large box   **$1,200**
  Boxed, small box   **$600**
  Dressed doll only, no accessories
    $225-$250
Russian Infantry Man:
  Boxed, large box   **$1,200**
  Boxed, small box   **$600**
  Dressed doll only, no accessories
    $225-$250
British Commando:
  Boxed, large box   **$1,250**
  Boxed, small box   **$500**
  Dressed doll only, no accessories
    $200-$225
French Resistance Fighter:
  Boxed, large box   **$900**
  Boxed, small box   **$500**
  Dressed doll only, no accessories
    $200-$225
Australian Jungle Fighter:
  Boxed, large box   **$750**
  Boxed, small box   **$400**
  Dressed doll only, no accessories
    $150-$175

**Hair must be in excellent condition.

G.I. Joe Action Marine, boxed. *McMasters Harris Premier Doll Auctions.*

Japanese Imperial Soldier (unique model used only for this type):

Boxed, large box	**$1,300**
Boxed, small box	**$800**
Dressed doll only, no accessories	**$250-$275**

Talking Action Soldier: Boxed   **$400**
Talking Action Sailor: Boxed   **$600**
Talking Action Marine: Boxed   **$475**
Talking Action Pilot: Boxed   **$800**

Nurse Action Girl:

Boxed	**$3,000**
Dressed doll only	**$1,500**
Naked doll	**$400**

Adventurer: (lifelike hair), Black, boxed   **$300**
Man of Action: (lifelike hair), boxed   **$250**
Man of Action with Kung-Fu Grip: (lifelike hair), boxed   **$225**
Talking Man of Action: (lifelike hair), boxed   **$225-$250**
Land Adventurer: (lifelike hair and beard), boxed   **$175-$190**
Air Adventurer: (lifelike hair and beard), boxed   **$240-$265**
Sea Adventurer: (lifelike hair and beard), boxed   **$225-$250**
Talking Astronaut, (lifelike hair):

Boxed	**$400-$425**
Dressed doll	**$225-$250**

Accessories:

Footlocker: green	**$40**
Space Capsule: boxed	**$350**
Five Star Jeep: boxed	**$500-$550**
Desert Patrol Jeep: boxed	**$1,900**
Motorcycle: boxed	**$250**

Outfits in unopened packages:

#7532 Green Beret Special Forces	**$600**
#7521 Military Police (brown)	**$400**
#7521 Military Police (aqua)	**$1,350**
#7531 Ski Patrol	**$250**
#7620 Deep Sea Diver	**$300**
#7710 Dress Parade Set	**$225**
#7537 West Point Cadet	**$1,500**
#7624 Annapolis Cadet	**$1,400**
#7822 Air Cadet	**$1,400**
#7612 Shore Patrol	**$300**
#7807 Scramble Set	**$275**
#7823 Fighter Pilot	**$1,000**

Space Capsule. *McMasters Harris Premier Doll Auctions.*

Eagle Eye Land Commander. *McMasters Harris Premier Doll Auctions.*

Ginny-Type Dolls*

Prices are for dolls in excellent overall condition with perfect hair, pretty coloring and original outfits. All dolls are hard plastic and about 7-8in (18-20cm) tall. Ca. 1950-1960.

A & H Doll Mfg. Corp.:
Gigi	$45-$50
Boxed	$100-$125
Outfits	$10-$15
Boxed outfits	$25-$30
Julie	$35-$40

Doll Bodies, Inc.:
Mary Lu	$40-$50

Fortune Doll Co.:
Pam	$65-$75
Outfits	$10-$15
Boxed Outfits	$25-$30
Pam Ballerina: (pointed toes)	
	$85-$90
Ninette	$40-$50

Hollywood Doll Mfg. Co.:
Girl	$40-$45

Miss Rosebud: England $30-$35

Stashin Doll Co.:
Andrea: Molded white strap shoes	
	$50-$60

Unidentified:
Black	$100-$125

Virga (Beehler Arts): Molded white strap shoes.
Lolly-Pop: Colored hair	$90-$100
Boxed	$150-$175
Lucy	$75-$80
Play-Mates	$75-$80
Boxed	$150-$175
Schiaparelli (GoGo)	$150-$175
Twinkle Ballerina: Boxed	
	$175-$200

*See separate entries for Cosmopolitan Ginger, Vogue Ginny, Nancy Ann Storybook Muffie and Alexander Wendy.

8in (20cm) *Miss Rosebud*, all original, in costume of Rattvik, Sweden. *H & J Foulke, Inc.*

8in (20cm) *Ginny*-type, all original. *Connie Blain Collection.*

Girl Scout

Prices are for dolls in excellent overall condition with perfect hair and original clothes, including hat, scarf, belt, shoes and socks.

Georgene Novelties, Inc.: 1930s and 1940s. All cloth.
Girl Scouts and Brownies:
Flat face: 15in (38cm)	**$350-$400**
Molded cloth face:	
13in (33cm)	**$225-$250**
Molded plastic face:	
13in (33cm)	**$100**

Terri Lee Sales Corp.: Ca. 1950. Hard plastic.
Girl Scouts and Brownies:
Terri Lee: 16in (41cm)	**$400**
Dress and hat only	**$125-$135**
Tiny Terri Lee:	
10in (25cm)	**$175-$200**
Ginger: 8in (20cm)	**$175-$200**
Outfit only	**$75-$85**

Vogue Dolls, Inc.: Ca. 1956. Hard plastic.
Girl Scouts and Brownies:
Ginny: Painted eyelash walker,	
8in (20cm)	**$275-$325**
Outfit only	**$100-$125**
80th Anniversary, 8in (20cm):	
Boxed	**$75-$100**
Black, boxed	**$125**

Uneeda Doll Co.: Ca. 1960. Vinyl head/hard plastic body, "U" on head.
Janie: 8in (20cm)	**$125-$150**
Carry Case	**$100**

Effanbee Doll Co.: Ca. 1960 through 1970s. Vinyl.
Patsy Ann: 15in (38cm):	
Girl Scout	**$350-$400**
Brownie	**$500**
Blue Bird, Camp Fire	**$550****
Suzette: 15in (38cm):	
Girl Scout	**$500 up**
Brownie	**$500 up**
Blue Bird, Camp Fire	**$550****
Fluffy: 8in (20cm):	
Girl Scout, Brownie	**$100-$125**

Boxed	**$125-$150**
Camp Fire, Blue Bird	**$200-$225**
Camp outfit or bathing suit sold	
separately	**$50-$75**
Punkin: 11in (28cm):	
Girl Scout, Brownie	**$125-$135**
Camp Fire, Blue Bird	**$175-$200**

Jesco, Inc.: Ca. 1985. Vinyl.
Katie: 9in (23cm)	**$75-$85**

Madame Alexander: 1992. Hard plastic. 8in (20cm)
(blonde harder to find)	**$100-$125**

Pleasant Co.: 1999.
American Girl of Today Girl Scout	
	$100-$125
Outfit only	**$50-$60**
Brownie outfit only	**$50-$60**

Avon:
Tender Memories: Bisque,	
14in (36cm) boxed	**$25**

**Not enough price samples to compute a reliable range.

13in (33cm) Georgene Novelties *Brownie*, all original. *Kathy & Terris's Dolls.*

Godey's Little Lady Dolls

Ruth Gibbs Doll: Pink or white china head; cloth body with china limbs and painted slippers; original clothes; excellent condition.

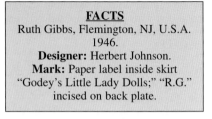

FACTS
Ruth Gibbs, Flemington, NJ, U.S.A. 1946.
Designer: Herbert Johnson.
Mark: Paper label inside skirt "Godey's Little Lady Dolls;" "R.G." incised on back plate.

7in (18cm)	**$90-$110**
Boxed	**$150-$165**
Little Women: set of five	**$850**
Trousseau: boxed set (four outfits)	**$575**
Fairy Tale: boxed set	**$575**
Williamsburg:	
boxed set (two outfits)	**$500**
Black, boxed	**$300-$350****
10in (25cm) skin wig	**$295**
Boxed	**$395**

12in (31cm)	**$145-$160**
Boxed	**$215-$235**

**Not enough price samples to compute a reliable range.

10in (25cm) Ruth Gibbs 1951 *The Good Fairy Queen,* with skin wig, all original and boxed. *H & J Foulke, Inc.*

Hallmark

Tagged Hallmark Cloth Doll: Printed on cloth with an article of separate clothing, usually a coat or skirt; stitch-jointed shoulders, hips and knees; shaped shoes and hats; all original and excellent.

6½-7½in (17-19cm)

1976 Bicentennial Commemorative Series:

George Washington, Martha Washington, Betsy Ross, Benjamin Franklin: Boxed **$15-$20 each**

1979 Series I:

Amelia Earhart, Annie Oakley, G. W. Carver, Chief Joseph, Babe Ruth, Susan B. Anthony:
Boxed **$12 each**

FACTS
Hallmark Cards, Inc., Kansas City, MO. 1976-1979.
Mark: Cloth label on each doll.

Holiday Dolls:

Little Drummer Boy, Santa Claus, Winifred Witch, Indian Maiden:
Boxed **$12 each**

1979 Series II:

Davy Crockett, Molly Pitcher, Mark Twain, P. T. Barnum, Clara Barton:
(never had boxes) **$5-$6 each**

Juliette Low: (founder of the Girl Scouts) **$65-$75**

Hallmark *George Washington* with original box. *H & J Foulke, Inc.*

Hard Plastic Dolls

Marked "Made in U.S.A." or with various letters: Ca. 1950s. All-hard plastic; sleep eyes, perfect wig; original clothes; all in excellent condition with very good coloring.

14in (36cm)	**$240-$265**
18in (46cm)	**$300-$350**
24in (61cm)	**$350-$400**

Miscellaneous Specific Dolls: All original clothes including underwear, shoes and socks; excellent condition with lovely complexion and perfect hair; unmarked except as indicated.

Answer Doll: 1951. Block Doll Corp., toddler with yes/no button.

10in (25cm)	**$75-$85**
Boy	**$140-$155**

Baby Walker: 1950s. Block Doll Corp., toddler, 10in (25cm) **$65**

Artisan Doll Co.: 1951-1955.

Raving Beauty: 1951. Open mouth, tag on some clothing: "Original Michelle//California;" separate clothing was available.

19-20in (48-51cm)	**$275-$325**

Miss Gadabout: 1953. Open mouth walker, marked with "Heady-Turny" label.

20in (51cm)	**$200-$225**

Duchess Doll Corp.: 1950s. Slender storybook and fashion dolls in various costumes, marked on back.

7-8in (18-20cm)	**$10-$12**
Boxed	**$15-$20**
Walt Disney's Peter Pan and Tinker Bell	**$20-$25 each**
Boxed	**$95-$100**

Eugenia Doll Co.:

Juliette: 1953. 21in (53cm) **$450**

Personality Pla-Mate: 1949.

16-18in (41-46cm)	**$350-$400**

Gigi Perreau: 1952. Goldberger Doll Mfg. Co.; portrait doll of the movie star with smiling mouth and teeth, Dynel hair, vinyl head, excellent face color; hard plastic body.

20in (51cm)	**$600 up****

Haleoke: 1950s. Roberta Doll Co., 18in (46cm), with accessories and additional clothing **$450**

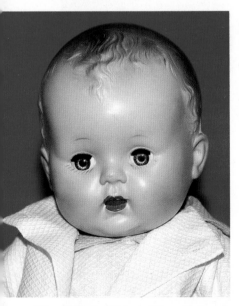

15in (38cm) USA toddler. *Kathy & Terri's Dolls.*

18in (46cm) unmarked bride, all original. *Kathy & Terri's Dolls.*

Heddi Stroller: 1952. Belle Doll & Toy Corp., walker, Saran braids,
   20in (51cm)   **$165-$195**

Hollywood Doll Mfg. Co.: 1947 on. Storybook and fashion dolls in various costumes; marked on back:
   4½-5½in (12-14cm), boxed **$15-$20**
   Boxed   **$30-$40**
   Ballerina: 5in (12cm) boxed **$65-$75**
   Rock-a-Bye Baby: Boxed **$50-$60**

LuAnn Simms: 1953. Roberta, Horsman & Valentine; **Mark:** "Made in U.S.A." or "180," walker.
   16in (41cm)   **$275-$325**

Marion: 1949. Monica Studios, rooted hair, sleep eyes, 18in (46cm) **$400****

Mary Jane: 1955. G.H.&E. Freydberg, Inc., **Terri Lee**-type doll:
   17in (43cm)   **$275-$300**

Rita: 1952. Paris Doll Co., walker.
   27-29in (69-74cm)   **$250**

Roxanne, Beat the Clock:
   16in (41cm) boxed   **$450**

Susan Stroller: 1953. Goldberger Doll Mfg. Co., walker, Saran hair; **Mark:** "Eegee."
   23in (58cm)   **$165-$195**

Wanda the Walking Wonder: 1950s. Advance Doll Co.:
   17-19in (43-48cm)   **$150-$200**

Italian Hard Plastic: Ca. 1950 on. Bonomi, Ottolini, Ratti, Furga, Magda and others. Heavy fine quality hard plastic; human hair wig, sleep eyes, sometimes flirty; original clothes; all in excellent condition.
Mark: Usually on head.
   12in (31cm)   **$125-$135**
   15-17in (38-43cm)   **$150-$200**
   19-21in (48-53cm)   **$225-$250**
   25in (64cm) fashion   **$275**

English Black Hard Plastic Characters: 1950s. Pedigree and others. Curly black wig, sometimes over molded hair.
   16in (41cm)   **$150-$175**
   21in (53cm)   **$225-$275**

**Very few price samples available for comparison.

15in (38cm) unmarked girl, all original. *H & J Foulke, Inc.*

21in (53cm) Italian hard plastic Oriental, all original. *H & J Foulke, Inc.*

Hasbro

Himstedt, Annette

Little Miss No Name: 1965. Large round eyes, molded tear, forlorn expression; original ragged clothes; all in excellent condition, with tear.

15in (38cm)	**$125-$150**
Boxed	**$250-$300**

Aimee: 1972. All-vinyl; original clothing; all in excellent condition **$45-$55**

Charlie's Angels: 1977. 8½in (21cm).

Boxed	**$40-$50**
Gift set, boxed	**$200-$250**

Jem Series: 1986-1987. 12½in (32cm) all-vinyl fashion dolls; original clothing; all in excellent condition; in original box. Deduct one-third for an out-of-box doll.

Jem	**$40-$45**
Kimber	**$45-$50**
Aja	**$50-$55**
Synergy	**$60-$70**
Roxy	**$60-$65**
Pizazz	**$65-$75**
Stormer	**$65-$75**
Rio	**$35-$40**
Boxed outfits	**$25-$35**

G.I. Joe: See page 266.
Raggedy Ann: See page 163.

FACTS

1986 on. Hard vinyl and cloth.
Designer: Annette Himstedt
Distributor: Mattel, Inc., Hawthorne, CA, U.S.A. Dolls made in Spain.
Mark: Wrist tag with doll's name; cloth signature label on clothes; signature on lower back plate and on back of doll's head under wig.

Marked Himstedt Doll: Hard vinyl head swivels on long shoulder plate, cloth lower torso, vinyl arms and curved legs; inset eyes with real eyelashes, painted feathered eyebrows, molded upper eyelids, open nose, human hair wig; original cotton clothing, bare feet; all in excellent condition with original box and certificate.

Barefoot Children: 1986. 26in (66cm):

Ellen	**$425-$475**
Kathe	**$425-$475**
Paula	**$425-$475**
Fatou	**$450-$550**
Lisa	**$425-$475**
Bastian	**$425-$475**

American Heartland Dolls: 1987. 19-20in (48-51cm):

Timi and Toni	**$250-$300 each**

The World Children Collection: 1988. 31in (79cm):

Kasimir	**$650-$750**
Malin	**$700-$800**
Michiko	**$600-$700**
Friederike	**$800-$900**
Makimura	**$525-$575**

Reflections of Youth: 1989. 26in (66cm):

Adrienne	**$425-$475**
Janka	**$375-$425**
Ayoka	**$425-$475**
Kai	**$350-$400**

Little Miss No Name. Miriam Blankman.

1990:
Fiene   **$550-$600**
Taki (baby)   **$800-$900**
Annchen (baby)   **$450-$550**
1991:
Liliane   **$450-$500**
Neblina   **$525-$550**
Tinka   **$550-$600**
Shireem   **$350-$375**
1993:
Kima   **$325-$350**
Lona   **$325-$350**
Tara   **$325-$350**
Jule   **$600-$650**
1994:
Panchita, Pancho, Melvin, Elke
                        $200-$250
1998:
Baby Leischen (club doll)
                        $350-$400
1999:
Mia Yin   **$650-$750**
Mirte & Little Mirte (club doll)
                        $500-$525
2002:
Annika   **$1,000**
Midori   **$800-$900**
Krinchen   **$700-$750**

26in (66cm) *Paula* from the *Barefoot Children* series, 1986. *Sidney Jeffrey Collection.*

Horsman

FACTS
E.I. Horsman Co.,
New York, NY, U.S.A.
Manufacturer; also distributor of
French and German dolls. 1878-on.

EARLY COMPOSITION DOLLS:
Original or appropriate old clothes; all in good condition.

Billiken: 1909. Composition head, velvet or plush body. **Mark:** cloth label.
12in (31cm)   **$350-$400**

"Can't Break 'Em" Characters: Ca. 1911. Character head; hard stuffed cloth body. **Mark:** "E.I.H. 1911."
11-13in (28-33cm)   **$200 up**
Polly Pru: 13in (33cm)   **$350-$375****

Little Mary Mix-Up:
15in (31cm)   **$350-$375****

Cotton Joe: Black:
13in (33cm)   **$425-$475**

Uncle Sam's Kid: 1917. Composition/cloth; all original:
16in (41cm)   **$400-$450**

Baby Bumps   **$250**
Black   **$300**

Puppy & Pussy Pippin: 1911. Grace G. Drayton. Plush body; composition head; cloth label.
8in (20cm) sitting:
Puppy Pippin   **$400-$450****
Pussy Pippin   **$500-$600****

Peek-a-Boo: 1913-1915. Grace G. Drayton. Composition head, arms, legs and lower torso, cloth upper torso. **Mark:** cloth label on outfit.
7½in (19cm)   **$150-$175**

Baby Butterfly: 1911-1913. Oriental doll; composition head; cloth body; original costume.
13in (33cm)   **$500****

Peterkin: 1914-1930. All-composition; various boy and girl clothing or simply a large bow.
11in (28cm)   **$325-$375**
Boxed, at auction   **$500**

**Not enough price samples to compute a reliable range.

18cm (46cm) *Ella Cinders. H & J Foulke, Inc.*

12½in (31cm) baby. *H & J Foulke, Inc.*

Gene Carr Characters: 1916. Composition/cloth. Snowball (black boy); **Mike** and **Jane** (eyes open); **Blink** and **Skinney** (eyes closed). Designed by Bernard Lipfert from Gene Carr's cartoon characters.

    13-14in (33-36cm)   **$325-$375**
    Black Snowball   **$450-$550**

Jackie Coogan: 1921. Composition/cloth; appropriate old clothes:

    14in (36cm)   **$550-$650**

HEbee-SHEbee: 1925. All-composition; blue shoes indicate a **HEbee;** pink ones a **SHEbee.**

    11in (28cm)   **$600-$650**
    Fair condition, some peeling
        $325-$375
    Mint, all original   **$800-$900**
    All-Bisque. See page 28.

Ella Cinders: 1925. Composition/cloth. From the comic strip by Bill Conselman and Charlie Plumb for Metropolitan Newspaper Service. **Mark:** "1925©MNS."

    18in (46cm)   **$650-$750**

Baby Dimples: 1928. Composition/cloth; appropriate old clothes.
Mark:

             "©
        E.I.H. CO. INC."
    16-18in (41-46cm)   **$300-$350**
    22-24in (56-61cm)   **$400-$450**

Mama Dolls: Late 1920s on. Composition/cloth.
Mark: "HORSMAN" or "E.I.H. CO. INC."

    Babies, including **Brother** and **Sister:**
        12-14in (31-36cm)   **$175-$200**
        18-20in (46-51cm)   **$275-$300**
    Girls, including **Rosebud** and **Peggy Ann:**
        14-16in (36-41cm)   **$250-$275**
        22-24in (56-61cm)   **$350-$400**

Tynie Baby: 1924. Slightly frowning face; cloth/composition; appropriate clothes. Designed by Bernard Lipfert.
Mark:

        "© 1924
        E.I. Horsman Inc.
        Made in
        Germany"
    Bisque head:
        14–16in (36-41cm)   **$650-$750**

Composition head:
  15in (38cm) long   **$250-$275**
  19-21in (48-53cm) **$375-$400**
All-bisque: swivel neck, glass eyes, wigged or molded hair,
  8-10in (20-25cm) **$2,200-$2,500**
Vinyl: 1950.
  15in (38cm), boxed   **$90-$110**

ALL-COMPOSITION   DOLLS:
1930s and 1940s. Original clothes; all in very good condition; may have "Gold Medal Doll" tag.
Mark: "HORSMAN"
  Slender Girl:
    13-14in (33-36cm) **$200-$225**
    16-18in (41-46cm) **$250-$275**
Chubby toddler:
    16-18in (41-46cm) **$250–$300**
Jo-Jo: 1937, 12in (31cm) **$250-$275**
Jeanie: 1937. 14in (36cm) **$225-$250**
Naughty Sue: 1937.
    16in (41cm)   **$425-$475**
Roberta: 1937.
    16in (41cm)   **$425-$475**
Bright Star: 1937.
    13in (33cm)   **$250-$300**
    17-20in (43-51cm) **$450-$550**

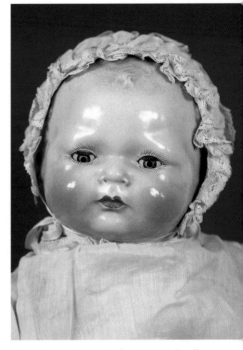

19in (48cm) *Tynie Baby. H & J Foulke, Inc.*

13in (33cm) *Jo-Jo*, all original. *H & J Foulke, Inc.*

25in (64cm) *Jackie*, all original. *H & J Foulke, Inc.*

Sweetheart: 1938. Teenager.

21in (53cm)	**$600****
24in (61cm)	**$700****
28in (71cm)	**$850****

ALL-HARD PLASTIC DOLLS:
1950s. Original clothing; perfect hair; good coloring; all in excellent condition.

Cindy: 1950-1955. Open mouth with teeth and tongue, synthetic wig; walker body. **Mark:** "160 [or "170" or "180"] Made in U.S.A."

16-18in (41-46cm) **$250-$300**

LuAnn Simms: Ca. 1953. Long brunette wig with front and side hair pulled to back, blue eyes; mold number 180 or 170.

18in (46cm) **$350-$400**

VINYL DOLLS: Original clothing; all in excellent condition with perfect hair and excellent color.

Rene Ballerina: 1957. Fully-jointed with high-heeled feet, rooted hair:
Mark: "82//HORSMAN"

19in (48cm) **$150-$165**

Cindy: 1957. Fashion Doll:

19in (21cm) **$200-$225**

Cindy Strutter: Child,

23in (58cm) boxed **$135**

Tweedie: 1958. Slender limbs, short hair:
Mark: "38 Horsman."

14½in (37cm)	**$50-$100**
Boxed	**$195**

Couturier Doll: 1958. Fashion doll with stuffed vinyl body:

20in (51cm) boxed **$225-$250**

Jackie Kennedy: 1961. Rooted black hair, blue sleep eyes; pearl jewelry.
Mark: "HORSMAN//19 © 61//JK25."

25in (64cm) **$165-$185**

Poor Pitiful Pearl: 1963. Cartoon character.
Mark: "1963//Wm Steig//Horsman"

11-12in (28-31cm)	**$100-$115**
Boxed	**$200-$225**
16in (41cm)	**$165**
Boxed	**$250-$275**

Hansel & Gretel: 1963. Character faces.
Mark: "Michael Meyerberg, Inc."

15in (38cm) **$200-$225**

Walt Disney's Cinderella Set: 1965. Extra head and costume for "poor" doll.
Mark: "H"

11½in (29cm), boxed **$150-$165**

Mary Poppins: 1964. Several different costumes.

12in (31cm)	**$30-$40**
Boxed set with 7in (18cm) Jane and Michael	**$150-$165**

Flying Nun: 1965. 12in (31cm) **$95**

Boxed **$175-$185**

Patty Duke: 1965. Gray flannel pants, red sweater.

12in (31cm)	**$75-$85**
Boxed	**$150-$175**

Elizabeth Taylor: 1976.

11½in (29cm) **$45-$55**

Angie Dickinson, Police Woman:
1970s. 9in (23cm) boxed **$35-$45**

Princess Peggy: 1959.

36in (91cm) **$300-$350**

Ruthie: 1962. 28in (71cm) **$200-$225**

**Not enough price samples to compute a reliable range.

12in (31cm) *Patty Duke*, all original. *Rosemary Kanizer.*

Mary Hoyer

Ideal

FACTS
The Mary Hoyer Doll Mfg. Co.,
Reading, PA, U.S.A. Ca. 1925-on.
Mark: Embossed on torso:
"The Mary Hoyer Doll"
or in a circle:
"ORIGINAL Mary Hoyer Doll"

FACTS
Ideal Novelty & Toy Co.,
Brooklyn, NY, U.S.A.
1907-on.

Marked Mary Hoyer: Original tagged factory clothes or garments made at home from Mary Hoyer patterns; all in excellent condition.
Composition: 14in (36cm) **$350-$450**
Hard plastic:
14in (36cm):

In knit outfit	**$400-$425**
In tagged Hoyer outfit	**$425-$525**
In tagged gown	**$500-$600**

14in (36cm) boy with caracul wig
$500-$550
18in (46cm), **Gigi:**

In tagged outfits	**$850-$1,250**
Boxed	**$1,250-$1,650**

Vinyl Play doll: 14in (36cm) **$95-$110**

18in (46cm) Mary Hoyer *Gigi*, all original. *Sidney Jeffrey Collection.*

Early Composition Dolls: 1910-1929. Composition heads; cloth bodies, composition lower arms; some with molded composition shoes; original or appropriate old clothes; all in good condition; some wear acceptable.
Head Mark:

Happy Hooligan: 1910. Comic character, 21in (53cm) **$500****
Snookums: 1910. Plush body, 14in (36cm) **$500-$600**
Ty Cobb: 1911. Baseball outfit **$500****
Naughty Marietta (Coquette): 1912. Molded hair with ribbon band **$350-$400**
Captain Jenks: 1912. Khaki uniform **$275-$325**
Uneeda Kid: 1914-1919. Molded black boots; original bloomer suit, yellow slicker and rain hat, carrying a box of Uneeda Biscuits, showing some wear.
16in (41cm) **$475-$500**
Bronco Bill: 1915. Cowboy outfit with gun and holster **$325**
ZuZu Kid: 1916-1917. Original clown suit, National Biscuit Co.:
16in (41cm) **$375-$425**
Liberty Boy: 1917. Molded clothes, cloth hat, some wear:
12in (31cm) **$275-$325**
Soozie Smiles: 1923. Two faces, crying and smiling **$400-$425**
Flossie Flirt: 1924-1931. Eyes move side to side.
14in (36cm) **$225-$250**
20in (51cm) **$300-$350**

**Not enough price samples to compute a reliable range.

Buster Brown: 1929. Red suit with hat, 17in (43cm)   **$325-$375**

Peter Pan: 1929. Original felt suit and hat, 18in (46cm):

    Excellent with label   **$550-$600**

    Good, some wear   **$300-$400**

Early Children:

    12-15in (31-38cm)   **$225-$250**

Early Babies: Baby Mine, Prize Baby and others: 15-16in (38-41cm)   **$225**

Composition Babies: 1930s and 1940s. Composition heads and lower limbs, cloth bodies; original or appropriate clothes; all in good condition with nice coloring; light crazing acceptable.

Tickletoes: 1930-1947, soft rubber arms and legs, flirty eyes:

    16in (41cm)   **$300-$350**

Baby Smiles: 1931. Toddler with rubber arms, 17in (43cm)   **$250-$275**

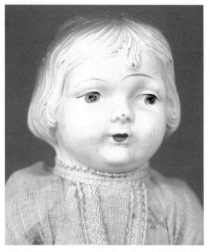

15in (38cm unmarked early child of the type made by Ideal, all original. *H & J Foulke, Inc.*

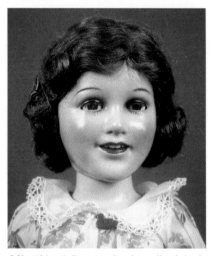

25in (64cm) *Deanna Durbin*, all original. *H & J Foulke, Inc.*

12in (31cm) *Betsy Wetsy*, all original. *Kathy & Terri's Dolls.*

Snoozie: 1933. Designed by Bernard Lipfert. Yawning mouth, may have rubber arms.

Mark: "©
            By B. LIPFERT"
16-20in (41-51cm)   **$325-$375**
Cuddles: 1933. Rubber limbs,
22in (56cm)   **$350-$400**
Bathrobe Baby: 1933. Rubber body,
12in (31cm)   **$100-$125**
Princess Beatrix: 1938. Magic eyes.
16in (41cm)   **$250-$300**
22in (56cm)   **$350-$400**

Betsy Wetsy: 1937-on. Drink-and-wet baby.
Head Mark: "IDEAL"
    Composition or hard rubber head/ rubber body:
        14-16in (36-41cm)   **$275-$300**
    Hard plastic head/rubber body:
        12-14in (31-36cm)   **$225-$250**
    Hard plastic head/vinyl body:
        14-16in (36-41cm)   **$210-$235**
        15in (38cm) original box and layette, mint   **$450**
    All-vinyl:
        8in (20cm) boxed   **$85**
        12in (31cm)   **$75-$100**
Composition Children: 1935-1947. All-composition in excellent condition with perfect hair and good cheek color; original clothes.
Shirley Temple: 1935. See page 301.
Snow White: 1937. Black wig, gown with rayon skirt showing figures of seven dwarfs.
Torso Mark: "SHIRLEY TEMPLE"
Dress tag: "An Ideal Doll"
    13in (33cm)   **$500-$550**
    18in (46cm)   **$650-$750**
    All-cloth: 16in (41cm)   **$525-$575**
        Mint-in-box   **$750**

Deanna Durbin: 1938. Smiling mouth with teeth, metal button with picture.
Head Mark:
"Deanna Durbin
Ideal Doll, USA"
    14in (36cm)   **$650**
    20-21in (51-53cm)   **$900-$1,000**
    24in (61cm)   **$1,300-$1,400**

Judy Garland as Dorothy from *The Wizard of Oz:* 1939.
Head Mark:
            "IDEAL DOLL
            MADE IN USA"
    16in (41cm)   **$1,500-$1,650**
    Replaced clothes   **$1,000-$1,100**

Betty Jane, Little Princess, Pigtail Sally, Ginger, Cinderella: 1935-1947.
    14in (36cm)   **$275-$325**
    18in (46cm)   **$375-$425**
Soldier: Ca. 1942. Character face; army uniform with jacket and hat,
    13in (33cm)   **$275-$325**
Miss Curity: Ca. 1945. Nurse uniform.
    14in (36cm)   **$325-$375**
    All original, with nurse kit, at auction   **$725**
Miss Liberty: Judy Garland mold,
    21in (53cm) at auction   **$700**
Flexy Dolls: 1938 on. Wire mesh torso, flexible metal cable arms and legs:
12in (31cm):
    Baby Snooks (Fanny Brice)
            $250-$275
    Mortimer Snerd   **$250-$275**
    Soldier   **$200-$225**
    Children   **$200-$225**

13in (33cm) *Little Princess,* all original. *H & J Foulke, Inc.*

10in (25cm) *Pinocchio. Kay Jensen Antique Dolls.*

14in (36cm) P-90 *Toni*, all original. *H & J Foulke, Inc.*

Judy Garland from *Strike up the Band:* 1940. (For photograph, see *14th Blue Book,* page 283.)
Head Mark: "MADE IN U.S.A."
Body Mark:
"IDEAL DOLL
[backwards 21]"
21in (53cm)   **$1,000-$1,200**

Composition and Wood Segmented Characters: 1940. Label on front torso.
Pinocchio:
10½in (27cm)   **$475-$525**
20in (51cm)   **$800-$900**
King Little: 14in (36cm) **$275-$325**
Jiminy Cricket:
9in (23cm)   **$450-$500**
Gabby: 11in (28cm)   **$375-$425**
Ferdinand the Bull:
9in (23cm)   **$425**

Magic Skin Dolls: 1940-on. Stuffed latex rubber body in very good condition (subject to easy deterioration); original clothes; all in excellent condition. **Head Mark:** "IDEAL."
Magic Skin Baby: 1940.
14-15in (36-38cm)   **$95-$110**
Plassie: 1940.
16in (41cm)   **$95-$110**

Toddler: All-hard plastic,
14in (36cm)   **$165-$195**
Sparkle Plenty: 1947.
15in (38cm) baby   **$200-$225**
Joan Palooka: 1953.
14in (36cm)   **$125-$135**
Baby Coos: 1948-1952. Sounds like a baby when squeezed,
14-16in (36-41cm)   **$110-$135**
Brother or **Sister Coos:**
25-30in (64-76cm), dressed like toddlers   **$200-$300**

Howdy Doody: 1947-1955. Hard plastic head, movable jaw; stuffed body; all original:
21in (53cm)   **$300-$325**
25in (64cm)   **$400-$450**

Toni Family: 1948-on. Hard plastic "Toni" home permanent doll and derivatives; nylon wig, perfect hair, pretty cheek color; original clothes; all in excellent condition.
Head Mark: "IDEAL DOLL"
Body Mark:
"IDEAL DOLL
P-90
Made in USA"

Toni:
  14-16in (36-41cm):
    P-90 & P-91   **$350-$400**
    Naked, untidy hair   **$70-$80**
    Mint-in-box   **$550-$650**
  19-21in (48-53cm) P-92 & P-93
         $600-$650
    Mint-in-box   **$1,300**
  22½in (57cm) P-94   **$950****
  Playwave Box and contents   **$75**
  Tagged dress   **$65-$85**
  Shoes   **$45-$60**
Mary Hartline:
  14in (36cm)   **$350-$400**
  22½in (57cm)   **$1,100-$1,200****
Harriet Hubbard Ayer: Vinyl head makeup doll.
  14in (36cm)   **$200-$225**
    Mint-in box with accessories
         $400-$450
  21in (53cm)   **$400-$450****
Miss Curity: Nurse.
  14in (36cm)   **$350-$400**
  Mint-in-box with accessories   **$650**
Sara Ann: Saran hair.
  14in (36cm)   **$350-$400**
  21in (53cm) Bride   **$600****

Hopalong Cassidy: 1949-1950.
  24in (61cm)   **$375**

Saucy Walker: 1951-1955. All-hard plastic with walking mechanism; original clothes; excellent hair and cheek color.
Mark: "IDEAL DOLL"
  16-17in (41-43cm)   **$150-$200**
  20-22in (51-56cm)   **$225-$250**
  Mint-in-box   **$350-$400**
Posie: 1954-1956. Vinyl head,
  17in (43cm)   **$185-$210**
Saralee: 1950. Black vinyl/cloth body. Designed by Sarah Lee Creech; modeled by Sheila Burlingame. Original clothes; excellent condition:
  17-18in (43-46cm)   **$300-$350**
  Undressed   **$125**
Bonny Braids: 1951. Vinyl character head; hard plastic body; original clothes; excellent condition:
  13in (33cm)   **$150-$200**
  Mint-in-comic strip-box   **$350-$400**

**Not enough price samples to compute a reliable range.

15in (38cm) *Toni Walker,* all original and boxed. *Rosemary Kanizer.*

18in (46cm) *Miss Revlon,* all original. *Kathy & Terri's Dolls.*

Revlon Dolls: 1955-1959. Vinyl head with rooted hair, perfect hair, bright cheek color; hard plastic body with jointed waist, high-heeled feet; original clothing; excellent condition.

Miss Revlon:

18-20in (46-51cm)	**$225-$275**
Mint-in-box, dress	**$400 up**
Mint-in-box, gown	**$475 up**

Little Miss Revlon:

10½in (27cm)	**$135-$165**
Boxed	**$225-$250**

Patti Playpal Family: 1959-1962.

Patti: 35in (89cm)	**$500-$600**
Mint-in-box	**$1,100**
Peter: 38in (97cm)	**$750-$850**
Mint-in-box, at auction	**$1,925**
Daddy's Girl:	
42in (107cm)	**$1,000-$1,200**
Miss Ideal:	
25in (64cm)	**$225-$250**
30in (76cm)	**$275-$325**
Patti: 18in (46cm)	**$350-$450**
Bonnie & Johnny:	
24in (61cm) babies	**$225-$250**
Penny: 32in (81cm)	**$275-$325**
Saucy Walker:	
32in (81cm)	**$325-$350**
Patti: 1982. Mint-in-box	**$125-$150**
Black: Mint-in-box	**$225**

Tammy Family: 1962-1966. Mint-in-box; deduct 50 percent for an out-of-box doll:

Tammy: 12in (31cm)	**$135-$150**
Pos'n Tammy:	
12in (31cm)	**$275-$300**
Glamour Misty (Miss Clairol)	
	$95-$110
Ted (big brother):	
12½in (32cm)	**$135-$150**
Mom: 12½in (32cm)	**$185-$200**
Dad: 13in (33cm)	**$150**
Pepper (sister): 9in (23cm)	**$75-$85**
Pete (little brother):	
7¾in (20cm)	**$200 up**
Patti (*Pepper's* friend):	
9in (23cm)	**$250 up**
Dodi (*Pepper's* friend):	
9in (23cm)	**$85**
Salty (*Pepper's* friend):	
7¾in (20cm)	**$200**
Bud (*Tammy's* boyfriend):	
12½in (32cm)	**$200**
Boxed outfits	**$60-$85**
Tammy Car, boxed	**$225**

Miscellaneous Vinyl Dolls: All original; excellent coloring; perfect condition.

Lori Martin (National Velvet):	
1961. 38in (97cm)	**$750-$850**
Magic Lips: 1955.	
24in (61cm)	**$145-$165**

30in (76cm) *Miss Ideal,* all original. *H & J Foulke, Inc.*

8½in (21cm) *Tearie Dearie. Kathy & Terri's Dolls.*

Thumbelina: 1961. Vinyl and cloth; wriggles like a real baby:
19-20in (48-51cm)	**$250-$350**
Tiny Thumbelina:	
14in (36cm)	**$225-$250**
Newborn Thumbelina:	
9in (28cm)	**$125-$150**

Kissy: 1961-1964. Toddler.
22in (56cm)	**$110-$135**
Mint-in-box	**$225-$250**

Tearie Dearie: 1963-1967.
9in (23cm)	**$40**

Bam Bam: 1963.
12in (31cm)	**$60-$70**
16in (41cm)	**$90-$100**

Pebbles: 1963.
8in (20cm)	**$40-$50**
12in (31cm)	**$80-$90**
16in (41cm) boxed	**$225-$250**

Betty Big Girl: 1968.
32in (81cm)	**$125-$150**

Little Lost Baby: 1968. Three faces,
22in (56cm)	**$95-$110**

Flatsy: 1968-1970.
Each with accessory	**$20-$25**
Boxed	**$40-$50**
Early style, boxed with frame	**$75-$95**

Joey Stivic: 1976. Archie Bunker's grandson, 15in (38cm), boxed **$65**

Dorothy Hamill: 1977.
11½in (29cm) boxed	**$25-$35**

Honey Moon: 1965. From Dick Tracy comic strip, mint, boxed **$100**

Diana Ross: 1969.
17½in (45cm)	**$300-$350**
Boxed, at auction	**$635**

Giggles: 1966. 18in (41cm) **$75-$85**
Boxed	**$110**

Crissy and Family: 1968-1974. Growing hair dolls, all original and excellent.
Crissy, Beautiful Crissy	**$40-$50**
Black Crissy	**$100-$110**
Velvet	**$40-$50**
Black Velvet	**$65-$75**
Cinnamon	**$30-$40**
Black Cinnamon	**$75**
Mia	**$55**
Kerry	**$50-$60**
Tressy	**$70-$80**
Brandi	**$50-$60**
Dina	**$50-$60**
Cricket	**$225-$275**
Baby Crissy	**$85-$95**
Black Baby Crissy:	
Boxed	**$125-$175**
Packaged clothes	**$25-$50**

Tiffany Taylor: 1974.
19in (48cm)	**$40-$45**
Boxed	**$55-$65**
Black	**$75-$85**

Flatsy, boxed. *Rosemary Kanizer.*

Velvet, all original. *Kathy & Terri's Dolls.*

Blythe: 1972. Changes eye color. Excellent and all original

	$1,200-$1,600
Boxed	$1,800-$2,200
Red hair	$1,800-$2,000
Boxed, at auction	$3,600

Dusty: 1974. Smiling face, freckles.

12in (31cm), boxed	$25-$35
Outfits	$10-$15

Skye: 1974. Black skin.

12in (31cm), boxed	$25-$35
Outfits	$10-$15

Cover Girls: 1978-1980. Fashion dolls with bendable elbows and knees, jointed wrists; 12in (31cm):

Darci	$55-$65
Erica (auburn)	$150-$175
Dana (black skin)	$75-$85
Outfits	$30-$40

Hardy Boys: 1978. Mint-in-box dolls:
Shaun Cassidy, Parker Stevenson
$35-$45

Hardy Boys, boxed. *Rosemary Kanizer.*

Star Wars: 1974-1978. Mint-in-box dolls. For excellent out-of-box dolls, deduct 50 percent.

Darth Vader:
15in (38cm)	$125-$150
Han Solo: 12in (31cm)	$450-$475

Luke Skywalker:
12in (31cm)	$175-$200

Princess Leia:
11½in (29cm)	$125-$150

Stormtrooper:
12in (31cm)	$125-$150

Obi Wan Kenobi:
12in (31cm)	$75-$100
R2D2: 7½in (19cm)	$125-$135
C3PO: 12in (31cm)	$85-$95
Boba Fett: 13in (33cm)	$175-$200
Jawa: 8½in (22cm)	$65-$75
IG88: 12in (31cm)	$400
Chewbacca: 15in (38cm)	$100-$125
Yoda: 9in (23cm)	$65-$75

Six Million Dollar Man: 1975-1978. 13in (33cm) boxed figures.

Bigfoot Bionic, at auction	$225
Steve Austin	$65-$85
Jaime Sommers	$55-$65
Bigfoot	$55-$65
Fembot	$100-$125
Oscar Goldman	$60-$70

Strawberry Shortcake: 1980-1986.

Vinyl doll with pet	$35 up

Boxed and complete:

Plum Pudding	$120-$130
Peach Blush	$125-$135
Raspberry Tart	$50-$60
Lemon Meringue	$50-$60
Lime Chiffon	$45-$55
Blueberry Muffin	$50-$60
Huckleberry Pie	$50-$60
Orange Blossom	$50-$60
Mint Tulip	$55-$65
Almond Tea	$55-$65
Berry Happy Home Dollhouse with furniture	$250-$350
Attic Playset: boxed	$200-$225
Cloth Dolls: 16in (41cm)	$45-$65

Knickerbocker

Composition Snow White: 1937. All-composition; black mohair wig with hair ribbon; original clothing; all in very good condition:

15in (38cm)	**$425-$475**
20in (51cm)	**$550-$650**

With molded black hair and blue ribbon: 13-15in (33-38cm) **$350-$450**
Set: 15in (38cm) Snow White and seven 9in (23cm) Dwarfs **$2,750**

Composition Seven Dwarfs: All-composition; individual character faces; original velvet costumes and caps with identifying names: Sneezy, Dopey, Grumpy, Doc, Happy, Sleepy and Bashful; very good condition.

9in (23cm) **$225-$250 each**
Additional composition dolls:

Jiminy Cricket:	
10in (25cm)	**$450-$550**
Pinocchio: 14in (36cm)	**$550-$650**
Figero the Cat	**$500-$550**
Blondie: 11in (28cm) all original and boxed, at auction	**$1,680**
Dagwood: 13in (33cm)	**$650-$750**
Alexander: 9in (23cm)	**$400-$450**

Additional cloth dolls:

Seven Dwarfs:	
14in (36cm)	**$200-$225 each**
Snow White:	
16in (41cm)	**$375-$425**
Donald Duck	**$500-$600**
Mickey Mouse: 1935.	**$550-$650**
Mickey Bandleader: At auction	**$1,680**
Minnie Mouse	**$500 up**

Raggedy Ann & Andy: See page 165.

Little Lulu:	
18in (46cm)	**$400-$500****

Child Doll: 1935. Mask face (washable), original clothes,

12-14in (31-36cm)	**$125-$150**
Little Orphan Annie and Sandy:	
1977. 16in (41cm)	**$25-$35**

**Not enough price samples to compute a reliable range.

> **FACTS**
> Knickerbocker Doll & Toy Co., New York, NY, U.S.A. 1937-on.
> **Head Mark:**
> "WALT DISNEY KNICKERBOCKER TOY CO."

9in (23cm) *Dopey. Kay Jensen Antique Dolls.*

Krueger

FACTS
Richard G. Krueger, Inc.,
New York, NY, U.S.A. 1917-on.
Mark: Cloth tag or label.

All-Cloth Doll: Ca. 1930. Mask face; oilcloth body with hinged shoulders and hips; original clothes; in excellent condition.

7in (18cm)	**$50-$60**
12in (31cm)	**$100-$125**
16in (41cm)	**$150-$165**
20in (51cm)	**$200-$225**

Pinocchio: Ca. 1940. Mask character face; cloth torso, wood jointed arms and legs; original clothes, all in good condition.

15in (38cm)	**$400-$450****

Kewpie: See page 128.
Dwarfs: Ca. 1937.
  All-cloth, mask face:

12in (30cm)	**$175-$200**
Set of seven, with Snow White	**$2,200**

Scootles: 1935. Rose O'Neill. All-cloth, mask face, yarn hair.

10in (25cm)	**$450****
18in (46cm)	**$850****

**Not enough price samples to compute a reliable range.

12in (31cm) child with mask face of the type made by Krueger, all original. *H & J Foulke, Inc.*

Mattel, Inc.

Condition: Unless otherwise indicated, all dolls should be in excellent unplayed-with condition, in original clothes with all accessories, perfect hair, excellent coloring.

Chatty Cathy Family: 1960-1965.
  Chatty Cathy:

20in (51cm)	**$250-$300**
Boxed	**$375-$475**
Black, at auction	**$1,700**
Speaks French, at auction	**$2,000**
Gift Set: 1962. At auction	**$2,600**

  Charmin' Chatty:

25in (64cm)	**$135-$150**
Boxed	**$175-$200**

  Chatty Baby:

18in (46cm)	**$95-$115**
Boxed	**$150**

  Tiny Chatty Baby:

15in (38cm)	**$75-$80**
Black	**$110-$125**

  Tiny Chatty Brother:

15in (38cm)	**$70-$75**

  Singing Chatty:

17in (43cm)	**$100-$125**

Buffy & Mrs. Beasley: 1967. All-vinyl **Buffy**, vinyl/cloth **Mrs. Beasley.**

6in (15cm) boxed	**$200**
10in (25cm) boxed	**$350-$375**

Mrs. Beasley: Vinyl and cloth, with glasses.

16in (40cm)	**$250-$300**
Boxed	**$450-$550**

Skediddles: 1966. Mint-in-package

	$65-$85

Star-Spangled Dolls: 1976.
  New England Girl, Pioneer Daughter, Southern Belle **$20-$30**
Sunshine Family: 1977.

Boxed set	**$100-$125**

Toddlers and Babies: All original and excellent, unplayed-with, in working condition.
  Baby Secret: 1966.

18in (46cm)	**$80-$90**

  Baby First Step: 1966.

18in (46cm)	**$65-$75**
Boxed	**$175**

Baby Pattaburp: 1964.
  16in (41cm)   **$40-$50**
Baby Tenderlove: 1970-1972.
  Newborn: 13in (33cm)   **$45-$55**
  Living: 20in (51cm)   **$65-$85**
  Brother (sexed):
    12in (31cm) boxed   **$50-$65**
Cheerful, Tearful: 1966.
  7in (17cm) with play case **$45-$50**
  13in (33cm)   **$45-$50**
Dancerina: 1970.
  12in (31cm)   **$30-$35**
  16in (41cm)   **$60-$70**
  24in (61cm)   **$125-$150**
Hi Dottie: 1969.
  17in (43cm) boxed   **$50-$60**
Sister Belle: 1961.
  17in (43cm)   **$65-$75**
Matty Mattel: 1961.
  17in (43cm)   **$65-$75**
Timey Tell: 1964.
  17in (43cm) with watch   **$45-$55**
  Boxed   **$125**
Tippy Toes: 1967.
  17in (43cm) with tricycle or horse,
  good face   **$50-$60**
  Boxed, at auction   **$165**

Dolls from Television Shows: All prices
are for mint-in-box or package dolls.
  Charlie's' Angels: 1978.
    11½in (29cm)   **$50-$60**
  Debbie Boone: 1978.
    11½in (29cm)   **$50-$65**
  Dick Van Dyke: 1969.
    25in (64cm), talks   **$125**

Donny Osmond: 1978.
  12in (31cm)   **$35-$40**
Marie Osmond: 1978.
  12in (31cm)   **$35-$40**
Jimmy Osmond: 1979.
  10in (25cm)   **$45-$50**
Grizzly Adams: 1971.
  10in (25cm)   **$35-$40**
Herman Munster: 1965.
  Hand puppet   **$125**
  Full body   **$200-$225**
How the West Was Won: 1971.
  10in (25cm)   **$25-$30 each**
Welcome Back Kotter: 1973.
  9in (23cm)   **$40-$50 each**

Little Kiddles: 1966. Mint-in-box or
package; deduct 50 percent for an out-
of-package doll with all accessories, in
excellent condition.
Body Mark:
"1965//Mattel, Inc.//Japan"
  Sleeping Biddle   **$125-$135**
  Liddle Biddle Peep   **$165**
  Peter Pandiddle   **$225**
  Liddle Middle Muffet   **$185-$210**
  Liddle Red Riding Hiddle
                                   $185-$210
  Sizzly Friddle   **$145**
  Freezy Sliddle   **$135**
  Howard Biff Boodle   **$135**
  Orange Ice Kone Kiddle   **$75-$80**
  Kologne Kiddle   **$50-$60**
  Locket Kiddle   **$55-$65**
  Heart Pin Kiddle   **$30-$35**
  Bracelet Kiddle   **$30-$40**

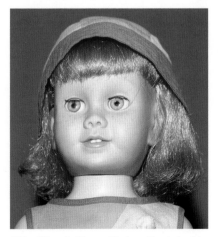

20in (51cm) *Chatty Cathy,* all original in
"Sunny Day." *Sidney Jeffrey Collection.*

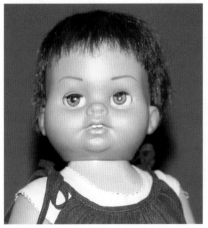

Chatty Baby, all original. *Sidney Jeffrey
Collection.*

Mawaphil Dolls

Mawaphil Stockinette Doll: One-piece stockinette dolls, some with attached limbs; hand-painted faces, rosy cheeks, painted hair; clothing usually an integral part of the body, but may have an added item; excellent condition.

    6-10in (15-25cm)   **$75-$95****

**Not enough price samples to compute a reliable range.

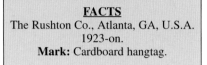

FACTS
The Rushton Co., Atlanta, GA, U.S.A.
1923-on.
Mark: Cardboard hangtag.

Mawaphil Cloth Character Doll: Mask face, painted features, rosy cheeks, mohair wig; cloth body; original clothing.

    15in (38cm)   **$165-195****

Small stockinette doll with Mawaphil tag. *Connie & Jay Lowe.*

15in (38cm) Mawaphil *Tommy Tucker. Kathy & Terri's Dolls.*

Mego Corporation

Television, Movie and Entertainment Dolls: All prices are for mint-in-box or package dolls.

Batman: 1974. 8in (20cm) **$125-$175**
Penguin: 1974. 8in (20cm) **$75-$85**
Captain & Tennille: 1977.
    12½in (32cm) **$50-$60 each**
Cher: 1976. 12in (31cm) **$65-$75**
    Sonny **$40**
CHiPs: 1977.
    8in (20cm) **$35-$40 each**
Diana Ross: 1977. 12½in (32cm) **$125**
Charlie's Angels: 1975.
    12½in (32cm) **$65-$70 each**
Happy Days: 1976.
    8in (20cm) **$40-$50 each**
KISS: 1978.
    12½in (32cm) **$125-$150 each**
Kojack: 1977. 9in (23cm) **$65-$70**
Laverne & Shirley: 1977.
    11½in (29cm) **$65-$70 each**
Joe Namath: 1971. 12in (31cm) **$125**
Our Gang: 1975.
    5in (13cm) **$20-$30 each**
Planet of the Apes: 1974.
    8in (20cm) **$100-$175 each**
Pirates: 1971.
    8in (20cm) **$100-$150 each**
Robin Hood Set: 1971.
    8in (20cm) **$35-$40 each**
Starsky & Hutch: 1976.
    8in (20cm) **$35-$40 each**
Suzanne Somers: 1978.
    12½in (32cm) **$50-$60**
The Waltons: 1975. 8in (20cm), two dolls in each box **$40-$50 per box**
Wild West: 1974.
    Buffalo Bill, Cochise, Davy Crockett, Sitting Bull, Wild Bill Hickok, Wyatt Earp $35-$40 each
Wonder Woman: 1976.
    12½in (32cm) **$150-$200**
Wizard of Oz: 1974.
    Dorothy, Glinda **$30-$35**
    Munchkins **$60-$65**
    Tin Man, Cowardly Lion **$30-$35**

Star Trek: 1975. Fully-jointed plastic; packaged on blister card. For unpackaged dolls, deduct 50 percent. 8in (20cm).
    Captain Kirk **$50**
    Mr. Spock **$35-$45**
    Dr. McCoy **$110-$125**
    Mr. Scott **$110-$135**
    Klingon **$40**
    Lt. Uhura **$50-$60**
    Andorian, at auction **$700**
    The Keeper **$175-$200**
    Romulan **$800-$1,000**
Star Trek: 1979. Mint-in-box, 12½in (32cm).
    Captain Kirk **$60**
    Mr. Spock **$50**
    Ilia **$50**

12in (30cm) *Cher*, all original and boxed. *H & J Foulke, Inc.*

Molly-'es

Molly-'es Composition Dolls: Beautiful original outfits; all in good condition.

Babies:
　　15-18in (38-46cm)　　**$225-$250**
　　Girls: 12-13in (31-33cm) **$175-$190**
Toddlers:
　　14-16in (36-41cm)　　**$275-$300**
Ladies:
　　18-21in (46-53cm)　　**$500-$550**
Internationals: All-cloth with mask faces; all original clothes; in excellent condition with wrist tag.
　　13in (33cm)　　　　　　**$65-$75**
　　Mint-in-box　　　　　**$100-$125**
Raggedy Ann & Andy: See page 164.
Thief of Baghdad Series: 1939. Orange hangtag.
　　Sabu: Composition:
　　　15in (38cm)　　　　　**$550-$600**
　　Sultan: 19in (48cm) cloth
　　　　　　　　　　　　　$650-$750
　　Princess: 15in (38cm) composition or 18in (46cm) cloth　　**$600-$650**
　　Prince: 23in (58cm) cloth　　**$750**

FACTS
International Doll Co., Philadelphia, PA, U.S.A. Made clothing only. Purchased undressed dolls from various manufacturers. 1920s-on.
Clothes Designer: Mollye Goldman.
Mark: A cardboard tag.

Hard Plastic: All original and excellent.
　　Stewardess: 14in (36cm)　　**$475**
Vinyl Dolls: All original and excellent.
　　Darling Little Women:
　　　8in (20cm)　　　　**$50-$60****
　　　12in (31cm)　　　　**$85-$95****
　　Internationals: 8in (20cm) **$25-$30**
　　Perky: 8in (20cm)　　　　**$25-$30**

**Not enough price samples to compute a reliable range.

20in (51cm) cloth toddler, all original. *Kathy & Terri's Dolls.*

15in (38cm) *Sabu*, all original. *H & J Foulke, Inc.*

Nancy Ann Storybook Dolls

Painted Bisque Marked Storybook Doll: Mohair wig, painted eyes; one-piece body and head, jointed legs and arms; original clothes; excellent condition with sticker or wrist tag and box. Deduct 25 to 30 percent for out-of-box dolls. 5½–7in (13-19cm).

1936: Babies only. Gold sticker on dress; sunburst box.
Mark: "88 Made in Japan" or "87 Made in Japan"
3½-4½in (8-10cm) **$450-$550**

1937-1938: Gold sticker on dress; sunburst box, gold label.
Mark: "Made in Japan 1146," "Made in Japan 1148," "Japan," "Made in Japan" or "AMERICA" **$700-$1,000**
Molded hair **$1,800**

"Made in Japan" *Storybook Doll* with molded hair, all original. *H & J Foulke, Inc.*

FACTS
Nancy Ann Storybook Dolls Co., South San Francisco, CA, U.S.A. 1936-on.

1938-1939: Gold sticker on dress; sunburst transition to silver dot box.
Mark: "JUDY ANN USA" (crude mark), "STORYBOOK USA" (crude mark); molded socks/molded bangs.
Mark: "StoryBook Doll USA"
$550-$750

Masquerade Series	**$800 each**
Topsy and Eva	**$1,200 pair**
Judy Ann	**$600-$700**
Oriental	**$1,700**
Gypsy	**$1,200**
Pirate	**$1,300**
Storybook Set	**$4,300**
Sports Series	**$1,200 each**
#179 Babes in the Woods: Pair, no box	**$2,235**

1940: Gold sticker on dress; colored box with white polka dots; molded socks.
Mark: "StoryBook Doll USA"
$250 up

Margie Ann	**$400-$500**
"Pudgies"	**$250-$350**

1941-1942: Gold wrist tag; white box with colored polka dots; jointed legs.
Mark: "StoryBook Doll USA"
$110-$125

White socks	**$135-$165**
"Pudgies"	**$250-$300**

1943-1947: Gold wrist tag; white box with colored polka dots; frozen legs.
Mark: "StoryBook Doll USA" (some later dolls with plastic arms) **$75-$95**

Socket head	**$95-$115**
Operetta Series	**$175-$225**
All Time Hit Parade Series	**$175-$200**
Powder and Crinoline Series	**$150-$175**
Holiday inserts	**$100-$125**

8in (20cm) *Muffie*, all original. *Rosemary Kanizer.*

18in (46cm) *Style Show*, all original. *Rosemary Kanizer.*

Hard Plastic Marked Storybook Doll: Swivel head, mohair wig, painted eyes; jointed legs; original clothes; gold wrist tag; white box with colored polka dots, excellent condition.
Mark: "Story Book Doll USA"

5½-7in (13-19cm)	**$50-$60**
Topsy: (black)	**$125-$150**
Holiday inserts	**$75-$85**

Storybook Doll Babies:

Bisque: Star hand	**$175-$200**
Bisque: Closed fist, open mouth	**$165-$185**
Bisque: Hard plastic arms	**$100-$125**
Hard plastic	**$100**
Boxed furniture	**$300 up**

Jesco Storybook Dolls: 1986.

Boxed	**$25-$35**

Muffie: All-hard plastic; wig, sleep eyes, 8in (12cm) tall.
Mark: "StoryBook Dolls USA" some with "Muffie"
1953: Straight-leg non-walker; painted eyelashes, no eyebrows, Dynel wig (side part with flip); 54 complete costumes; original clothes; excellent condition **$300-$400***
1954: Walker; molded eyelashes, eyebrows after 1955, side part flip or braided wig; 30 additional costumes; original clothes; excellent condition **$200-$250***
1955-1956: Hard plastic walker or bent-knee walker; rooted Saran wig (ponytail, braids or side part flip); vinyl head and hard plastic body; molded or painted upper eyelashes **$165-$185**

Nancy Ann Style Show:

18in (46cm) hard plastic	**$750-$1,250**

Miss Nancy Ann:

10½in (27cm) teenage body, high-heeled feet	**$125-$150**
Boxed	**$225-$250**
Boxed outfits	**$85 up**

Debbie: Hard plastic toddler.

10in (25cm)	**$160-$175**
Mint-in-box	**$350**

Little Miss Nancy Ann:

9in (23cm) boxed	**$225**

*Allow extra for red hair.

House of Nisbet

FACTS
House of Nisbet, Ltd., England.
1952-1995.
Designer: Peggy Nisbet
Mark: Black printed paper wrist tag.

Nisbet Portrait & Costume Doll: Historical personages and traditional characters of the United Kingdom. All-hard plastic; portrait face, painted eyes, styled wig; body jointed at arms only; painted shoes; original costume; excellent condition with box.

7½-8in (19-20cm)	**$25-$50**
Queen Guinevere	**$70**
St. Nicholas	**$65**
Joan of Arc	**$60**
Shah of Iran and Empress Farah	**$200**

9in (23cm) Old Cottage doll, all original. *H & J Foulke, Inc.*

Old Cottage

FACTS
Old Cottage Toys, Allargate, Rustington, Littlehampton, Sussex, Great Britain. 1948.
Designers: Greta Fleischmann and her daughter, Susi.
Mark: Paper label – "Old Cottage Toys – handmade in Great Britain"

Old Cottage Doll: Rubber compound or hard plastic head with hand-painted features, wig; stuffed cloth body; original clothing; excellent condition.

8-9in (20-23cm)	
Children and Storybook outfits	**$165**
Scotch, Pearlies	**$135**
12-13in (31-33cm), mint-in-box	**$350****

Tweedledee & Tweedledum:

9in (23cm), at auction	**$1,000 pair**

**Not enough price samples to compute a reliable range.

7½in (19cm) Nisbet Oriental girl. *Kathy & Terri's Dolls.*

Princess Diana Dolls

Dolls must be mint-in-box, complete with all accessories and have their certificates.

Madame Alexander: 1998. Hard plastic, 10in (25cm) **$75-$85**

Ashton-Drake: 1998. Porcelain, designed by Titus Tomescu, in blue, red or green evening gown. Edition of 5,000.
18in (46cm) **$75-$95**

Danbury Mint: 1982. Porcelain, wedding gown, 19in (48cm) **$125-$150**
Royal Wardrobe Collection: Doll with nine outfits **$150-$200**
Trunk **$70**

Effanbee: 1982. Vinyl, wedding gown **$100-$125**

Franklin Mint: 1998. Porcelain, beaded gown and others,
17in (43cm) **$100-$125**
People's Princess: 1998.
16in (41cm) vinyl, blue suit, doll only **$50-$55**
Boxed outfits **$15-$25**
Millennium Princess: Limited Edition of 2000 **$185**

Princess of Radiance: 2003. Limited Edition of 75 **$650-$750**

Gadco: 1998.
Young Diana: Red coat and hat, 35in (89cm) **$260-$310****
2001: Blue brocade gown, 16in (41cm) **$120-$125**

Royal Britannia Collection: 1997 reissue of 1982 doll. Wedding gown, 12in (31cm) boxed **$45-$55**

Royal Diana: Set of eight boxed dolls **$65-$75**

Society for Preservation of History, Inc.: 1997. Porcelain,
18in (46cm) blue satin gown **$60-$70**

Street Players Holding Corp.:
12in (31cm) vinyl:
1997. Wedding gown **$15-$20**
1998. Black dress **$15-$20**

Peggy Nisbet: 1982.
Wedding gown **$65-$75**
Engagement dress **$75**

**Not enough price samples to compute a reliable range.

Effanbee Club Limited Edition *Princess Diana.* *H & J Foulke, Inc.*

Raleigh

Ravca

FACTS
Jessie McCutcheon Raleigh,
Chicago, IL, U.S.A. 1916-1920.
Designer: Jessie McCutcheon Raleigh.
Mark: None.

Raleigh Doll: All heavy composition; appropriate clothes; all in good condition.
Child:
   11in (28cm) wigged   **$450-$500**
   13in (33cm) molded hair **$600-$650**
   18in (46cm) molded hair
                    $950-$1,050
   22-24in (56-61cm) shoulder head on cloth body, composition arms
                    $350-$450
Baby:
   12in (30cm)   **$400**
   18in (46cm)   **$600**

Bernard Ravca Doll: Paris, France, 1924-1939; New York, NY, U.S.A. 1939-on. Stockinette face individually needle-sculpted; cloth body and limbs; original clothes; all in excellent condition.
Mark: Paper label: "Original Ravca Fabrication Française"
   10in (25cm) French peasants
                    $85-$100
   13in (33cm)   **$135-$150**
   21in (53cm)   **$350-$400**
American Historical Figures:
George Washington, Betsy Ross, Ben Franklin and others,
   9in (23cm)   **$175-$225**
Circus Figures   **$85-$95**
Composition heads, bendable bodies:
   7½in (19cm)   **$50-$60**
Ravca-type fine quality peasant man or lady: 17in (43cm) **$225-$265 each**

Frances Diecks Ravca Doll: New York, 1935-on.
   Queen Elizabeth II and others:
   1952. 36in (91cm)   **$650-$850**
   "Easter Sunday": 1973.
      12in (30cm) black child   **$250**
   Little Women:
      12-13in (31-33cm)
                  $225-$250 each

13½in (34cm) Raleigh doll. *H & J Foulke, Inc.*

Right: 7in (18cm) Ravca circus figures. *Diane Costa.*

Reliable Toy Co.

FACTS
Reliable Toy Co., Toronto, Canada.
1920-on.
Mark: "RELIABLE//MADE
IN//CANADA"

Marked Reliable Doll: All-composition or composition shoulder head and lower arms, cloth torso and legs, sometimes composition legs; painted features; original clothes; all in good condition; some light crazing acceptable.

Barbara Ann Scott (Ice Skater):
15in (38cm) **$400-$500**
Canadian Mountie:
17in (43cm) **$300-$350**
Clicquot Club Soda Eskimo:
14in (36cm) **$250-$275**
Her Highness:
15in (38cm) **$350-$375**
Hiawatha or **Indian Maiden:**
13in (33cm) **$85-$110**
Military Man:
14in (36cm) **$225-$275**
Scots Girl or **Boy:**
14in (36cm) **$85-$110**
Shirley Temple: 22in (56cm) **$1,200**

Remco Industries

Littlechap Family: 1963. Basic doll, unplayed-with, in original box. Deduct 50 percent for out-of-box dolls.
Dr. John: 14½in (37cm) **$65-$75**
Lisa: 13½in (34cm) **$65-$75**
Judy: 12in (31cm) **$65-$75**
Libby: 10½in (27cm) **$65-$75**
Rooms **$200-$300**
Office **$200-$300**
Tagged clothes
(packaged outfits) **$30-$75**
Trunk **$75**

Television Programs & Personalities: All prices are for dolls that are mint, in original box.
Addams Family:
5½in (14cm) **$100-$125 each**
I Dream of Jeannie:
6in (15cm) **$40-$50**
Bottle Playset **$85-$95**
Laurie Partridge (Susan Dey):
1973. 19in (48cm) **$85-$95**
Orphan Annie: 1967.
15in (38cm) **$35-$45**
Beatles: 1964. 4½in (11cm) set of four with guitars **$350-$400**

17in (43cm) Reliable RAF Pilot. *H & J Foulke, Inc.*

Remco booklet showing *Littlechap* family. *Rosemary Kanizer.*

Santons

Sandra Sue

FACTS
1930s to present.
Simone Jouglas, J.P. Marinacei,
Syndicat de Satonniers de Provence
and others.
Provence, France.

Santons: Figures representing the elderly people of Provence. Clay character heads, clay hands and legs, wire armature bodies; authentic costumes, many representing various occupations and activities; all original, excellent condition.

7in (18cm)	**$55**
10-12in (25-31cm)	**$100-$125**

Sandra Sue: 1952 on. All-hard plastic, slender; Saran wig, molded eyelashes; unmarked.

8in (20cm) basic doll: (camisole, panties, half-slip, shoes and socks)

	$125-$140
Boxed	**$225-$250**
In street dresses	**$150-$175**
In gowns	**$200-$250**
Little Women	**$225**
Outfits, packaged	**$50-$100**
Bridal gown	**$125**
Communion dress	**$110**
Shoes	**$25**

Cindy Lou: 1951. All-hard plastic walker; Saran wig. Many outfits matched Sandra Sue's.

14in (36cm) basic doll: (camisole, panties, half-slip, shoes and socks)

	$300-$350
In street dresses	**$425-$475**

FACTS
Richwood
Toys, Inc.,
Annapolis, MD,
U.S.A. 1952-on.
Designer:
Ida H. Wood

12in (31cm) Santon, all original. *H & J Foulke, Inc.*

Right: 8in (20cm) *Sandra Sue*, all original. *Rosemary Kanizer.*

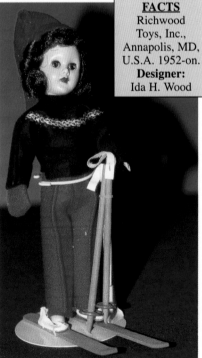

Sasha

Studio Model (from Sasha Morgenthaler's studio): 1940-1975.
Mark: "Sasha" with model numbers on foot.
  20-21in (51-53cm) child **$5,000 up**

"Course" Doll (made in Sasha Morgenthaler's studio): Cloth face and body **$2,000-$2,500**

Götz "Serie Sasha": 1964-1970.
Mark: "Sasha Serie" on head and torso.
  16in (41cm)
    All original   **$1,150-$1,450**
    Naked or later clothes **$850-$950**
    Boxed   **$2,000-$2,200**
    "No Nose"   **$1,350-$1,500**

Frido/Trendon Sasha or Gregor: 1965-1986. All-vinyl of exceptionally high quality, long rooted synthetic hair; original clothing, tiny circular wrist tag; excellent condition, unmarked.
  16in (41cm)
    1965-1971.*   **$300-$400**
    1974-1986. Boxed   **$175-$165**
      No box   **$135-$165**
    Cora: (black girl), boxed **$175-$200**
    Caleb: (black boy), boxed **$175-$200**

FACTS
Puppenfabrik Hans Götz, Rödental, Germany. 1964-1970; 1995-2001. Frido Ltd./Trendon Toys, Ltd., Reddish, Stockport, England. 1965-1986. **Designer:** Sasha Morgenthaler.

Black baby, boxed   **$125-$150**
White baby, boxed   **$100-$125**
Sexed baby, pre 1979, boxed **$165**
Packaged clothes   **$50-$85**
Wrist tag   **$10-$15**

Limited Edition Dolls, boxed:
  1980 **Velvet Dress**   **$250-$300**
  1982 **Pintucks Dress**   **$250-$300**
  1983 **Kiltie**   **$250-$300**
  1984 **Harlequin**   **$250-$300**
  1985 **Prince Gregor**   **$250-$300**
  1986 **Princess**   **$1,000-$1,500**
  1986 **Sari**   **$750-$800**

Götz: 1995-2001.   **$175-$225**

*White and/or striped elastic used for arms and legs.

Götz *Serie Sasha*, all original. *H & J Foulke, Inc.*

Trendon 1970 *Gregor London*, #4-304, all original. *H & J Foulke, Inc.*

Shirley Temple

All-Composition Child: 1934 through late 1930s. Marked head and body; jointed composition body; all original including wig and clothes; entire doll in excellent condition. Sizes: 11-27in (28-69cm).

Mark: On body:

On head: **SHIRLEY TEMPLE**

On cloth label:

Genuine SHIRLEY TEMPLE DOLL REGISTERED U.S. PAT OFF IDEAL NOVELTY & TOY CO	MADE IN U.S.A.

11in (28cm)	$900-$1,100*
13in (33cm)	$850-$900*
15-16in (38-41cm)	$850-$900*
18in (46cm)	$1,000-$1,100*

FACTS
Ideal Novelty & Toy Co.,
New York, NY, U.S.A. 1934-on.
Designer: Bernard Lipfert.

20-22in (51-56cm)	$1,200*
25in (64cm)	$1,400*
27in (69cm)	$1,800-$2,000*
16-18in (41-46cm) with trunk and wardrobe	$1,700-$1,900
Button	$110-$135
Dress, tagged	$175 up
Shoes	$75-$125
Trunk	$225-$250
Carriage	$650-$850

*Allow 50 to 100 percent more for mint-in-box doll. Allow extra for **Texas Ranger, Captain January** and other unusual outfits.

18in (46cm) composition *Shirley Temple*, all original. *H & J Foulke, Inc.*

Right: 12in (31cm) 1957 vinyl *Shirley Temple*, all original with box. *H & J Foulke, Inc.*

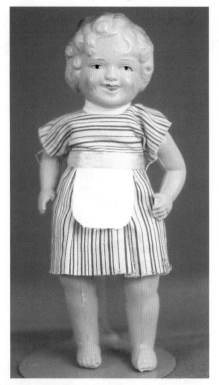

7in (18cm) celluloid "Made in Japan" *Shirley Temple. H & J Foulke, Inc.*

8in (20cm) 1982 vinyl *Shirley Temple. H & J Foulke, Inc.*

Hawaiian Shirley:

18in (46cm)	**$900-$1,000**

Baby Shirley: Composition/cloth; original clothing; good condition,

16-18in (41-46cm)	**$1,250-$1,500**

Shirley at Organ: Mechanical,

at auction	**$4,400**

Other Composition Shirley Temples:
Made in Japan:

7½in (19cm)	**$225-$275**

Reliable: (Canada), all original and boxed, 18-22in (46-56cm)   **$1,200**

Celluloid: (Japan)	**$200-$225**

Vinyl and Plastic: Excellent condition, original clothes.
1957.

12in (30cm)	**$185-$210**
Boxed	**$325-$375**
Boxed with trousseau	**$650**
15in (38cm)	**$250-$275**

17in (43cm)	**$325-$350**
19in (48cm)	**$375-$400**
36in (91cm)	**$1,200-$1,500**
Script name pin	**$40-$45**
Name purse	**$25**
Tagged or boxed dress	**$65 up**
Black Plastic Curler Box	**$80**

1973:

16in (41cm) size only	**$65-$85**
Boxed	**$125-$150**
Boxed dress	**$35**

1972, Montgomery Ward:

14in (36cm)	**$200-$225**

1982, 1983:

8in (20cm)	**$30-$40**
12in (30cm)	**$55-$65**

1984, Dolls, Dreams & Love:

36in (91cm)	**$175-$225**

Porcelain, all original and boxed:
Danbury Mint: Various models

	$75-$100

Skookum Indians

FACTS
Created and designed by Mary McAboy,
Missoula, MT and Denver, CO, U.S.A.
Dolls made by various companies
including Arrow Novelty Co.,
New York and H.H. Tammen Co.,
New York, Denver and Los Angeles.
1913-on.
Mark: Sometimes a paper label
on the sole of the foot.
Trademark:
Skookum (Bully Good)

Skookum Indian Doll: Composition character face, black mohair wig; Indian blanket folded to represent arms; cotton print dress or shirt and felt trousers, headband with feathers; beads; suede boots; all very colorful; excellent unplayed-with condition.

Mailer	**$20-$30**
6in (15cm)	**$35-$45**
9-10in (23-25cm)	**$85-$125**
14in (36cm)	**$200-$250**
16in (41cm)	**$300-$350**
20in (51cm)	**$500-$600**
36in (91cm)	**$1,600 up**

14in (36cm) *Skookum,* all original. *H & J Foulke, Inc.*

Sun Rubber Co.

Silly and Popo: 1937. Comic characters with molded clothes,
   10in (25cm)   **$55-$65****

Minnie Mouse: 1937. In red-and-white polka dot sundress,
   10½in (27cm)   **$125-$150****

Bonnie Bear, Wiggy Wags, Happy Kappy, Rompy: 1940s. One-piece squeeze dolls with molded clothes and hats. Designed by Ruth E. Newton.
   6-8in (15-20cm)   **$15-$25****

So-Wee: 1941. Designed by Ruth E. Newton with painted or sleep eyes, molded hair; excellent;
   10-12in (25-31cm)   **$65-$75**

Sunbabe: 1950. Drink-and-wet baby with painted eyes and molded hair; excellent:
   11-13in (28-33cm)   **$45-$55**

FACTS
Barberton, OH, U.S.A. 1930s-on.
Marks: "Sun Rubber Co." with various numbers, names and dates

---

In original box   **$110-$125**
Sewing set, boxed   **$150-$175**

Amosandra: 1940s. From "Amos & Andy" radio show.
Mark:
     "Amosandra©
Columbia Broadcasting System, Inc.
   Designed by Ruth E. Newton."

10in (25cm) naked   **$95-$125**
Boxed with accessories **$300-$400**

Baby Bannister: 1954. All-vinyl drink-and-wet doll based on the famous baby photographs by Constance Bannister; excellent;
   12in (31cm) naked   **$50-$60**
In original box   **$100-$135**

Gerber Baby: 1955. All-rubber with inset eyes and molded hair, open/closed mouth; excellent:
   11-13in (28-33cm)   **$100-$125**
   In original box   **$275-$325**

**Not enough price samples to compute a reliable range.

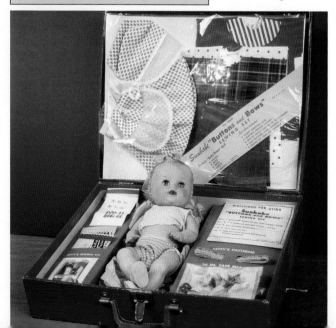

Sunbabe, all original and boxed. *H & J Foulke, Inc.*

Terri Lee

Terri Lee Child Doll: Original wig, painted eyes; jointed at neck, shoulders and hips; all original tagged clothing and accessories; very good condition. 16in (41cm).

Composition, stiff hair	**$500-$600****
Hard Plastic:	
Pat. Pending	**$525-$675**
Terri Lee only	**$375-$525**
Mint-in-box	**$650-$750**
With trunk and seven tagged outfits, at auction	**$3,383**
Talking Terri: Boxed	**$700-$750**
Push walker: at auction	**$975**
Vinyl head	**$600****
Patty-Jo: (black)	**$900-$1,100**
Bonnie Lou: (black)	**$1,300**
Jerri Lee: 16in (41cm)	**$525-$625**
Benji: (black)	**$700-$800****
Clothing:	
School dress	**$125-$150**
Party dress	**$150-$175**
Gown	**$150-$200**
Shoes	**$65-$75**
Majorette outfit with boots	**$225**
Cowgirl outfit with hat	**$175**
Holster and gun	**$130**

FACTS
TERRI LEE Sales Corp.,
V. Gradwohl, Pres. 1946-Lincoln, NE;
then Apple Valley, CA, U.S.A.,
from 1952-Ca. 1962.
Mark: First dolls:
"TERRI LEE PAT. PENDING"
raised letters.
Later dolls: "TERRI LEE"

Fur coat	**$125-$150**
Clothes rack	**$125**
Trunk	**$150**
Tiny Terri Lee: Inset eyes.	
10in (25cm)	**$185-$210**
Boxed	**$300**
Tiny Jerri Lee: Inset eyes.	
10in (25cm)	**$185-$210**
Connie Lynn	**$375-$425**
Gene Autry:	**$1,800-$2,000**
Linda Baby: 10in (25cm)	**$165-$185**
Ginger Girl Scout:	
8in (20cm)	**$175-$200**

**Not enough price samples to compute a reliable range.

16in (41cm) *Jerri Lee*, all original. *H & J Foulke, Inc.*

16in (41cm) *Terri Lee*, Patent Pending, all original. *H & J Foulke, Inc.*

Tiny Town Dolls

Uneeda Doll Co.

FACTS
Alma LeBlane dba Lenna Lee's Tiny Town Dolls, San Francisco, CA, U.S.A. Trademark registered January 11, 1949.
Mark: Some have a gold octagonal wrist tag with "Tiny Town Dolls" on one side and name of doll on the other.

FACTS
New York, NY, U.S.A. 1917-on.

Tiny Town Dolls: Molded felt faces with painted eyes and mouths, mohair wigs of various styles and colors; wrapped cloth bodies over wire armatures, felt hands; weighted white metal shoes; original clothes; excellent condition.

4in (10cm)*	$100-$150
Boxed	$165-$225

*Other known sizes are 5in (13cm) and 7¼in (19cm) but no prices are available.

Composition Dolls:
Lucky Lindy (Charles Lindbergh): 1927. Composition/cloth; brown aviator suit; good condition;
14in (36cm)	$350-$450**

Rita Hayworth: 1939. All-composition; red mohair wig; all original clothes; excellent;
14in (36cm)	$450-$500**

Toddler: Ca. 1940. All-composition; all original clothes; very good condition; 13in (33cm) $200-$225

**Not enough price samples to compute a reliable range.

Hard Plastic and Vinyl Dolls: Excellent, unplayed-with condition with original clothes, perfect hair, rosy cheeks.

4in (10cm) Tiny Town *Alice*, all original. *H & J Foulke, Inc.*

Uneeda composition toddler, all original. *H & J Foulke, Inc.*

Dollikin: 1957. Fully-jointed hard plastic:
8in (20cm) mint-in-box	**$45-$50**
11in (28cm) mint-in-box	**$75-$80**
19in (48cm)	**$250-$300**
Boxed	**$350-$400**

Baby Dollikin: 1958. Jointed elbows and knees, 21in (53cm) **$175-$185**

Saranade: 1962. With phonograph and record, 21in (53cm) **$175-$185**

Pollyanna: 1960. Hayley Mills in pink-and-white checked outfit:
10½in (27cm)	**$35-$40**
17in (43cm)	**$50-$60**
31in (79cm)	**$225-$250**

Wee Three: Mother, daughter and baby brother:
Set	**$125**
Boxed set	**$200**

Suzette: 1960. 12in (31cm) **$75-$85**
Bob: 1962. 12in (31cm) boxed **$90**
Annette Funicello: Ca. 1960.
10in (26cm)	**$75-$85**

Blue Fairy: 1959.
10½ in (25cm)	**$100-$110**

Miss Deb: 1972. 16in (41cm) growing hair, boxed **$100**

Tiny Teen: 1967. Mint-in-bubble package **$45-$50**

Vinyl Dolls

All dolls must be in excellent condition with perfect hair, excellent coloring, no discoloration and crisp original clothes.

14R Fashion Dolls: 1957-1965. All-vinyl, excellent quality ladies:
19-20in (48-51cm)	**$80-$90**
Boxed	**$135**

James Bond, Secret Agent 007: 1965. Gilbert Toys, movie character,
12½in (31cm) boxed	**$75-$100**

Angela Cartwright: 1961. Natural Doll Co., featured as Linda Williams on "The Danny Thomas Show,"
14in (36cm) smiling character face	**$40-$50**

Carol Channing: 1960. Nasco, all-vinyl, 11½in (29cm), costume from musical **$45-$55**

Dick Clark: 1958-1959. Juro Novelty Co., personality portrait doll, original clothes,
26in (66cm) at auction	**$400-$500**

Debutante: Ca. 1960. Goldberger, high-heeled fashion doll, vinyl and hard plastic, 29in (74cm) **$90-$110**

Hello, Dolly: 1961. Kaysam, all-vinyl, 21in (53cm), costume from musical **$75-$100**

Honey West: 1965. Gilbert Toys, hard plastic and vinyl, painted eyes,
11½in (29cm) boxed	**$125**
Packaged #16261 Secret Agent Outfit	**$90**

10in (25cm) Uneeda *Annette Funicello*, all original. *McMasters Harris Premier Doll Auctions.*

Left: 7½in (19cm) Flagg *Auto Driver & Auto Girl,* all original and boxed, $48. Unboxed, $25-$30. *Kathy & Terri's Dolls.*

Below: Flagg *Peter Pan Wendy* from "Nursery Rhymes Series," all original and boxed, $48. *Kathy & Terri's Dolls.*

Lonely Lisa: 1964. Royal Doll Co., vinyl and cloth, large painted eyes, 20in (51cm)   **$90-$100**

Man from U.N.C.L.E.: 1965. Gilbert Toys, characters from television series, 12½in (31cm) boxed   **$75-$100**

Miss America: 1957-1959. Sayco Doll Co., vinyl fashion doll:
10in (25cm)	**$55-$65**
18in (46cm)	**$90-$110**

Marilyn Monroe: 1983. World Doll Co., 18in (46cm) boxed, red dress   **$50-$60**

Puppetrina: 1963. Goldberger, vinyl head, cloth body, hand puppet doll, 22½in (57cm)   **$65**

Queen for a Day: 1957. Valentine, vinyl fashion doll, 20in (51cm) in taffeta gown and velvet cape   **$90-$110**

Ginger Rogers: 1983. World Doll Co., 18in (46cm) boxed   **$50-$60**

Roxanne, Beat the Clock: 1953. 16in (41cm) boxed   **$450**

Sally Starr: 1960s. Philadelphia television personality, 10½in (26cm) cowgirl outfit **$25-$35**

Lili: 1955. *Bild* (German Newspaper) promotional doll, **BARBIE**®-type.
11in (28cm)	**$1,000-$1,500**
In container	**$2,000-$3,000**

Vogue

All-composition Girl: 1940s. Original clothes; all in good condition, with perfect hair.
Mark: None on doll; round silver sticker on front of outfit. May have name stamped on sole of shoe.

13in (33cm)	**$400-$450**
19in (48cm)	**$525-$575**

All-composition Toddles: 1937-1948. Painted eyes looking to side; original clothes; all in good condition.
Mark: "VOGUE" on head
"DOLL CO." on back
"TODDLES" stamped on sole of shoe

7-8in (18-20cm)	**$275-$325***
Boxed	**$400-$500**

Hard Plastic Ginny: Original wig and tagged clothes; all in excellent condition with perfect hair and pretty coloring. 7-8in (18-20cm).
Mark:
On strung dolls: "VOGUE DOLLS"
On walking dolls: "GINNY//VOGUE DOLLS"
1948-1949:

Painted eyes	**$375-$425****
Half-Century Series	**$1,000**
Crib Crowd Baby	**$800-$900**
Easter Bunny Baby	**$1,200-$1,400**

1950-1953:
Painted eyelashes, strung, excellent
$500-$600**
Caracul wig, poodle cut excellent
$500-$600**

Beryl, Cheryl, Tiny Miss, Kindergarten: Boxed	**$1,500**
Queen Elizabeth II	**$900-$1,100**
Black **Ginny**	**$2,000-$2,500**

1954: Painted eyelashes, walks
$300-$350*

1955-1957:
Molded eyelashes, walks
$225-$275**

Davy Crockett	**$400-$450**
Girl Scout or **Brownie**	**$275-$325**
Bon Bon: Boxed	**$400-$450**
Tiny Miss, Debs: boxed	**$350-$400**
Nun	**$350**

FACTS
Vogue Dolls, Inc.,
Medford, MA, U.S.A.
Creator: Jennie Graves.
Clothes Designer:
Virginia Graves Carlson.
Clothes Label:
"Vogue," "Vogue Dolls" or
"VOGUE DOLLS, INC.
MEDFORD, MASS. USA
® REG U.S. PAT OFF"

1957-1962:
Molded eyelashes, walks, jointed
knees **$150-$200****
1962 on:
Vinyl head, hard plastic body with
jointed knees **$80-$90**

*Allow extra for unusual outfits, such as cowboy and **Uncle Sam.**
Allow extra for mint-in-box dolls and desirable outfits, such as **Tiny Miss Series and **Kindergarten Series.**

13in (33cm) WAAC, all original. *H & J Foulke, Inc.*

8in (20cm) *Toddles Oriental*, all original. *H & J Foulke, Inc.*

8in (20cm) hard plastic, painted eyes 1950 *Valentine Girl. H & J Foulke, Inc.*

8in (20cm) 1952 strung *Ginny. H & J Foulke, Inc.*

Accessories: All in excellent condition.

Ginny's Pup	**$200-$225**
Cardboard suitcase with contents	**$50**
Parasol	**$15-$18**
Gym set	**$350-$450**
Dresser, bed, rocking chair, wardrobe, vanity	**$55-$65 each**
Trousseau Tree	**$150-$175**
School bag	**$75-$85**
"Hi I'm Ginny" pin	**$75**
Ginny's First Secret book	**$125**
Swag bag, hatbox, auto bag and garment bag	**$35 each**
Roller skates in cylinder	**$35**
Hats	**$20-$30**
Headband	**$8-$10**
Dress and panties, tagged	**$50-$75**
Glasses	**$4-$5**
Shoes, center snap	**$75-$100**
Shoes, plastic	**$15-$20**
Boxed	**$30-$35**
Locket & chain	**$65**
Purse (Ginny)	**$6**
Boxed Clothing: 1950-1954.	
	$100-$200

Vinyl Ginny: 1972.

Children and internationals	**$25-$35**
Gift Set	**$65-$75**

10in (25cm) *Jill*, all original. *H & J Foulke, Inc.*

Vinyl Ginny: 1977-on.
8in (20cm) children	**$30-$40**
International costumes	**$25-$35**
Sasson	**$25-$35**
Black Ginnette	**$15-$20**

Other Dolls: All must be in excellent condition with perfect hair, excellent coloring and original clothes.

Jill: 1957. All-hard plastic, adult body,
10in (25cm)	**$175-$200**
Boxed outfits	**$75-$105**

Jeff: 1957. Vinyl head.
10in (25cm)	**$75-$95**
Boxed	**$125-$150**

Jan: 1958.
All-vinyl	**$95-$110**
Boxed	**$125-$150**

Ginnette: 1957. All-vinyl baby.
8in (20cm)	**$125-$135**
Nursing bottle	**$30-$40**
Baby Tender	**$50**
Crib	**$75**
Boxed outfits	**$50-$85**

Jimmy: 1958.
8in (20cm) painted eyes	**$135-$150**
Boxed	**$175-$200**

Lil Imp: 1959-1960. Vinyl head, hard plastic body with bent knees.
11in (28cm)	**$125-$150**
Boxed	**$250-$300**

Wee Imp: 1960. All-hard plastic, red hair, 8in (20cm) **$250-$300**

Baby Dear: 1960-1964. Designed by Eloise Wilken. Vinyl head and limbs, cloth body.
12in (31cm)	**$175-$195**
18in (46cm)	**$250-$300**

Baby Dear One: 1962-1963.
25in (63cm)	**$275-$325**

Baby Dear Two (toddler): 1963.
17in (43cm)	**$175-$225**
23in (59cm)	**$275-$325**

Miss Ginny: 1962.
16in (41cm)	**$65-$75**

Ginny: 1960.
36in (91cm)	**$300-$500****

Brikette: 1961.
16in (41cm)	**$100-$125**
22in (56cm)	**$150**

Love Me Linda: 1965. All-vinyl,
16in (41cm)	**$65-$75**

R. John Wright *Becky,* all original. *Pat Vaillancourt.*

Wright, R. John

Cloth Dolls: All boxed and in perfect condition.

Adult Characters: 1977-1981.
(no boxes)	**$800-$1,200**
Children	**$600-$1,100**

Snow White & Seven Dwarfs: 1989-1994. Matching numbered set
$3,750

Little Prince: 1983-1984. Premiere
$2,000

Pinocchio: 1992. (Disney) carved wood **$900**

Christopher Robin & Winnie the Pooh: 1985. Series I.
18in (46cm)	**$1,250-$1,500**
Pocket Pooh Characters	**$190-$225**
Pocket Christopher Robin:	
1998-1999. 12in (31cm)	**$650**

Winnie the Pooh:
14in (36cm) with honeypot,
1987-1989.	**$600-$700**

Lifesize: 1987-1988.
18in (46cm)	**$1,000-$1,200**

Kewpies: 1999 on. **$450-$500**
UFDC Boutonnier: 1999.
$135-$165

Peter Rabbit: 1998. **$400**

Golliwog: 1996-1998. Club exclusive, 11in (28cm) **$575-$625**

Bibliography

Anderton, Johana.
Twentieth Century Dolls. North Kansas City, Missouri: Trojan Press, 1971.
More Twentieth Century Dolls. North Kansas City, Missouri: Athena Publishing Co., 1974.

Angione, Genevieve.
All-Bisque & Half-Bisque Dolls. Exton, Pennsylvania: Schiffer Publishing Ltd., 1969.

Borger, Mona.
Chinas, Dolls for Study and Admiration. San Francisco: Borger Publications, 1983.

Cieslik, Jürgen and Marianne.
German Doll Encyclopedia 1800-1939. Cumberland, Maryland: Hobby House Press, Inc., 1985.

Coleman, Dorothy S., Elizabeth Ann and Evelyn Jane.
The Collector's Book of Dolls' Clothes. New York: Crown Publishers, Inc., 1975.
The Collector's Encyclopedia of Dolls, Volumes I & II. New York: Crown Publishers, Inc., 1968 & 1986.

Corson, Carol.
Schoenhut Dolls, A Collector's Encyclopedia. Cumberland, Maryland: Hobby House Press, Inc., 1993.

Foulke, Jan.
Blue Books of Dolls & Values, Volumes I-XV. Cumberland, Maryland: Hobby House Press, Inc., 1974-1997.
Doll Classics. Cumberland, Maryland: Hobby House Press, Inc., 1987.
Focusing on Effanbee Composition Dolls. Riverdale, Maryland: Hobby House Press, 1978.
Focusing on Gebrüder Heubach Dolls. Cumberland, Maryland: Hobby House Press, Inc., 1980.
Kestner, King of Dollmakers. Cumberland, Maryland: Hobby House Press, Inc., 1982.
Simon & Halbig Dolls, The Artful Aspect. Cumberland, Maryland: Hobby House Press, Inc., 1984.
Treasury of Madame Alexander Dolls. Riverdale, Maryland: Hobby House Press, 1979.
China Doll Collecting. Grantsville, Maryland: Hobby House Press, Inc., 1995.
German 'Dolly' Collecting. Grantsville, Maryland: Hobby House Press, Inc., 1995.
Doll Buying &Selling. Grantsville, Maryland: Hobby House Press, Inc., 1995.

Gerken, Jo Elizabeth.
Wonderful Dolls of Papier-Mâché. Lincoln, Nebraska: Doll Research Associates, 1970.

Hillier, Mary.
Dolls and Dollmakers. New York: G. P. Putnam's Sons, 1968.

The History of Wax Dolls. Cumberland, Maryland: Hobby House Press, Inc.; London: Justin Knowles, 1985.

Izen, Judith.
Collector's Guide to Ideal Dolls. Paducah, Kentucky: Collector Books, 1999.

Izen, Judith and Carol Stover.
Collector's Encyclopedia of Vogue Dolls. Paducah, Kentucky: Collector Books. 1999.

Jensen, Don.
Collector's Guide to Horsman Dolls. Paducah, Kentucky: Collector Books, 2002.

Judd, Polly and Pam.
Hard Plastic Dolls. Cumberland, Maryland: Hobby House Press, Inc., 1985.
Hard Plastic Dolls II. Cumberland, Maryland: Hobby House Press, Inc., 1989.
Glamour Dolls of the 1950s &1960s. Cumberland, Maryland: Hobby House Press, Inc., 1988.
Compo Dolls 1928-1955. Cumberland, Maryland: Hobby House Press, Inc., 1991.
Compo Dolls, Volume II. Cumberland, Maryland: Hobby House Press, Inc., 1994.

Mathes, Ruth E. and Robert C.
Dolls, Toys and Childhood. Cumberland, Maryland: Hobby House Press, Inc., 1987.

McGonagle, Dorothy A.
The Dolls of Jules Nicolas Steiner. Cumberland, Maryland: Hobby House Press, Inc., 1988.

Merrill, Madeline O.
The Art of Dolls, 1700-1940. Cumberland, Maryland: Hobby House Press, Inc., 1985.

Mertz, Ursula R.
Collector's Encyclopedia of American Composition Dolls, 1900-1950. Paducah, Kentucky: Collector Books, 1999.

Pardella, Edward R.
Shirley Temple Dolls and Fashions. West Chester, Pennsylvania: Schiffer Publishing, Ltd., 1992.

Richter, Lydia.
Heubach Character Dolls and Figurines. Cumberland, Maryland:Hobby House Press, Inc., 1992.

Schoonmaker, Patricia N.
Effanbee Dolls: The Formative Years 1910-1929. Cumberland, Maryland: Hobby House Press, Inc., 1984.
Patsy Doll Family Encyclopedia, Volumes I & II. Cumberland, Maryland: Hobby House Press, Inc., 1992.

Tabbat, Andrew.
Collector's World of Raggedy Ann & Andy. Volumes I & II. Annapolis, Maryland: Gold Horse Publishing, 1997.

Tarnowska, Maree.
Fashion Dolls. Cumberland, Maryland: Hobby House Press, Inc., 1986.

About the Author

The name Jan Foulke is synonymous with accurate information. As the author of the *Blue Book of Dolls & Values®*, she is the most quoted source on doll information and the most respected and recognized authority on dolls and doll prices in the world.

Born in Burlington, New Jersey, Jan Foulke has always had a fondness for dolls. She recalls, "Many happy hours of my childhood were spent with dolls as companions, since we lived on a quiet county road, and until I was ten, I was an only child." Jan received a B.A. from Columbia Union College, where she was named to the *Who's Who in American Colleges & Universities* and was graduated with high honors. Jan taught for 12 years in the Montgomery County school system in Maryland and also supervised student teachers in English for the University of Maryland where she did graduate work.

Jan and her husband, Howard, who photographs the dolls presented in the *Blue Book*, were both fond of antiquing as a hobby, and in 1972, they decided to open a small antique shop of their own. Their daughter, Beth, was quite interested in dolls and this sparked their curiosity about the history of old dolls. The stock in their antique shop gradually changed and evolved into an antique doll shop.

Early in the development of their antique doll shop, Jan and Howard realized that there was a critical need for an accurate and reliable doll identification and price guide resource. In the early 1970s, the Foulkes teamed up with Hobby House Press to produce (along with Thelma Bateman) the first *Blue Book of Dolls & Values*, originally published in 1974. Since that time, the Foulkes have exclusively authored and illustrated the 15 successive editions, and today the *Blue Book* is regarded by collectors and dealers as the definitive source for doll prices and values.

Jan and Howard Foulke now dedicate all of their professional time to the world of dolls: writing and illustrating books and articles, appraising collections, lecturing on antique dolls, acting as consultants to museums, auction houses and major collectors, and selling dolls by mail order, the internet and exhibits at major shows throughout the United States. Mrs. Foulke is a member of the United Federation of Doll Clubs, Doll Collectors of America and a past officer of the National Antique Doll Dealers Association. Her biography appears in *Who's Who in the East*.

Mrs. Foulke has appeared on numerous television talk shows and is often quoted in newspaper and magazine articles as the ultimate source for doll pricing and trends in collecting. Both *USA Today* and *The Washington Post* have stated that the *Blue Book of Dolls & Values* is "the bible of doll collecting."

In addition to her work on the 16 editions of the *Blue Book of Dolls & Values*, Jan Foulke has also authored: *Focusing on Effanbee Composition Dolls; A Treasury of Madame Alexander Dolls; Kestner, King of Dollmakers; Simon & Halbig, The Artful Aspect; Focusing on Gebrüder Heubach Dolls; Doll Classics; Focusing on Dolls; China Doll Collecting; German 'Dolly' Collecting* and *Doll Buying and Selling*. She has been a regular contributor to *Doll Reader®* magazine for 31 years. Her current column is the popular *Antique Q&A*.

Glossary

Applied Ears: Ears molded independently and affixed to the head. (On most dolls the ear is included as part of the head mold.)

Bald Head: Head with no crown opening, could be covered by a wig or have painted hair.

Ball-jointed Body: Usually a body of composition or papier-mâché with wooden balls at knees, elbows, hips and shoulders to make swivel joints; some parts of the limbs may be wood.

Bébé: French child doll with "dolly face."

Belton-type: A bald bisque head with one, two or three small holes for attaching a wig or stringing the body.

Bent-limb Baby Body: Composition body of five pieces with chubby torso and curved arms and legs.

Biscaloid: Ceramic or composition substance for making dolls; also called imitation bisque.

Biskoline: Celluloid-type substance for making dolls.

Bisque: Unglazed porcelain, usually flesh tinted, used for dolls' heads or all-bisque dolls.

Breather: Doll with an actual opening in each nostril, also called open nostrils.

Breveté (or Bté): Used on French dolls to indicate that the patent is registered.

Character Doll: Dolls with bisque or composition heads, modeled to look lifelike, such as infants, young or older children, young ladies and so on.

China: Glazed porcelain used for dolls' heads and *Frozen Charlottes*.

Child Dolls: Dolls with a typical "dolly face," which represents a child.

Composition: A material used for dolls' heads and bodies, consisting of such items as wood pulp, glue, sawdust, flour, rags and sundry other substances.

Contemporary Clothes: Clothes not original to the doll, but dating from the same period when the doll would have been a plaything.

Crown Opening: The cut-away part of a doll head.

DEP: Abbreviation used on German and French dolls claiming registration.

D.R.G.M.: Abbreviation used on German dolls indicating a registered design or patent.

Dolly Face: Typical face used on bisque dolls before 1910 when the character face was developed; "dolly faces" were used also after 1910.

Embossed Mark: Raised letters, numbers or names on the backs of heads or bodies.

Feathered Eyebrows: Eyebrows composed of many tiny painted brush strokes to give a realistic look.

Fixed Eyes: Glass eyes that do not move or sleep.

Flange Neck: A doll's head with a ridge at the base of the neck which contains holes for sewing the head to a cloth body.

Flapper Dolls: Dolls of the 1920s period with bobbed wig or molded hair and slender arms and legs.

Flirting Eyes: Eyes which move from side to side as doll's head is tilted.

Frozen Charlotte: Doll molded all in one piece including arms and legs.

Ges. (Gesch.): Used on German dolls to indicate design is registered or patented.

Googly Eyes: Large, often round eyes looking to the side; also called roguish or goo goo eyes.

Hard Plastic: Hard material used for making dolls after 1948.

Ichimatsu: Japanese play doll. See page 153 for full description.

Incised Mark: Letters, numbers or names impressed into the bisque on the back of the head or on the shoulder plate.

Intaglio Eyes: Painted eyes with sunken pupil and iris.

JCB: Jointed composition body. See *ball-jointed body*.

Kid Body: Body of white or pink leather.

Lady Dolls: Dolls with an adult face and a body with adult proportions.

Mama Doll: American composition and cloth doll of the 1920s to 1940s with "mama" voice box.

Mohair: Goat's hair widely used in making doll wigs.

Molded Hair: Curls, waves and comb marks which are actually part of the mold and not merely painted onto the head.

Motschmann-type Body: Doll body with cloth midsection and upper limbs with floating joints; hard lower torso and lower limbs.

Open-Mouth: Lips parted with an actual opening in the bisque, usually has teeth either molded in the bisque or set in separately and sometimes a tongue.

Open/Closed Mouth: A mouth molded to appear open, but having no actual slit in the bisque.

Original Clothes: Clothes belonging to a doll during the childhood of the original owner, either commercial or homemade.

Painted Bisque: Bisque covered with a layer of flesh-colored paint which has not been baked in, so will easily rub or wash off.

Paperweight Eyes: Blown glass eyes which have depth and look real, usually found in French dolls.

Papier-mâché: A material used for dolls' heads and bodies, consisting of paper pulp, sizing, glue, clay or flour.

Parian: Very fine quality white bisque with no complexion tint, usually used to make molded hair dolls.

S.G.D.G.: Used on French dolls to indicate that the patent is registered "without guarantee of the government."

Shoulder Head: A doll's head and shoulders all in one piece.

Shoulder Plate: The actual shoulder portion sometimes molded in one with the head, sometimes a separate piece with a socket in which a head is inserted.

Socket Head: Head and neck which fit into an opening in the shoulder plate or the body.

Solid-dome Head: Head with no crown opening, could have painted hair or be covered by wig.

Stationary Eyes: Glass eyes which do not move or sleep.

Stone Bisque: Coarse white bisque of a lesser quality.

Toddler Body: Usually a chubby ball-jointed composition body with chunky, shorter thighs and a diagonal hip joint; sometimes has curved instead of jointed arms; sometimes is of five pieces with straight chubby legs.

Topsy Turvy: Doll with two heads, one usually concealed beneath a skirt.

Turned Shoulder Head: Head and shoulders are one piece, but the head is molded at an angle so that the doll is not looking straight ahead.

Vinyl: Soft plastic material used for making dolls after 1950s.

Watermelon Mouth: Closed line-type mouth curved up at each side in an impish expression.

Wax-Over: A doll with head and/or limbs of papier-mâché or composition covered with a layer of wax to give a natural lifelike finish.

Weighted Eyes: Eyes which can be made to sleep by means of a weight which is attached to the eyes.

Wire Eyes: Eyes that can be made to sleep by means of a wire which protrudes from doll's head.

Index

Mold Numbers

Other Titles by Author:

Other Titles by Author:
Blue Book of Dolls & Values®
2nd Blue Book of Dolls & Values®
3rd Blue Book of Dolls & Values®
4th Blue Book of Dolls & Values®
5th Blue Book of Dolls & Values®
6th Blue Book of Dolls & Values®
7th Blue Book of Dolls & Values®
8th Blue Book of Dolls & Values®
9th Blue Book of Dolls & Values®
10th Blue Book of Dolls & Values®
11th Blue Book of Dolls & Values®
12th Blue Book of Dolls & Values®
13th Blue Book of Dolls & Values®
14th Blue Book of Dolls & Values®
15th Blue Book of Dolls & Values®

Focusing on Effanbee Composition Dolls
Focusing on Treasury of Mme. Alexander Dolls
Focusing on Gebrüder Heubach Dolls
Kestner: King of Dollmakers
Simon & Halbig Dolls: The Artful Aspect
Doll Classics
Focusing on Dolls
China Doll Collecting
Doll Buying & Selling
German 'Dolly' Collecting

Out-of-print editions of the ***Blue Book*® *of Dolls & Values*** have become collectors' items. Out-of-print books can be found at doll shows or auctions. The following prices are for clean books with light wear on covers and corners.

Blue Book® *of Dolls & Values* . . . . **$100-$135**
2nd Blue Book® *of Dolls & Values* . . . . . **$90-$110**
3rd Blue Book® *of Dolls & Values* . . . . . . **$50-$75**
4th Blue Book® *of Dolls & Values* . . . . **$50-$75**
5th Blue Book® *of Dolls & Values* . . . . **$40-$50**
6th Blue Book® *of Dolls & Values* . . . . **$35-$40**
7th Blue Book® *of Dolls & Values* . . . . **$35-$40**
8th Blue Book® *of Dolls & Values* . . . . **$35-$40**
9th Blue Book® *of Dolls & Values* . . . . **$25-$30**
10th Blue Book® *of Dolls & Values* . . . . . . **$25-$30**